Wigand / Seetharaman

Building AI Agents for Engineers

Tobias Wigand
Ram Dhiwakar Seetharaman

Building AI Agents for Engineers

Best Practices for Product Development

With contributions from Michael Finocchiaro, Felix Klutzny, Ryan McClelland, Patrick Schmidt and Eric Stähle

HANSER

About the authors:
Tobias Wigand, Sachsenheim
Ram Dhiwakar Seetharaman, Bremen

Print-ISBN: 978-1-56990-562-3
E-Book-ISBN: 978-1-56990-969-0
E-Pub-ISBN: 979-8-950184-14-7

Bibliographic information of the German National Library:
The German National Library lists this publication in the German National Bibliography; detailed bibliographic data are available on the Internet at http://dnb.d-nb.de.

Vilshofener Straße 10 | 81679 Munich | info@hanser.de
www.hanserpublications.com
www.hanser-fachbuch.de
Editor: Julia Stepp
Production Management: Melanie Zinsler
Cover concept: Marc Müller-Bremer, www.rebranding.de, Munich
Cover design: Max Kostopoulos
Cover picture: © Max Kostopoulos
Typesetting: le-tex publishing services GmbH, Leipzig

Contents

List of Co-Authors

Co-Author	Section
Michael Finocchiaro, Independent PLM and Engineering AI Consultant	Section 1.8 , "Guest Perspective: Why This Moment Is Different for Engineering AI"
Felix Klutzny, Consultant Digital Engineering, ARRK Engineering	Section 3.4.7, "Guest Perspective: Why Engineering Service Providers Need Automation Now"
Ryan McClelland, AI Infusion Lead and Mechanical Engineer, NASA Goddard Space Flight Center	Section 3.2.7, "Guest Perspective: From Generative Design to Intelligent Engineering at NASA"
Dr. Patrick Schmidt, Head of Systems and Process Engineering, Miele	Section 3.3.7, "Guest Perspective: Scaling Engineering Productivity with Context-Aware Agents"
Eric Stähle, Development Engineer at IMS Gear	Section 3.1.7, "Guest Perspective: Implementing Multi-Agent Systems in RFQ Engineering"

1 The Moment Engineering Changed

This book begins with a very concrete moment. When agents first became capable of calling tools rather than only generating text, we started to experiment. Not as a formal initiative or roadmap item, but as a side project on weekends. The initial motivation was simple curiosity. What happens when language models are no longer confined to explanations, but can actually trigger actions in real systems?

The results were overwhelming.

Until then, AI in engineering had largely been split into two separate worlds. On the one side stood classic rule-based automation. It was powerful and reliable but limited to processes that follow fixed logic with clearly defined decision criteria. On the other side were isolated AI applications. These included assistants that could analyze documents, classify data, or support individual tasks, but remained detached from the actual engineering workflow.

Tool-calling agents removed this boundary almost overnight. For the first time, fuzzy reasoning, experience-based judgment, and contextual interpretation could be combined with deterministic execution. This was precisely the gap where traditional automation always struggled. Edge cases were hard to encode. Exceptions were painful to handle. Anything that normally required discussion, trade-off evaluation, or human judgment was out of scope. With agents, this limitation began to dissolve.

We did not explore this through demos or toy problems. From the beginning, we applied it to real engineering workflows. Together with a small group of technology enthusiasts inside companies with an early innovator mindset, we started side projects that addressed concrete, operational problems. The setups were far from perfect. Integrations were brittle. Processes were incomplete. Yet even the earliest results exceeded expectations by a wide margin.

The potential was visible from day one.

Encouraged by this, we began to push the topic more deliberately with a small set of customers. At the same time, our own organization gave us the opportunity to spend a meaningful share of our working time exploring the technology hands-on. This combination mattered. We were not experimenting in isolation. Every insight was shaped by real constraints: on-premise environments, legacy CAx tools, strict security requirements, fragmented data landscapes. This was the same reality most engineering organizations face every day.

One of the biggest surprises was the capability of the language models themselves. Even though they could not directly operate CAx tools or interpret native result files, their reasoning abilities were remarkable. Once engineering outputs were converted into interpretable formats, plots, tables, images, or structured summaries, the models demonstrated a level of physical intuition that often caught us off guard. More than once, an agent identified an engineering mistake we had introduced ourselves. Not because it calculated better, but because it questioned an assumption we had implicitly made.

At that point, one thing became clear. The question was no longer whether large language models could support engineering. They clearly could. The real challenge lay elsewhere, namely in connecting these models to fragmented, on-premise engineering toolchains in a way that was reliable, traceable, and safe.

Another insight followed quickly and proved even more important. The real impact was not automation. It was coordination. In every agentic system we built, the core engineering execution remained deterministic, whether it involved scripts, solver runs, meshing rules, or geometry operations. That foundation did not disappear. Engineering does not exist in isolation, though. It exists to enable decisions, evaluate trade-offs, manage risk, and create business value. This is where agents changed everything. They became the connective tissue between engineering execution and decision-making. They orchestrated tasks, synchronized information across domains, preserved context, and made implicit assumptions explicit. The value did not come from replacing engineering logic. It came from coordinating it.

That realization is the foundation of this book. What follows is not a theoretical discussion of AI. It is a practitioner's perspective on how agentic systems transform engineering work when they are treated not as smarter tools, but as a new coordination layer between people, processes, and technology.

1.1 The Impossible Equation Facing Engineering

Engineering organizations are entering a phase where familiar improvement levers no longer add up. The pressure they face is not driven by a single factor. It is the combination of several forces that reinforce each other and create a structural tension that traditional operating models can no longer resolve.

The first and most visible force is speed. Across industries, expectations for time to market have shifted dramatically. Development cycles that once spanned several years are now expected to shrink by 30 to 50 percent. These targets are not aspirational slogans. They are embedded in product roadmaps, investor expectations, and competitive benchmarks. Faster iteration, earlier validation, and quicker decisions are no longer optional. They determine whether a product is still relevant when it reaches the market.

At the same time, engineering organizations face sustained cost pressure. Head counts are not growing with ambition. In many cases, they are shrinking. Reductions of 10 to 20 percent have become common, driven by margin pressure, restructuring programs, or the expectation that digitalization should compensate for fewer people. The implicit assumption is clear. Engineering output must increase while engineering capacity decreases.

Complexity adds a third dimension to this equation. Products are becoming more configurable, not less. Variants multiply. Regulatory requirements expand across regions and domains. Safety, sustainability, cybersecurity, compliance considerations, and software now intersect with traditional mechanical and electrical design. Processes that were once sequential span multiple disciplines in parallel, each with its own tools, data models, and validation logic.

Taken together, these forces create a contradiction for traditional engineering models.

Faster delivery requires more parallel work, more iterations, and earlier decisions. Fewer people reduce available capacity and increase individual workload. Higher complexity increases the number of interfaces, assumptions, and dependencies that must be managed. If execution effort was the main constraint, productivity gains through better tools or automation might compensate. In practice, execution is no longer the bottleneck.

The bottleneck has shifted. In many organizations, the limiting factor is no longer calculation, modelling, or simulation time. Modern CAx tools are powerful, solvers are fast, compute capacity scales, and AI-based prediction models add further acceleration. What slows engineering down is coordination, waiting for input, aligning assumptions across teams, reconciling conflicting constraints, and preparing decisions that can be defended across technical, commercial, and regulatory dimensions.

This shift often remains hidden. It does not show up as idle time in task lists. Engineers are busy and calendars are full. An increasing share of effort is spent synchronizing rather than creating, though. Meetings replace modelling. Emails replace analysis. Decisions are delayed not because data is missing, but because context is fragmented.

Traditional optimization approaches focus on execution efficiency. Faster solvers, better templates, or more automation scripts. These improvements still matter, but they target the wrong constraint. When coordination dominates execution, incremental gains stop compounding. They are absorbed by the overhead of alignment and decision preparation.

This is why incremental optimization is no longer sufficient. The challenge engineering organizations face is structural, not local. It requires a different way of organizing work, preserving context, and preparing decisions. Without addressing this shift explicitly, the gap between expectations and reality will continue to widen, regardless of how advanced individual tools become.

This pressure is not temporary. It is the new baseline. And it sets the stage for why agentic systems are not a nice-to-have innovation, but a response to a fundamental change in how engineering work must be organized.

1.2 From Drawing Boards to CAD to Simulation

Engineering has undergone several profound transformations over the past decades. Each reshaped daily work, improved productivity, and expanded what was technically possible. Yet despite their impact, these shifts shared a common characteristic. They changed the tools, not the nature of engineering work itself.

The first major transition was the move from hand drawings to 2D CAD. Drafting tables, pencils, and erasers were replaced by digital lines and layers. Drawings became cleaner. Revisions became faster. Reuse became practical. Errors could be corrected without starting over, and scaling or copying became trivial. Yet the underlying activity remained unchanged. Engineers still translated ideas into drawings, defined dimensions, and communicated intent through geometry. The medium changed. The work did not.

The transition from 2D CAD to 3D parametric modeling marked the next step. Instead of describing geometry through projections, engineers began defining parts and assemblies as digital objects with parameters, constraints, and relationships. This was a major leap in capability. Design intent could be encoded directly. Variants became easier to generate. Interferences could be detected automatically. Assemblies scaled to a level that was previously unmanageable.

Still, the core task remained the same. Engineers designed parts, reasoned about geometry, and decided how components fit and function together. Parametric models did not make decisions. They executed precisely what engineers defined, faster and more consistently, but never independently.

The rise of simulation-driven development followed the same pattern. Physical testing was complemented and, in some cases, replaced by numerical methods. Finite element analysis, CFD, and multi-physics simulations enabled virtual exploration long before hardware existed. Costs dropped. Iteration cycles shortened. Optimization became feasible at a scale physical testing could never support.

Yet simulation did not change the structure of engineering work either. Engineers still defined load cases, boundary conditions, materials, and acceptance criteria. They interpreted results, judged trade-offs, and decided what to change next. Simulation accelerated feedback. It did not replace reasoning, coordination, or responsibility.

Looking across these revolutions, a clear pattern emerges. Each step improved speed, precision, and scale. Each step reduced manual effort and error rates. Each step enabled engineers to manage greater complexity. All of them were tool-centric, though. They assumed that the essence of engineering work remains stable. A human defines the problem, applies expertise, coordinates with others, and makes decisions. Tools assist by executing calculations, managing geometry, or visualizing results.

This assumption held for decades. It shaped organizational structures, role definitions, and productivity strategies. When pressure increased, the response was consistent: introducing better tools, adding more automation, and improving individual efficiency.

The limitation of this approach becomes visible once coordination, not execution, becomes the bottleneck. Tools excel at accelerating well-defined tasks. They struggle when work depends on interpretation, prioritization, negotiation, and cross-functional alignment. As long as engineering could be decomposed into mostly independent tasks, tool-centric revolutions delivered continuous gains.

The next shift breaks this pattern.

Agentic systems do not simply make existing tasks faster. They challenge the assumption that engineering work itself is fixed. To understand why this matters and why it represents a fundamentally different kind of transformation, we need to look beyond tools and focus on how engineering work is actually organized today.

1.3 Why Agentic Systems Represent a Different Kind of Change

Agent-based systems matter not because they automate more tasks, but because they change what engineers actually do during a working day. This distinction may seem subtle at first, but its consequences are fundamental.

Traditional engineering tools, no matter how advanced, assume a stable division of labor. Humans think, decide, and coordinate. Tools execute. CAD systems draw what engineers specify. Simulation tools calculate what engineers define. Automation scripts accelerate steps that are already clearly structured. Even highly sophisticated workflows follow this logic. The engineer remains the central operator, moving from tool to tool, preparing inputs, checking outputs, and deciding what happens next.

Agentic systems break this pattern. With agents, the primary task of engineering shifts from executing steps to defining goals. Instead of manually preparing every model, configuring every analysis, or coordinating every handover, engineers increasingly specify what should be achieved and under which constraints. Agents then navigate the space between intent and outcome. They execute sequences of actions, evaluate intermediate results, and iterate until conditions are met or escalation is required.

This does not remove engineers from the loop. It changes the loop itself. Engineers move from manual setup to supervision of decision loops. They review proposals instead of constructing them step by step. They validate outcomes instead of assembling inputs. They intervene when assumptions are wrong, constraints are unclear, or trade-offs require judgment. The center of gravity shifts upward from tool operation toward decision quality.

As a result, engineers increasingly act as orchestrators rather than operators. Their expertise is no longer consumed by repetitive preparation work. It is applied where it creates the most value, namely by defining objectives, setting boundaries, evaluating alternatives, and resolving conflicts between competing requirements. These activities were always part of engineering. What changes is how much time and attention they receive.

This type of shift has historical precedents, but not in the usual engineering tool narrative. A closer analogy can be found in coordination revolutions rather than tool revolutions. The steam engine did not merely provide more power. It reorganized labor. Work moved from small, independent workshops to coordinated factories. Productivity gains came not only from mechanical efficiency but also from new ways of structuring tasks, timing, and responsibility.

Assembly lines followed a similar pattern. The core activities of manufacturing did not disappear. Cutting, shaping, and assembling still happened. What changed was how these activities were coordinated. Tasks were decomposed, sequenced, and synchronized at a scale no individual could manage manually. The result was not just faster production but a fundamentally different organization of work.

More recently, algorithmic logistics and planning systems introduced comparable shifts. Routing trucks, managing inventories, or scheduling fleets is not primarily a calculation problem. It is a coordination problem under uncertainty. The breakthrough came when systems could continuously adapt plans, react to change, and balance trade-offs dynamically. Humans moved from micromanaging routes to supervising objectives and exceptions.

Agentic systems apply this logic to engineering. They make coordination scalable—not by eliminating complexity, but by managing it continuously. Agents can maintain context across steps, remember assumptions, compare alternatives, and synchronize work across domains without fatigue. They do not replace engineering judgment. They create the conditions under which judgment can be applied more effectively.

This is the key qualitative difference. Execution was already scalable through tools and automation. Coordination was not. It remained bound to human attention, meetings, emails, and informal agreements. As product complexity and organizational coupling increased, coordination became the limiting factor. Agentic systems directly address this constraint.

For the first time, engineering organizations gain a mechanism to scale not only calculations or geometry handling but decision preparation itself. This changes how work is structured, how roles evolve, and how value is created. It is not an incremental improvement in existing tools. It is a shift in how engineering work is organized.

1.4 Why Deterministic Automation Reaches Its Limits

Rule-based automation has delivered major productivity gains in engineering for decades. Scripts, macros, templates, and workflow engines work extremely well where processes are stable, inputs are clear, and decision criteria are known in advance. In these contexts, deterministic automation is fast, predictable, and reliable.

The limitation is not technical but structural. Engineering workflows are rarely stable. Requirements change late. Data is incomplete or inconsistent. Interfaces shift. Edge cases are common, not exceptional. Many decisions must be made under uncertainty and must be revised as constraints evolve. These conditions violate the core assumption of rule-based systems: that relevant situations can be fully anticipated and encoded upfront.

When cases deviate from the predefined path, rule-based automation becomes brittle. Either it fails outright or it requires manual intervention. To compensate, organizations add more rules, exceptions, and special cases. Over time, rule sets grow complex, opaque, and difficult to maintain. Small changes ripple through many dependencies. Debugging turns into guesswork.

More importantly, rule-based systems do not scale judgment. They execute predefined steps efficiently, but they cannot question whether those steps are still appropriate. They cannot weigh incomplete information, resolve conflicting constraints, or adapt priorities dynamically. As a result, engineers remain deeply involved in decision-making, even as execution is automated.

This creates a paradox. Automation reduces effort in individual tasks but increases coordination and maintenance overhead at the system level. The more dynamic the environment becomes, the faster this overhead grows. This is the ceiling rule-based automation hits. It is excellent at doing things right. It is poor at deciding what the right thing is when conditions change.

Rule-based automation remains essential for deterministic execution, but it cannot carry the coordination burden of modern engineering on its own. To operate effectively under today's pressure, automation must extend beyond static rules and begin to support reasoning, adaptation, and coordination. That is the gap agentic systems are designed to fill.

1.5 Why "AI-Enhanced Automation" Is Not Enough

The first wave of AI adoption in engineering has already happened. Long before agents could plan, reason, or call tools, AI models were introduced as local accelerators. Geometry classifiers, document readers, prediction models, and optimization heuristics improved individual steps across many toolchains. In isolation, these capabilities often worked well. Specific tasks became faster, more consistent, and less manual.

At first, this looked like meaningful progress—and it was. Over time, though, a structural limitation became apparent. The problem was not the quality of the models. It was their isolation. Most AI-enhanced solutions were embedded into single tools or narrow process steps. Each model optimized its own task with little awareness of upstream context or downstream consequences. Assumptions had to be reconstructed at every handover. Results were copied, reinterpreted, or manually reconciled. Context did not persist. The consequence was counterintuitive. While individual steps accelerated, overall workflows often did not. In some cases, they slowed down.

Engineering throughput is rarely constrained by task execution speed. It is constrained by coordination. Decisions depend on multiple inputs. Changes propagate across domains. Uncertainty is resolved through comparison, iteration, and alignment. Improving isolated steps without addressing this coordination layer simply moves the bottleneck.

Faster silos do not produce faster outcomes.

In practice, local intelligence often increases global friction. Results arrived earlier, but without shared assumptions. Different tools produced outputs that were individually plausible, yet inconsistent with each other. Engineers then spent additional time explaining, aligning, and validating, offsetting the gains from faster execution.

Our own experiments made this clear. Performance improved noticeably, analyses ran faster, and data extraction became more reliable. When embedded into real workflows, though, engineers spend more time contextualizing results than before. The missing element was not better models. It was shared context. Engineering workflows are not linear task chains. They are networks of interdependent decisions. What matters is not only what a result says but also why it says it, under which assumptions, and how it relates to other results. Without a mechanism to preserve and evolve this context across steps, intelligence remains local and fragile.

This is where orchestration becomes decisive. Someone, or something, must manage information flow, maintain assumptions, coordinate actions, and decide when iteration is required. In traditional workflows, humans fill this role implicitly. In AI-enhanced automation, it is often left unaddressed.

Multi-agent systems close this gap. They do not replace local intelligence. They connect it. Agents share context, reason about dependencies, and coordinate actions across tools and domains. Intelligence moves from isolated features to the system level. This marks the boundary between AI-enhanced automation and agentic systems. One accelerates steps. The other transform processes.

1.6 Multi-Agent Systems as the Next Step

The limitations described in the previous sections all point in the same direction. The central challenge engineering organizations face today is not a lack of intelligence at individual steps. It is the absence of a system that can coordinate intelligence across steps, disciplines, and decisions. Multi-agent systems (MAS) emerge precisely at this intersection.

At a high level, a multi-agent system is defined by three structural elements. First, it consists of specialized agents. Each agent is responsible for a clearly scoped role. This may include interpreting requirements, classifying geometry, preparing simulations, evaluating results, or checking compliance. The key is not the specific task but the clarity of responsibility. Agents do not attempt to solve everything. They contribute deliberately to a shared decision process.

Second, agents operate on shared context. Inputs, assumptions, intermediate results, and decisions are no longer passed implicitly through meetings, emails, or spreadsheets. They are represented explicitly and remain accessible throughout the workflow. This shared context allows agents to build on one another's work instead of repeatedly reconstructing information from scratch.

Third, multi-agent systems rely on orchestration rather than linear workflows. Instead of executing a fixed sequence of steps, the system decides which agents need to be involved, in which order, and under which conditions. Iteration is not treated as a failure or exception. It is a first-class mechanism. When assumptions change or result in conflicts, the system can deliberately revisit earlier steps without losing context.

These characteristics change what actually scales. Traditional automation scales tasks. It executes predefined steps faster and more often. Multi-agent systems scale coordination. They reduce the effort required to align information, manage dependencies, and prepare decisions across complex workflows. This distinction is subtle, but decisive. In most engineering environments, coordination effort grows faster than execution effort as complexity increases. That is why productivity gains from classical automation eventually plateau.

Another defining aspect of agentic systems is learning through usage. Each execution produces more than an output. It generates feedback: Which assumptions held? Which decisions were accepted or rejected? Where did humans intervene? Over time, this feedback accumulates. Rules are refined. Prompts are clarified. Edge cases are captured. The system becomes more robust not because it was redesigned but because it was used.

This learning effect changes the economics of automation. Early deployments often feel incomplete. Coverage is limited. Human oversight remains high. That is not a failure mode. It is a natural starting point. The value does not come from immediate replacement of work. It comes from reuse. As the same agents, logic, and orchestration patterns are applied repeatedly, marginal effort decreases while quality improves. What begins as support gradually becomes infrastructure.

This is also why agentic systems should not be understood as software in the classical sense. They are not installed and finished. They are built, governed, and evolved. Their value depends less on initial feature completeness and more on how deeply they are embedded into real engineering work. In this sense, an agentic system is an organizational capability. It captures how an organization reasons, decides, and coordinates.

The technical mechanics of agent communication, orchestration, and tool integration matter, but they are not the core message of this chapter. These aspects will be addressed in detail in Chapter 2. What matters here is the structural role multi-agent systems play. They are not an incremental improvement to existing automation. They are a response to a structural mismatch. Engineering organizations are expected to move faster, with fewer people, under rising complexity. Task-level optimization cannot resolve this tension. Coordination-level scaling can.

1.7 Why Now?

Technological shifts often look obvious in hindsight. In the moment, they feel incremental. What makes the current moment different is that several independent developments have crossed a threshold at the same time. Each of them alone would not be sufficient. Together, they change what is realistically possible in engineering automation.

The most decisive change is that agents can now act, not just reason. For a long time, AI systems were confined to analysis, prediction, or text generation. They could explain, summarize, or recommend, but they could not reliably execute actions. Engineering work, however, is not only about thinking. It is about triggering tools, preparing models, running simulations, collecting results, and handing them off to the next step. Once agents gained the ability to call tools in a controlled and repeatable way, this boundary disappeared. AI moved from being an external advisor to becoming an active participant inside the workflow. That shift fundamentally changed the relevance of AI systems for real engineering work.

This capability only matters because the surrounding ecosystem is ready. A few years ago, even acting agents would have been constrained by missing infrastructure. Today, automation platforms can reliably control CAD systems, solvers, preprocessors, and reporting pipelines. Orchestration layers coordinate actions across tools and domains. Engineering software exposes usable APIs. These components are no longer experimental. They are already in productive use. Agentic systems do not require a new technology stack. They emerge by connecting existing capabilities into a coherent whole.

In parallel, engineering data has become more digital and accessible. CAx models, simulation results, requirements, cost data, and quality records increasingly reside in structured or semi-structured systems. The data is rarely perfect, but it is locatable and machine-readable enough to serve as shared context. This shared context is essential. Without it, agents remain isolated. With it, coordination becomes possible.

There is also a non-technical factor that matters just as much. Organizational pressure has reached a point where experimentation is no longer optional. Engineering teams are expected to deliver faster with fewer people and higher complexity. Incremental optimization cannot close this gap. Many traditional levers have already been exhausted. Outsourcing, specialization, and additional tools no longer provide relief. This creates openness for approaches that would previously have been considered too risky. Agentic systems benefit from this shift. They are no longer competing with comfortable alternatives. They are competing with an unsustainable status quo.

This leads to a final and often underestimated point. Waiting is no longer neutral. In earlier technology cycles, delaying adoption mainly meant missing early efficiency gains. With agentic systems, delay has a different cost. These systems improve through use. They accumulate knowledge, refine rules, and adapt to organizational reality over time. Organizations that start earlier do not just gain short-term productivity. They build a capability that compounds. Organizations that wait do not stand still. They fall behind relative to those learning curves. This is why the question is no longer whether agentic systems will matter for engineering. The question is who will have real experience with them when they do. That answer is being shaped right now.

1.8 Guest Perspective: Why This Moment Is Different for Engineering AI

Michael Finocchiaro

The Architectural Debt of Engineering Software

The problems holding back engineering workflows today are not primarily technical. They are architectural, economic, and historical. Three decades of decisions have crystallized into structural pain that most engineers accept as simply how engineering works.

CAD and CAE systems were designed in the 1990s when files were the atomic unit of work. This made sense for UNIX workstations with limited memory. Today, it means every design lives in isolated silos: a CATIA file here, an ANSYS mesh there, a STEP translation somewhere else. The digital thread everyone talks about is actually millions of broken threads held together by file references, hardcoded paths, and manual version reconciliation.

On top of this, design engineers use CAD, analysis engineers use CAE, and manufacturing engineers use CAM. Each speaks a different data language. The handoffs between disciplines are where knowledge dies, not from malice, but from structure. When a stress analyst receives a STEP file stripped of design intent, they are not collaborating. They are archaeologically reconstructing what the designer meant.

Vendor boundaries compound the problem. Each major vendor optimizes for their silo, not for the engineer's workflow. The integrations they provide are bridges designed to maintain ecosystem lock-in, not to solve the actual coordination problem. Legacy tools were built for expert users willing to invest years becoming proficient. Modern engineers expect consumer-grade usability. Instead, they get interfaces requiring tribal knowledge to decode.

Why Integration Has Remained So Hard

The integration challenge is not fundamentally about data formats or standards. STEP, JT, and OpenUSD exist. The deeper issue is an incentives problem layered on top of architectural debt. Vendors profit from lock-in, and every integration they build preserves their data gravity.

More importantly, CAD, CAE, and PLM were built on fundamentally incompatible foundations. CAD thinks in parametric feature trees and geometry kernels. CAE thinks in meshes, boundary conditions, and load cases. PLM thinks in bills of materials, change workflows, and approvals. These are not just different data models. They are different ontologies for what a product is. Bridging them requires translating not just data but entire worldviews.

The industry mistake was treating integration as a plumbing problem, connecting System A to System B, instead of a cognitive problem: helping engineers maintain context across tools. Vendors integrated data formats when they should have been integrating context and intent. When a design change propagates from CAD to CAE, the geometry transfers, but the reasoning does not. The analyst rediscovers constraints the designer already knew. This happens millions of times daily across the industry.

Knowledge That Never Gets Captured

The most valuable engineering knowledge is procedural, contextual, and negative, which is exactly what traditional digitalization cannot encode. Every experienced engineer knows dozens of rules of thumb, such as not making ribs thinner than a certain dimension in a specific material because they crack during injection molding. None of this is in the CAD system. When that engineer retires, the knowledge vanishes, relearned one failure at a time by the next generation (Figure 1.1).

Equally important is the graveyard of ideas that seemed promising but failed for subtle reasons. A company tried topology optimization on a part that looked great in simulation but failed in production due to residual stresses. This is documented somewhere, perhaps in an email from years ago, if you even know where to search for it.

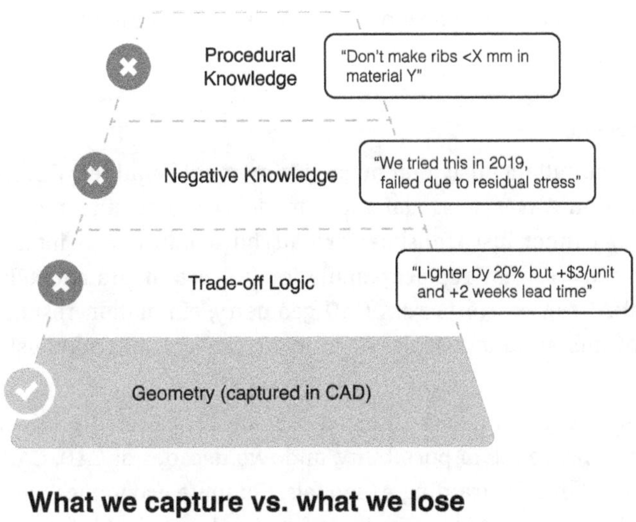

Figure 1.1 Traditional engineering data capture preserves only what exists in CAD geometry, while the most valuable institutional knowledge—procedural rules, failure history, and trade-off logic—remains undocumented and at risk of being lost when engineers leave (© Iryna Novoseletska).

Design is fundamentally about negotiating conflicting objectives. A part could be lightened significantly by adding ribs, but manufacturing says it adds cost per unit and supply chain says it increases lead time. The final geometry captures the decision but not the trade-off logic that led there. Traditional approaches tried to capture knowledge as rules and data. Engineering knowledge is contextual and experiential, though, and it resists being encoded in relational databases.

What Previous Waves Got Right and Where They Stopped

Previous digitalization waves achieved important things. CAD adoption in the 1990s eliminated drafting tables and enabled parametric design. Simulation democratization in the 2000s brought FEA and CFD from supercomputers to desktops, reducing physical testing costs dramatically. PLM rollouts in the 2010s established that product data is strategic and created change management discipline.

Where they stopped short was consistent. They digitized artifacts, geometry, meshes, and bills of materials, but not reasoning: why this shape, why this load case, why this supplier? They optimized tool performance but not workflow coherence. They focused on capturing the current state of a design but not preserving the context of how it got there and why alternatives were rejected.

Most critically, previous waves assumed humans would remain the integration layer. Engineers would maintain context in their heads, translating between tools, reconciling conflicts, remembering why. This worked when one engineer could own the full lifecycle. It breaks when products require dozens of engineers across multiple time zones using many different tools.

Why This Moment Is Different

Five factors have converged simultaneously that make this moment genuinely different from previous digitalization waves. Large language models can now understand engineering language. They cannot just translate formats but comprehend intent. Physics-informed neural networks can replace simulation solvers at dramatically higher speeds. Multimodal AI can reason across CAD geometry, simulation results, and manufacturing constraints simultaneously. Agentic AI can act autonomously within bounded domains.

At the same time, cloud PLM adoption has centralized previously scattered product data, open standards have improved data portability, and two decades of CAD, CAE, and PLM history are now available for training AI models. Compute economics have shifted as well, with GPU clusters becoming affordable for simulation and inference costs dropping enough to make AI copilots viable for large engineering populations.

Organizational maturity has also evolved. Remote work forced companies to move from tools in a room to workflows in the cloud. A generational handoff is underway as engineers who grew up with smartphones demand modern user experiences. And expectations reset after the ChatGPT moment showed everyone what AI could do, raising the bar across the industry. Five years ago, LLMs could not reason reliably, cloud PLM was not mature, and organizations were not ready. Five years from now, the competitive window will have closed.

Agents as a New Computational Paradigm

AI agents are not a new tool category and not merely a new integration layer. They represent a fundamentally different computational paradigm. Tools are passive: Engineers use CAD, run simulations, and query PLM. Agents are active collaborators that observe context, maintain goals, and take initiative.

What distinguishes agents from scripting is that scripts execute predefined logic while agents adapt to context. What distinguishes them from automation is that automation removes manual steps while agents maintain continuity of reasoning across steps, understanding why they are doing things, not just what they are doing. What distinguishes them from rules engines is that rules encode expert knowledge statically while agents learn dynamically, observing patterns, updating models, and suggesting improvements to their own rules.

The paradigm shift is this: Previous digitalization assumed humans as the integration layer, with systems providing data and humans making sense of it. AI agents invert this relationship. Systems maintain context, and humans provide judgment at decision points. Instead of an engineer pulling data from five systems, making a decision, and pushing updates to three systems, the agent presents a synthesized recommendation with a confidence level, the engineer approves or modifies it, and the agent executes across systems.

Where Agents Add Value First

Agents add realistic value in the near term where problems are bounded, success criteria are measurable, and humans remain in the loop. Change impact analysis is a prime example: When a designer proposes a modification, an agent can immediately analyze affected assemblies, flag interference issues, check simulation dependencies, query manufacturing rules, and identify supplier lead-time risks, synthesizing a recommendation that would otherwise take weeks of manual coordination.

Other near-term applications include simulation setup assistance, where agents prepare meshes, boundary conditions, and load cases based on similar parts, and design standards enforcement, where agents flag manufacturability violations and corrosion risks in real time. Search and retrieval agents can surface similar designs from organizational history along with the lessons learned from those projects.

Expectations are overhyped where agents are positioned as general problem-solvers or human replacements. Fully autonomous design, where AI designs products end-to-end without human input, remains far off. Design requires navigating ambiguous, conflicting objectives with incomplete information. The realistic path is specialized agents, a simulation setup agent, a design-for-manufacturing agent, a change impact agent, coordinated by orchestration layers rather than a single general model.

The Cognitive Load Problem

If agents succeed, the problem they are actually solving is not speed, coordination, or knowledge preservation individually. It is the cognitive load problem at the intersection of all three. Modern products require understanding across hundreds of interdependent design decisions, dozens of analysis domains, manufacturing processes spanning continents, regulatory requirements across jurisdictions, and real-time supply chain dynamics. No single engineer can hold this complexity in their head.

Teams distribute the cognitive load but then face coordination overhead. Knowledge gets lost in handoffs. Decisions fragment across silos. Agents address this by maintaining context that no human could, tracking thousands of parts, relationships, constraints, and history simultaneously. When design passes to analysis and then to manufacturing, agents preserve not just the what but the why. Context does not die at boundaries. It flows with the work.

Institutional memory also stops retiring. The knowledge that a particular approach was tried years ago and failed for specific reasons no longer walks out the door when an engineer leaves. Agents learn from every decision, building organizational intelligence that compounds over time.

The Mindset Shift

The mindset shift that matters more than any specific AI technology is moving from thinking of tools that do tasks to thinking of colleagues that maintain context. Engineers have spent three decades thinking in terms of using CAD to make geometry, FEA to analyze it, and PLM to manage it. The new framing is collaborating with an agent that maintains continuity across these tasks while the engineer focuses on the engineering decisions that require human judgment.

This requires unlearning deeply held beliefs. Engineers trust processes they can watch step by step, but demanding full visibility into every neural network computation kills the value of speed and scale. The shift is from demanding to see every step to asking for confidence levels and uncertainty estimates. Automation does not mean removing humans. It means reducing cognitive load and improving decision quality. Waiting for perfect data before starting with AI means waiting forever.

Organizations that succeed with agents will be those that embrace imperfection and iteration over perfectionism and planning. Start small, learn fast, expand gradually. AI agents will not replace engineering judgment. They will make it scalable. The engineers who thrive will be those who learn to think with agents, not just use tools.

1.9 Between Hype and Reality

Before moving into the theoretical, practical, and organizational foundations in the following chapters, it is important to set expectations clearly. Agentic systems are surrounded by hype, strong opinions, and exaggerated promises. This book deliberately takes a different path.

This is not a hype-driven AI book. It does not promise fully autonomous engineering organizations, instant productivity miracles, or the near-term replacement of engineers. We have seen firsthand how quickly such narratives collapse when they meet real processes, real constraints, and real accountability. The goal of this book is not to impress. It is to be useful.

This is also not a purely technical architecture manual. Architecture, orchestration, and tooling matter, but they are only part of the picture. Many technically sound agent systems fail because they ignore how engineering organizations actually work. Decisions are distributed. Responsibilities are negotiated. Trust is earned slowly. Focusing on architecture alone misses the real challenge.

Instead, this book is a practitioner's guide to agentic engineering. It is written from the perspective of people who experimented early, connected agents to real engineering tools, struggled with integration, faced organizational resistance, and learned what actually makes these systems work in practice. The focus is on real workflows, not toy examples, and on decision-making, not demos. The focus is also on building long-term capability, not short-term automation wins.

Throughout the book, the central question is not what agents can theoretically do, but how they change the way engineering work is organized. We examine where agentic systems create real leverage, where they introduce new risks, and how organizations can adopt them without breaking trust, governance, or existing structures. Economic impact, adoption, learning effects, and organizational readiness are treated as first-class concerns.

The structure of the book reflects this intent. Chapter 2 explains why agentic systems have become relevant now, why previous automation paradigms are reaching their limits, and how different agentic approaches can be understood conceptually. They establish a shared mental model rather than diving into implementation details. In Chapter 3 we explore concrete use cases across engineering domains, showing how multi-agent systems operate in practice and where industry-specific challenges emerge. Chapter 4 focuses on implementation, change management, operating models, risks, and limitations. The progression is deliberate: foundations first, practice second, scaling and governance last.

If you are looking for a catalogue of AI features, this book is not for you. If you are looking for a realistic, experience-based guide to understanding when and how agentic systems can become a durable engineering capability, you are in the right place.

One additional point is worth keeping in mind. Agentic systems are a young and rapidly evolving technology. Some techniques considered state of the art today may look different by the time you read this book. For that reason, both the theoretical and practical chapters stay conceptual where possible. The goal is not to document transient implementation details, but to convey patterns, principles, and ways of thinking that remain relevant over time. Read this book as guidance for finding your own path, not as a fixed recipe.

If you are wondering whether AI agents were used to writing this book, the answer is yes. Of course they were, but that does not mean the book was written by AI. We used AI to brainstorm, to refine structure, and to improve clarity and flow. The content itself comes from experience. And, as you will see throughout the book, this is exactly where agentic AI creates value. It handles repetitive and tedious tasks, surface alternatives, and makes suggestions. **Humans decide. Humans take responsibility**.

2 Foundations of AI Agents

Every engineering leader has encountered this moment: A vendor walks into the room, drops the phrase "AI-powered automation," and promises to cut development cycles in half. Your team nods politely. The procurement department starts asking about ROI. And somewhere in the back of your mind, a question nags: Do I actually understand what's under the hood well enough to know if this is real or theatre?

You're not alone. The gap between AI hype and engineering reality has never been wider, and it's never been more expensive to get wrong. Companies are committing millions to agent-based systems that sometimes amount to little more than a chatbot with a fancy wrapper, while others are quietly deploying AI agents that are genuinely transforming how products get designed, costed, and manufactured. The difference between the two isn't magic—it's architecture, and architecture is something engineering leaders can learn to read. This chapter gives you that literacy.

2.1 Conceptual Framework

Before we dive into transformers, tool integration, and memory architectures, we need a shared mental model for what an AI agent actually is and, just as importantly, what it isn't. The terminology in this space is a mess. "Agent," "copilot," "assistant," and "autonomous system" get used interchangeably by people selling very different things. If you and your team don't share a precise vocabulary, every architectural decision becomes a debate about definitions instead of trade-offs.

The conceptual framework in this section draws a clear line between three things that often get conflated: language models that generate text, assistants that respond to requests within a single turn, and agents that pursue goals across multiple steps by reasoning, using tools, and adapting when things go wrong. Each has its place in engineering workflows. Understanding where each capability starts and stops is what lets you make smart build-versus-buy decisions, set realistic timelines, and perhaps most critically know when someone on your team or across the table is overselling what their system can actually do.

2.1.1 Understanding Agentic AI for Engineering

To work effectively with agentic AI systems, engineering leaders need to understand what makes them work. One doesn't necessarily need to learn it at a depth that you need to derive backpropagation equations or debug transformer attention mechanisms. You do need sufficient technical literacy, though, to ask the right questions when engineers pitch agent solutions, to evaluate architectural choices when your team proposes implementations, and to set realistic expectations about what these systems can and cannot do.

This chapter demystifies the technology behind AI agents. We'll examine the large language models that provide agents with reasoning capability, and focus on their practical strengths and limitations rather than their internal mechanics. We'll explore how agents transform from chatbots that discuss problems into systems that solve them through tool integration, memory architecture, and coordination mechanisms. We'll understand what distinguishes true agentic systems from traditional automation, and why this distinction matters for engineering applications.

The goal is pragmatic understanding. When someone tells you their agent system uses "RAG with vector embeddings for context retrieval," you'll know they're describing how the agent finds relevant information from your past projects. When they mention "agentic workflows with tool orchestration," you'll recognize they're talking about agents that can actually run simulations and modify CAD models, not just suggest that you should. When they discuss "LLM-based reasoning with structured planning," you'll understand the trade-offs between flexibility and predictability that choice entails.

This understanding matters because the decisions you make now which models to use, how to integrate tools, what context to capture, which autonomy levels to permit will shape your organization's agent capabilities for years. The technology landscape changes rapidly, but the fundamental concepts remain stable. Understanding these foundations allows you to navigate the hype, evaluate options objectively, and build systems that deliver sustained value rather than impressive demos.

Modern engineering organizations operate with powerful software tools: CAD systems for modeling, simulation engines for behavior prediction, PLM platforms for revision tracking, and costing tools for detailed calculations. However, integrating these tools remains largely manual, time-consuming, and dependent on tacit knowledge held by individual engineers. This additionally represents a context problem along with a technology limitation. Agentic AI systems promise to bridge this gap by encoding organizational knowledge and orchestrating tool integration autonomously.

How We Got Here: A Brief History

Before examining agentic AI systems in detail, we need to understand how we arrived at this point. The application of computational intelligence to engineering has evolved through distinct eras, each building on the foundations of the last. Understanding this evolution clarifies both the capabilities of today's agent systems and their place in the engineering toolkit.

Statistics and Quality Control (1920s – 1980s)

The first wave of computational intelligence in engineering came through statistics. In the 1920s and 1930s, pioneers like Ronald Fisher and Walter Shewhart brought mathematical rigor to experimental design and quality control. Engineers learned to extract signal from noise, to design experiments that efficiently explored design spaces, and to quantify uncertainty in their predictions.

Statistical methods gave mechanical and industrial engineering several foundational capabilities. Design of experiments (DOE) allowed engineers to understand how multiple variables interacted to affect outcomes, identifying optimal operating conditions without exhaustively testing every combination. Response surface methodology enabled the creation of mathematical models relating inputs to outputs, allowing prediction and optimization within bounded regions. Statistical process control brought discipline to manufacturing, detecting when processes drifted out of specification before defects accumulated.

These methods were fundamentally about learning from data, but the learning was explicit and interpretable. An engineer could look at a regression model or a factorial design and understand exactly what it meant. The relationships were linear or low-order polynomial. The number of variables was manageable typically dozens, not thousands. The engineer remained firmly in control, using statistics as a tool to augment human reasoning, not replace it.

The limitations became apparent as systems grew more complex. Statistical methods struggled with high dimensionality when hundreds or thousands of variables interacted. Traditional experimental designs became impractical. They assumed relatively simple functional relationships, failing when the underlying physics was highly nonlinear or discontinuous. They required careful experimental design upfront, making them poorly suited for learning from messy historical data. In addition, they provided little capability for pattern recognition in unstructured data like images or sensor streams.

Machine Learning (1990s – 2000s)

The second wave emerged in the 1990s and 2000s as machine learning algorithms matured and computational power grew. Neural networks, support vector machines, decision trees, and ensemble methods brought new capabilities that statistical methods couldn't match. These algorithms could learn complex, nonlinear relationships directly from data without requiring engineers to specify the functional form. They could handle high-dimensional spaces, finding patterns among hundreds of input variables. They excelled at classification and pattern recognition tasks, identifying defects in manufacturing or predicting equipment failures.

For mechanical engineering, machine learning enabled surrogate modeling of expensive simulations. Instead of running thousands of finite element analyses to explore a design space, engineers could run a strategic sample, train a neural network on the results, and use that trained model for rapid what-if exploration. Manufacturing operations used machine learning for predictive maintenance, learning the signatures of impending failures from sensor data. Quality systems employed it for automated defect detection, training vision systems to identify problems that once required human inspectors.

Industrial engineering found perhaps even more applications. Production scheduling systems used reinforcement learning to optimize complex job shops. Supply chain models employed machine learning to forecast demand and optimize inventory. Facility layout problems used genetic algorithms and other ML-inspired optimization methods to search vast solution spaces.

Yet machine learning brought new challenges alongside its capabilities. Models became black boxes. A neural network with thousands of parameters might make excellent predictions, but explaining why it made a particular prediction was difficult or impossible. This created problems for safety-critical applications where explainability mattered. The models required substantial amounts of training data, which wasn't always available for novel designs or rare failure modes. They learned correlations but not causation, sometimes producing nonsensical predictions when extrapolating beyond training data. In addition, they had no inherent understanding of physical laws, occasionally violating conservation of energy or other fundamental principles.

Most critically for engineering applications, traditional machine learning operated in isolation from the engineering tools and workflows. You extracted data from CAD, simulation, or manufacturing systems, trained a model offline, and then manually integrated insights back into the design process. The model couldn't interrogate the CAD system directly, run its own simulations, or reason about broader engineering context. It was a powerful tool, but still just a tool requiring human orchestration.

Deep Learning (2010s)

The third wave began in the 2010s with the deep learning revolution. Convolutional neural networks achieved superhuman performance on image recognition. Recurrent networks handled sequential data like time series and text. Generative models learned to create novel designs, not just classify existing ones. Transfer learning allowed models trained on massive general datasets to be adapted to specific engineering tasks with relatively little domain data.

Deep learning enables new engineering applications. Computer vision applications that were impossible with traditional machine learning became routine detecting microscopic defects on machined surfaces, identifying weld quality from thermal images, reading and interpreting engineering drawings automatically. Generative design systems could propose novel geometries optimized for specific performance criteria, exploring topologies human designers might never consider. Time series models predicted equipment degradation and remaining useful life with high accuracy, thus changing maintenance strategies.

For mechanical engineering, deep learning enabled analysis of complex physical phenomena. Convolutional networks could be trained to predict stress distributions or fluid flow patterns directly from geometry, orders of magnitude faster than simulation. This enabled real-time design feedback that was previously impossible. Industrial engineering applied deep learning to process optimization, learning to control complex manufacturing processes with many interacting parameters.

Deep learning also amplified some of machine learning's challenges, though. Models grew even larger and more opaque. Training required massive datasets and computational resources, creating barriers to adoption. The models were brittle. A deep learning system trained to inspect parts from one production line might fail completely on parts from another line with slightly different lighting or surface finish. And like earlier ML approaches, deep learning systems remained isolated tools, not integrated participants in engineering workflows.

Physics-Informed Machine Learning

Recognizing the limitations of pure data-driven approaches, researchers developed physics-informed machine learning methods that combine the pattern-learning capabilities of ML with the fundamental constraints of physical laws. Physics-Informed Neural Networks (PINNs) embed differential equations describing physical behavior directly into the loss function during training, ensuring the learned model respects conservation laws and boundary conditions. Hybrid models combine physics-based simulation with data-driven corrections, using ML to capture phenomena the physics model approximates or omits. Multi-fidelity approaches blend expensive high-fidelity simulations with cheap low-fidelity models and empirical data, using ML to optimally combine information sources.

These methods address key weaknesses of pure ML approaches. By incorporating physical constraints, they require less training data, and the model doesn't need to learn conservation of mass from examples. It's built in. They extrapolate more reliably beyond training data because physics provides guardrails against nonsensical predictions. They're more interpretable because the physics component is transparent even if the data-driven component is opaque.

For mechanical engineering, physics-informed methods have enabled rapid solution of inverse problems determining what material properties or boundary conditions must exist to produce observed behavior. They've accelerated multi-scale modeling, using ML to bridge between atomic-scale material behavior and component-scale structural response. In industrial engineering, they've improved production models by combining theoretical queuing models with empirical data about actual system behavior, capturing effects the theory alone misses.

Yet physics-informed methods still share a fundamental limitation with all previous approaches: They remain tools to be wielded by human engineers. A physics-informed neural network can predict stress distributions, but it can't decide whether those stresses are acceptable, can't modify the geometry to reduce them, can't check if the new geometry is manufacturable, and can't update the cost estimate to reflect the changes. It operates within its narrow domain, waiting for a human to interpret results and orchestrate the next step.

Agents: Where We are Now

This brings us to the current moment: the emergence of multi-agent systems powered by large language models. The distinguishing characteristic of this era is the integration of multiple capabilities into systems that can perceive, reason, act, and learn across the full engineering workflow.

Agents can understand natural language instructions and engineering documents, translating ambiguous requirements into concrete tasks. They can reason about problems that don't have clear precedent, combining retrieval of past solutions with logical inference about new situations. They can operate engineering tools directly reading CAD models, running simulations, querying databases, updating PLM systems by not just consuming extracted data but actively participating in workflows. They can communicate with each other and with humans to maintain context across complex multi-step processes. In addition, they can learn from experience and improve their performance as they accumulate organizational knowledge.

This integration enables capabilities that previous approaches lacked. Previous AI systems optimized within domains a better surrogate model, a more accurate defect detector, and a faster topology optimizer. Agent systems can orchestrate across domains, coordinating geometry generation, simulation, cost estimation, manufacturability assessment, and documentation in an integrated workflow. They can handle the messy, context-dependent decisions that dominate real engineering work—not just the clean optimization problems, but the judgment calls about what's "good enough," what risks are acceptable, or what trade-offs align with business priorities.

The statistical era taught us to learn from data rigorously. The machine learning era taught us to find complex patterns. The deep learning era taught us to see and generate. The physics-informed era taught us to marry data and domain knowledge. The agent era is teaching us to build systems that integrate these capabilities into workflows that mirror how engineering organizations actually operate, collaborative, context-aware, and adaptive.

Agents differ from previous AI technologies not because they're smarter at any individual task, but because they can bridge between tasks, maintain context, and participate in the full complexity of engineering work.

The CAD systems, PLM platforms, and simulation packages available today are powerful, but they are also widely available. Any organization with sufficient budget can acquire the same tools. What differs between organizations is not the tools themselves but the accumulated knowledge about how to use them effectively, the lessons learned from past projects, the understanding of specific customer requirements, and the awareness of manufacturing capabilities and supply chain constraints.

This organizational knowledge has traditionally been difficult to capture systematically. It resides in the experience of senior engineers, in informal processes, in institutional memory that walks out the door when people retire or change jobs. Multi-agent systems offer a new approach: They provide an architecture for encoding this contextual knowledge in a form that software systems can access and apply.

This chapter covers the foundational concepts. We examine what autonomy means in the context of engineering agents, how multiple agents coordinate their activities, and how communication patterns preserve context across complex workflows. These principles inform the practical implementation decisions covered in later chapters.

2.1.2 What Is an Agent?

Understanding what makes software "agentic" requires examining both the technical components and the conceptual foundations. This section establishes a comprehensive view of agents by exploring the underlying technologies, the transformation from language models to action-taking systems, and the essential components that every agent requires.

Large Language Models

At the heart of today's AI agents sit large language models or LLMs—neural networks trained on massive amounts of text data to understand and generate human language. LLMs function as sophisticated pattern-matching systems that learned the statistical structure of language by processing billions of documents, books, websites, and conversations.

When you write a prompt to an LLM, say, "Analyze this stress concentration and suggest design modifications," the model doesn't "understand" stress or geometry in the way a mechanical engineer does. Instead, it recognizes patterns in your prompt that match patterns it saw during training. It's encountered thousands of discussions about stress concentrations during its training in engineering textbooks, technical papers, design guidelines, online forums. It learned that when discussing stress concentrations, certain concepts tend to appear together: fillet radii, stress concentration factors, material properties, failure modes. It learned the mathematical relationships, the design principles, and the common solutions.

The model generates its response token by token one word or word-fragment at a time by predicting what would most likely come next based on all the context it has seen. This prediction isn't random guessing, it's informed by the patterns learned from billions of examples. The model has internalized that after someone mentions a sharp internal corner causing high stress, the next logical discussion typically involves suggesting increased fillet radii, showing the calculation of stress concentration factors, or recommending finite element analysis.

Modern LLMs achieve their capabilities through their size: billions or even trillions of parameters that capture nuanced patterns and their training on diverse, high-quality data. They can discuss mechanical engineering principles, write code, interpret specifications, draft reports, and reason through multi-step problems. They demonstrate what appears to be understanding even though they're fundamentally pattern-matching machines.

However, LLMs have important limitations that engineering leaders must understand. They sometimes "hallucinate," generating confident-sounding information that's completely wrong. They learned patterns from their training data, which might include incorrect information or outdated practices. They don't inherently know your company's specific context, design standards, or engineering heritage. They can't perform precise calculations reliably. Although they understand the concept of calculating a stress concentration factor, asking them to compute one numerically may yield incorrect results. And crucially, they have no way to verify their outputs against physical reality, unless given tools to do so.

The Transformer Architecture

The technical foundation enabling LLMs is called the transformer architecture, introduced in a seminal 2017 paper titled "Attention Is All You Need." While mathematical details aren't essential for engineering leaders, understanding the core concept is valuable.

Previous neural network architectures processed text sequentially one word at a time, maintaining a running summary of what came before. This created problems with long-range dependencies. If a critical detail appeared at the beginning of a long document, the model might "forget" it by the time it processed text at the end.

Transformers solve this through a mechanism called "attention." Rather than processing text strictly sequentially, the transformer can look at all parts of the input simultaneously and determine which parts are most relevant to understanding each element. When processing the word "it" in a sentence, the attention mechanism figures out which earlier noun "it" refers to. When analyzing a design requirement, attention allows the model to connect that requirement to specifications, constraints, and context mentioned thousands of words earlier in the conversation.

This attention mechanism enables transformers to handle much longer contexts than previous architectures. Modern LLMs can process tens or even hundreds of thousands of words at once, to maintain coherent understanding across entire documents. For engineering applications, this means an agent can read a complete design specification, remember all requirements simultaneously, and generate responses that account for constraints mentioned anywhere in the document.

The transformer architecture also enables parallel processing during training, allowing these massive models to be trained on enormous datasets using clusters of powerful GPUs. This computational efficiency made modern LLMs economically feasible to develop.

From Language Models to Agents

A language model alone is just a sophisticated text generato. It can discuss engineering problems but can't actually do engineering work. The transformation from language model to agent requires adding several critical capabilities.

First, tool use. Modern LLMs can be taught to invoke external tools functions that perform actions outside the model itself. When properly designed, the LLM learns to recognize when a tool would be helpful and how to call it with appropriate parameters. For engineering applications, these tools might include CAD system APIs, simulation launchers, database queries, calculation functions, or any other software capability you want the agent to access.

The workflow typically looks like this: The agent receives a request ("Check if this bracket design meets strength requirements"). The LLM reasoning component recognizes that this requires several steps: retrieving the CAD geometry, extracting material properties, running stress analysis, and comparing results to requirements. It formulates tool calls to perhaps invoke a CAD reading function to get geometry, a database query to get material allowables, and a simulation API to run finite element analysis. Each tool returns results, which the LLM processes and incorporates into its reasoning. Finally, the agent synthesizes findings and communicates them back.

Second, memory and state management. Unlike a simple chat where each interaction is independent, agents need to remember context across conversations and even across sessions. They need working memory what's been discussed in the current interaction and long-term memory knowledge accumulated from past projects, decisions, and lessons learned. Implementing this requires infrastructure beyond the LLM itself: databases to store conversation history, vector databases to enable semantic search of past experiences, and systems to selectively retrieve relevant memories when needed.

Third, structured reasoning and planning. While LLMs can reason through problems in natural language, complex engineering tasks often benefit from more structured approaches. Modern agent frameworks implement reasoning patterns like "chain of thought" (explicitly breaking down problems into steps), "tree of thought" (exploring multiple solution paths), and "reflection" (having the agent critique its own proposed solutions). These patterns help agents tackle problems that require extended, systematic reasoning.

What Makes AI "Agentic"

The term "Agentic AI" distinguishes systems that can act autonomously from traditional AI that merely provides recommendations. The key difference is agency, which is the ability to take action, not just generate text.

A traditional AI chatbot might respond to "Optimize this design for manufacturing cost" with suggestions: "Consider reducing the number of unique fasteners, simplifying this geometric feature, or changing to a more standard material." That's helpful, but it requires a human to implement each suggestion, verify the impact, and iterate.

An agent with true agency would actually perform those optimizations. It would access the CAD model, systematically explore modifications, run cost estimates for each variation, check that performance requirements still hold, and present optimized options ready for human review. Human's role shifts from doing the optimization to directing it and evaluating results.

This autonomy requires several capabilities working together. The agent must decompose high-level goals into actionable subtasks understanding that "optimize for cost" implies exploring material alternatives, geometry simplifications, and manufacturing process changes. It must sequence these subtasks appropriately, recognizing that some explorations can run in parallel while others depend on earlier results. It must handle failures gracefully. If a proposed modification creates a geometric error, the agent should recognize this and try alternative approaches rather than simply reporting failure. And critically, it must know when to escalate to humans when uncertainty is high, when stakes are significant, or when the problem exceeds its capabilities.

The progression from passive AI tools to agentic systems represents a different approach in how we interact with computation. Instead of tools that require human orchestration at every step, these systems can orchestrate themselves, with humans providing high-level direction and oversight. This shift delivers measurable efficiency gains. Tasks that previously required four hours of manual coordination as gathering CAD screenshots, extracting simulation results, compiling cost estimates, and checking compliance against standards can be reduced to fifteen minutes of agent execution with human review. Engineers who spend 30 percent of their time on routine documentation and data gathering can redirect that effort toward creative problem-solving and innovation. The automation doesn't eliminate engineering judgment. It eliminates the repetitive mechanics that consume time without requiring expertise.

The Five Components

Every AI agent contains five core components (Figure 2.1):

1. the brain (large language model)
2. the hands (tools)
3. the memory (context storage)
4. the senses (input processing)
5. the voice (output generation)

Some implementations add more components planning modules, reflection mechanisms, and specialized reasoning engines but these five are the foundation. Let's examine each one.

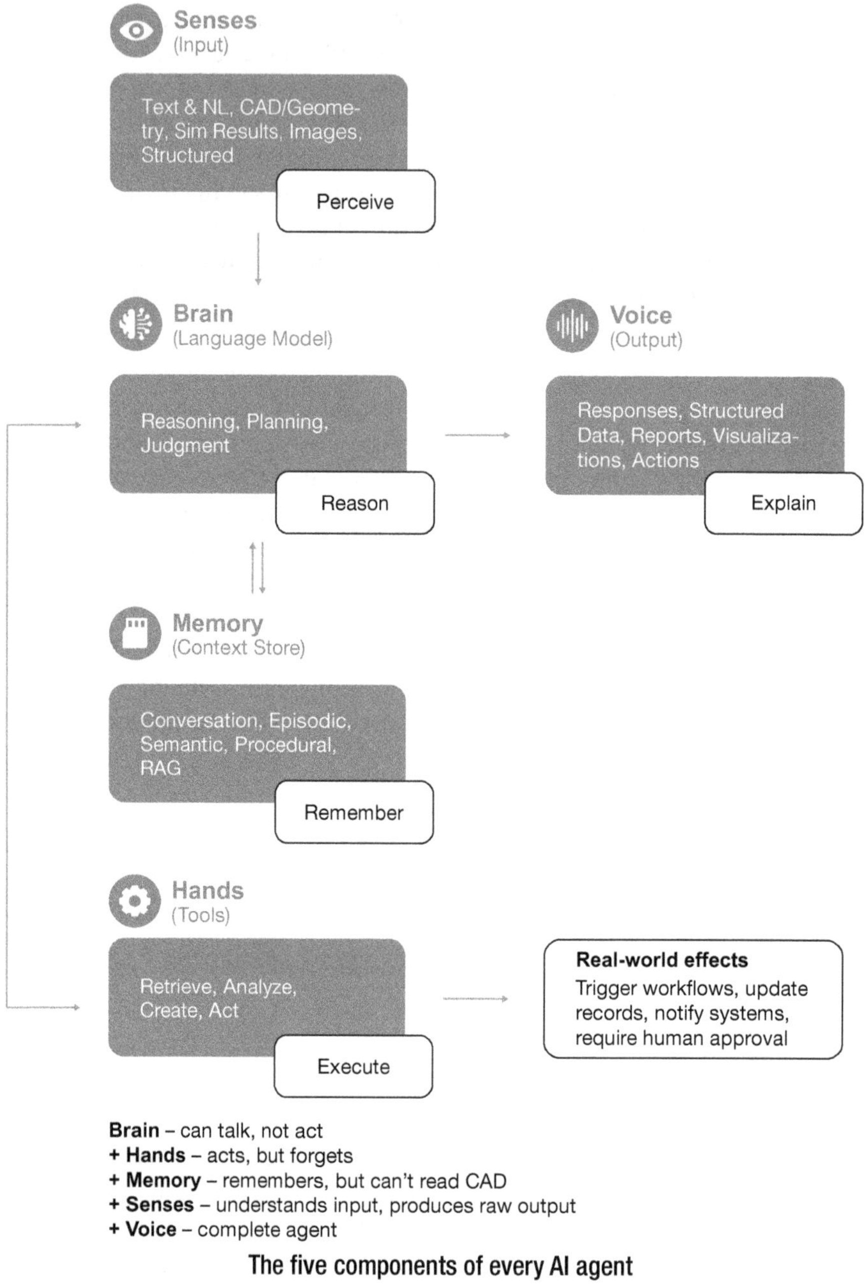

Figure 2.1 The five foundational components of every AI agent—senses for perceiving diverse engineering inputs, a language model brain for reasoning and planning, memory for context retention, tools as hands for real-world execution, and voice for communicating outputs—progressively combined to form a complete agent (© Iryna Novoseletska)

The Brain (Language Model)

The large language model provides modern agents with flexibility and natural language capability. It's the component that understands requests, reasons about problems, and generates responses. However, calling it "the brain" can be misleading. A better analogy might be "the intern."

Consider a talented new hire. They're smart, well-educated, and capable of learning quickly. They have general knowledge about many topics. They can understand what you're asking and attempt to help. However, they don't know your specific systems, your company's history, your customers, or your unwritten rules. They need guidance, supervision, and context.

An LLM operates similarly. It has broad capabilities but no specific expertise in your domain. It can reason about problems but doesn't know your constraints. It can generate plausible answers but doesn't know which answers are actually correct for your situation. This is why the other components are necessary. The LLM alone is insufficient. Without tools, it can only discuss actions rather than execute them. Without memory, it forgets everything between conversations. Without proper input, it doesn't understand the situation. Without appropriate outputs, its insights don't translate into action.

Engineering applications impose specific requirements on language models that differ from general-purpose chatbot applications. First, reasoning capability matters because engineering problems require multi-step logical chains. Models must maintain coherent thought processes across complex analyses and understanding that stress concentration depends on geometry, which affects factor of safety, which determines whether the design meets the requirements. Second, tool use ability determines whether the model can actually invoke CAD systems, simulation engines, and databases effectively. This capability varies significantly across models. Some reliably call tools with correct parameters while others struggle with complex function signatures. Third, context window size constrains how much information the model can consider simultaneously. Engineering documents specifications with hundreds of requirements, simulation reports with detailed results, or design reviews spanning multiple components can be large. Larger context windows allow the model to maintain awareness of all relevant information without losing critical details. Fourth, instruction following ensures the agent adheres to procedures precisely. Engineering workflows often have mandatory steps, required checks, and specific sequences that cannot be skipped or reordered. Finally, domain knowledge varies considerably across models. Some have strong foundational understanding of engineering principles, physics, and mathematics from their training data, while others lack this grounding and produce technically nonsensical suggestions.

The LLM landscape evolves rapidly. Current leading models include GPT-4, Claude, and others. By the time you read this, there may be new options. The key is understanding what capabilities you need and evaluating the models against those requirements.

For CAD engineers beginning to work with agents, a practical starting point is testing the agent's understanding of geometric relationships. Ask it to explain how fillet radii affect stress concentration or how draft angles impact moldability. If the agent can discuss these concepts correctly, it likely has sufficient domain knowledge. If it produces confused or contradictory responses, the underlying model may lack engineering fundamentals necessary for reliable operation.

The Hands (Tools)

An agent without tools is limited to text generation. Tools provide interfaces between the agent and external systems, enabling the agent to read information from databases and files, execute operations in software systems, run calculations and simulations, communicate with other systems and agents, and perform actions that have real-world effects.

Engineering agents require four broad categories of tools, each serving distinct purposes in the workflow. Information retrieval tools provide access to data scattered across the organization with querying databases for parts, materials, costs, and specifications; reading files containing CAD models, documents, and drawings; searching knowledge bases that capture standards, best practices, and past projects; and accessing external sources like supplier catalogs and material databases. These tools function like a research assistant who knows where every piece of information lives and can retrieve it on demand.

Analysis tools enable agents to evaluate designs and predict behavior. They run simulations for stress, thermal, fluid dynamics, and multi-physics analyses; perform calculations for weight, cost, and performance metrics; check compliance against design rules, standards, and regulations; and evaluate manufacturability through process checks and tolerance analysis. For simulation engineers, accustomed to manually setting up every analysis, agents with these tools can automate routine setup while escalating unusual cases for human review letting you focus your expertise where it matters most.

Creation tools allow agents to generate artifacts rather than just analyze existing ones. They generate geometry through parametric models and configurations, create documents including reports, specifications, and work instructions, produce 2D drawings from 3D models, and build visualizations such as renderings and animations. This generative capability transforms agents from passive evaluators to active contributors in the design process.

Action tools give agents the ability to affect real workflows and data systems. They submit workflows for engineering changes and approvals, update records in PLM systems and bills of materials, send communications through notifications and requests, and trigger downstream processes like releases and manufacturing orders. These tools carry the most risk because they create consequences beyond the agent's immediate scope, which is why they typically require human approval before execution.

Tools require contextual information to function effectively beyond their core functionality. Consider a tool that queries your cost database. A basic implementation returns raw numbers such as material cost per kilogram, machining time per feature, or assembly labor rates. A context-aware implementation provides much more: current cost model assumptions explaining which overhead factors are included, typical accuracy expectations at this design stage (conceptual estimates might be ±30 percent while detailed designs achieve ±10 percent), commonly underestimated cost elements specific to your manufacturing processes (setup time for small batches, tooling amortization for custom features), historical benchmark comparisons showing how similar components actually cost versus initial estimates, and product line margin expectations that determine whether a cost figure is acceptable or requires redesign.

The tool itself might just be a simple database query, but the wrapper that the agent uses should provide context. This requires encoding organizational knowledge into the tool interface. For product development engineers who implement agent tools should start by documenting what experienced engineers know, that novices don't, about each tool's outputs. When a senior engineer looks at a cost estimate, what questions do they ask? What red flags do they look for? What contextual factors do they consider? Encoding these insights into tool wrappers makes agents behave more like experienced team members and less like interns blindly reading numbers.

The Memory

Humans remember things. We remember past conversations, previous decisions, lessons learned, and relationships between concepts. This memory is essential for intelligent behavior. Without it, we'd have to start from scratch every time.

Early AI systems had limited memory to whatever fit in a single prompt. This made them feel stateless and shallow. Modern multi-agent systems use several types of memory, each serving distinct purposes. Conversation memory maintains the record of the current interaction, and what has been discussed, decided, and planned. This enables coherent multi-turn conversations where the agent remembers earlier points without requiring the user to repeat context. Session memory persists across conversations within a session or project, allowing the agent to remember decisions from earlier in the day even across multiple separate conversations. This prevents the frustrating experience of explaining the same context repeatedly.

Episodic memory captures records of past experiences, enabling the agent to recall that "last time we tried this approach on a similar bracket, and it didn't work because the weld access was insufficient." Learning from history prevents repeating mistakes and surfaces relevant precedents. Semantic memory contains structured knowledge about the domain. Not specific episodes, but general facts and relationships. The agent knows that aluminum alloys typically have density around 2.7 g/cm^3, that certain heat treatments affect hardness predictably, and that particular failure modes correlate with specific loading conditions. It learned these relationships from accumulated experience without necessarily remembering every individual instance. Procedural memory captures knowledge about how to do things such as workflows, best practices, and standard approaches. The agent knows that for a structural analysis of a bracket, you typically start by identifying load paths, establishing boundary conditions, selecting appropriate mesh density, and validating results against analytical approximations. Finally, retrieval memory through RAG (Retrieval-Augmented Generation) systems provides the ability to search and retrieve relevant information from large document collections, extending the agent's knowledge without requiring every detail to reside in the base model.

Memory needs to be both persistent and retrievable. Storing everything is insufficient. You need to find the right memories at the right time. This is where embedding technologies and vector databases prove valuable, enabling semantic search that finds memories conceptually related to the current situation, not just keyword matches. When an agent encounters a design challenge with a cast aluminum housing, it should retrieve experiences with similar housing even if they used different terminology or part numbers.

For engineering applications, memory should include past projects and their outcomes (which designs succeeded, which required expensive rework, etc.), design decisions and their rationales (why particular materials were selected, why certain features were shaped as they are, etc.), lessons learned and best practices (what approaches work reliably, what pitfalls to avoid, etc.), standard approaches and procedures (how your organization typically solves recurring problems), and company-specific knowledge and policies (manufacturing constraints, supplier relationships, regulatory interpretations, etc.). This represents a direct encoding of your organizational context into the agent's memory. The completer and more accurate this memory is, the more the agent behaves like an experienced member of your team rather than a generic AI. For engineering leaders, the practical implication is clear: budget time for knowledge capture, not just for software integration. The smartest agent with an empty memory provides generic advice. An adequate agent with rich organizational memory provides specific, contextually appropriate guidance.

The Senses (Input)

Agents need to understand inputs from multiple sources and in multiple formats. Text inputs include natural language from users, documents, emails, and specifications. While LLMs excel at natural language processing, engineering text poses unique challenges through domain-specific abbreviations (FOS for factor of safety, DFMEA for design failure mode and effects analysis), specialized terminology with precise technical meanings, and references to standards and drawings that require contextual knowledge to interpret correctly.

Structured data arrives as database records, spreadsheets, configuration files, and API responses. The agent needs to interpret structure and understand what the data means, not merely parse fields. A bill of materials isn't just a list of part numbers and quantities. It encodes design intent, manufacturing sequences, and assembly relationships that context-aware processing must recognize. CAD and geometry present particular challenges because LLMs don't natively understand spatial relationships. A 3D model, assembly, or drawing requires specialized interfaces or tools that translate geometric information into representations. The language model can reason about extracting features, relationships, dimensions, and design intent from spatial data.

Images and visualizations including photographs, renderings, diagrams, and screenshots become increasingly accessible as multi-modal LLMs mature. These models can now interpret images directly, opening possibilities for agents that can "see" designs identifying features in photographs, reading dimensions from drawings, or detecting anomalies in inspection images. Simulation results from FEA, CFD, and other physics-based analyses can be complex multi-dimensional datasets requiring specialized interpretation. An agent must understand not just that maximum stress is 450 MPa, but where that stress occurs, whether it's at a geometric feature or a mesh artifact, how it compares to material yield strength, and whether the analysis assumptions remain valid at that stress level.

Input processing must convert these diverse formats into representations the agent can understand while preserving relevant context and metadata. It must filter noise and extract signals, knowing that a CAD model's construction history matters less than its current geometric features, or that simulation convergence warnings require attention while routine solver messages don't. The processing must handle errors and inconsistencies gracefully, neither failing completely when encountering malformed data nor proceeding blindly with corrupted information. Finally, input processing connects new information to the agent's existing knowledge and recognizing when current inputs relate to past experiences or established patterns.

The Voice (Output)

Agents produce outputs that need to be understood by humans and consumed by systems. Natural language responses include answers to questions, explanations of analyses, and recommendations for decisions. These need to be clear, accurate, and appropriately detailed for the audience. A response to a senior engineer can assume deep technical knowledge and skip basic explanations, while a response to a program manager should focus on implications and trade-offs rather than technical minutiae.

Structured data outputs serve as parameters for tool calls, records for databases, and inputs for other systems. Here precision and format compliance matter critically. A slight mismatch in data structure can cause downstream system failures that manual outputs would avoid through human interpretation. Reports and documents including summaries, analyses, specifications, and proposals may need to follow organizational templates and standards. An agent-generated design review report should match the structure your team expects: the same sections, the same level of detail, and the same terminology so reviewers can find information where they're accustomed to looking.

Visualizations such as charts, graphs, and annotated images help communicate complex information quickly. An agent explaining stress distribution benefits from highlighting the maximum stress location on a color contour plot rather than describing it in text. Actions and triggers which include commands to other systems, workflow initiations, and notifications have real-world effects and need appropriate safeguards, as triggering a manufacturing release or updating a PLM record affects downstream processes and people.

Output generation must match the output to the audience in technical depth, terminology, and format. It should provide appropriate confidence levels and caveats rather than presenting all conclusions with equal certainty. Stating "based on preliminary analysis, the factor of safety appears adequate" differs meaningfully from "this design meets all structural requirements." Output should be actionable, providing not just information, but guidance about what to do with it. They must be traceable, connecting recommendations to evidence so engineers can understand the reasoning and verify the basis. Finally, output should be consistent. Similar situations produce similar outputs. This builds trust, while erratic behavior erodes confidence even when individual outputs are technically correct. For CAE engineers working with analysis agents, a practical guideline is requiring agents to cite specific result values, supporting their conclusions. If an agent claims a design is acceptable, it needs to reference the actual stress levels, safety factors, and acceptance criteria rather than making assertions without evidence.

How They Work Together

The components don't operate in isolation. They work together in a continuous cycle where each component enables the next. Input arrives and the senses process it into understandable form, converting raw CAD files, simulation results, or natural language into structured representations. Context is loaded from memory, providing relevant background about similar past situations, applicable design rules, and organizational constraints. Reasoning happens as the brain considers the input in context, determining what the request actually requires and what approach would be appropriate. Actions are determined as the brain decides what tools to use and in what sequence to address the request. Tools execute, performing actual operations like querying databases, running simulations, or modifying geometries. Results return and the senses process these tool outputs, interpreting what the simulation revealed or what the database query found. Memory updates with new information, stored for future reference: This design approach worked, that constraint proved binding, this analysis uncovered an issue. Output generates as the voice produces a response appropriate to the situation and audience. The cycle continues as needed until the task is completed, with each iteration building on previous results.

This cycle can repeat many times for complex tasks, with intermediate results informing subsequent reasoning and actions. A design optimization might iterate dozens of times, each cycle proposing a modification, analyzing its effects, comparing to requirements, and deciding whether to continue refining or present results. Understanding this cyclical nature helps engineering leaders recognize why agent responses sometimes take longer than simple database queries. The agent isn't just retrieving information, it's reasoning, acting, and learning in repeated cycles until it reaches a satisfactory conclusion.

The Agent Equation: Model + Tools + Context

When engineering leaders ask "what exactly is an agent?," the clearest answer is deceptively simple: An agent is the integration of a large language model, tools that enable action, and context that makes those actions meaningful. Understanding why each component is essential and what happens when any is missing clarifies both what agents can accomplish and what they cannot.

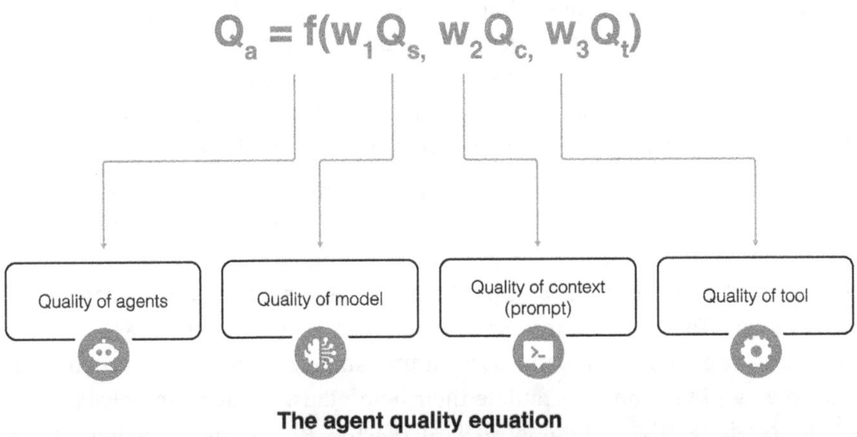

Figure 2.2 Agent output quality is a weighted function of four interdependent variables—the quality of the agent architecture, the underlying model, the context and prompts provided, and the tools available to act on the world (© Iryna Novoseletska).
Where:
Q_a = agent quality (overall system performance)
Q_s = quality of model (LLM capabilities, reasoning, accuracy)
Q_c = quality of context (organizational knowledge, prompt engineering)
Q_t = quality of tools (integration depth, reliability, coverage)
w_1, w_2, w_3 = weighting factors (task-dependent)

Key Insight:

- Agent quality is a multiplicative function, not additive.
- Weakness in any component degrades the entire system.
- Excellence in all three is necessary; no single component suffices.

The equation looks straightforward at first glance, but like many elegant formulas, its power lies in the interactions between components rather than the components themselves. This is not a simple sum, it's a multiplicative relationship where weakness in any dimension degrades the whole. A language model without tools can discuss engineering problems eloquently but cannot solve them. Tools without language models require explicit programming for every possible task. Context without tools remain locked in documents, inaccessible when decisions need to be made. Only the combination creates something genuinely useful for engineering work.

Consider what happens when you remove each component in turn. An LLM alone, GPT-4, Claude, Gemini, or any other model accessed through a simple chat interface can answer engineering questions impressively. Ask it about stress concentration factors, and it explains the theory, describes common causes, and suggests mitigation strategies. Ask it to review a design specification, and it identifies potential issues, questions ambiguities, and proposes improvements. This is valuable, but it's passive assistance. The LLM cannot retrieve the actual CAD geometry to examine. It cannot run a finite element analysis to quantify the stress concentration. It cannot update the PLM system to reflect design changes. It can advise but not act, which limits its utility for engineering workflows where action matters as much as advice.

Tools without LLM APIs to CAD systems, simulation engines, databases, and manufacturing systems provide automation but not intelligence. You can write scripts that invoke these tools in predefined sequences, and such automation delivers enormous value when workflows are stable and predictable. These scripts cannot adapt when situations change. They cannot interpret ambiguous requirements, reasons about novel problems, or explain their actions in natural language. They follow instructions they've been given but cannot formulate their own plans. In the terminology we've established, this is Level 1 autonomy, at best reactive execution of predetermined logic, not genuine agency.

Context without LLM and tools is perhaps the most frustrating situation of all. Your organization possesses decades of engineering knowledge such as design guidelines, lessons learned, material selection rationale, manufacturing constraints, supplier qualifications, and customer preferences. This knowledge lives in documents, emails, CAD files, simulation reports, and engineers' memories. Without an LLM, this context remains locked in its various formats, accessible only through manual search and human interpretation. Without tools to act on that context, even if you could retrieve relevant information, you'd still need humans to apply it manually. The knowledge exists but cannot be deployed effectively.

The combination creates capabilities that none of the components provide individually. The LLM brings reasoning and natural language understanding, which is the ability to interpret ambiguous requirements, make contextual judgments, explain decisions, and adapt to novel situations. Tools bring action, which is the ability to read CAD models, run simulations, query databases, update systems, and generate reports.

Context brings specificity, which is the knowledge of your manufacturing capabilities, your customer requirements, your design heritage, your hard-won lessons. Together, these components enable an agent to receive a high-level goal like "optimize this bracket for cost while maintaining strength," retrieve relevant design precedents from your project history, explore geometry modifications using CAD tools, evaluate each option through simulation, estimate costs using your costing models, identify the best solution while considering your specific constraints, and explain its recommendation in terms your engineers understand.

The quality of each component directly affects the agent's utility. A more capable LLM reasons better, handles more complex instructions, and makes fewer errors. More comprehensive tool integration expands what an agent can do. There is a fundamental difference between an agent that can only read CAD files and one that can modify them, run analyses, and update downstream systems. Richer context enables more sophisticated decisions. An agent with access to ten years of design history makes different choices than one working only from generic engineering principles.

This explains why "context is your competitive advantage" isn't mere rhetoric. Every organization will have access to the same LLMs. They are increasingly commoditized services available to anyone. Most engineering tools provide APIs or can be wrapped with modest effort. Tool integration is engineering work, but it's not proprietary insight. Context, however, is unique to your organization: the specific manufacturing processes your facilities support, the particular customer requirements your products must meet, the design approaches that have succeeded or failed in your product lines, the supplier relationships that affect your sourcing decisions, the regulatory interpretations that guide your compliance strategies. All this context cannot be purchased or downloaded. It must be captured, structured, and encoded deliberately.

The interaction between components creates emergent capabilities worth examining explicitly. When an LLM has tools but limited context, it can perform engineering tasks but in generic ways that may not align with your organization's realities. It might suggest a design optimization that's theoretically optimal but requires manufacturing processes your facilities don't support. It might recommend a material that's excellent on paper but that you've deliberately avoided due to past supply chain problems. The actions are technically correct but contextually inappropriate.

When an LLM has context but limited tools, it can provide highly specific advice but cannot implement it. It might tell you exactly how to modify a design based on your organization's specific constraints and history, but you still must manually open the CAD system, make the changes, run the simulations, update the documentation. The advice is valuable, but the process remains labor-intensive. This situation characterizes many early deployments of LLMs in engineering as sophisticated chatbots that engineers consult for guidance but that don't reduce the manual effort of actually executing engineering tasks.

When tools and context exist but the LLM is insufficiently capable, the agent struggles with reasoning tasks that require nuanced judgment. It might successfully execute simple workflows to retrieve a design, to run a standard analysis, or to generate a report but fail when situations require adaptation. Faced with an unexpected simulation failure, a weak LLM might simply report the error rather than diagnosing the cause and adjusting the setup. Presented with conflicting requirements, it might not recognize the conflict or might propose solutions that don't actually resolve the tension. The infrastructure exists, but the intelligence to use it effectively doesn't.

This component framework also clarifies what different types of agents require. A simple retrieval agent needs primarily LLM capability and context which is the ability to understand questions and find relevant information from your knowledge base. Tools matter less because the agent isn't taking action beyond search. A workflow automation agent needs primarily tools and limited context because it's executing well-defined sequences where the LLM mainly handles error conditions and edge cases. A design optimization agent needs all three components working together: LLM reasoning to explore the design space strategically, tools to actually modify geometry and run analyses, and context to ensure optimizations respect your organization's specific constraints and preferences.

The equation also helps diagnose agent failures. When an agent produces poor results, the question becomes: Which component is inadequate? Did the LLM misunderstand requirements or reason incorrectly? Did the tool integration fail, providing bad data or executing commands wrong? Did context gaps lead the agent to make decisions that don't reflect organizational realities? Each failure mode requires different remediation as improving prompts, fixing integrations, or capturing more context.

Looking forward, the relative importance of components will shift as technology evolves. LLM capabilities are advancing rapidly. Models from eighteen months ago seem primitive compared to today's frontier models, and the pace isn't slowing. This means the LLM component of the equation will become increasingly powerful and, paradoxically, less of a differentiator. Every organization will have access to excellent language models. Tool integration will standardize as patterns mature and vendors provide better APIs, designed explicitly for agent access. What remains differentiating is context, the unique knowledge of how your organization operates, what your products require, what your customers value, and what you've learned through experience.

The agent equation is simple in form but profound in implications. Building effective agents requires deliberate investment in all three components, with particular attention to the one that provides enduring competitive advantage. You can buy the LLMs. You can integrate the tools. However, you must capture, structure, and maintain the context. That work which is unglamorous, often difficult, definitely time-consuming, separates agents that impress in demonstrations from agents that deliver sustained value in production.

2.1.3 Deterministic vs. Autonomous Agents

The Spectrum of Agent Control

When engineering organizations first encounter "agentic AI," a common question arises: How is this different from the automation we've been implementing for years? The answer lies in understanding the fundamental distinction between deterministic, flow-based agents and non-deterministic, autonomous agents powered by large language models.

This distinction shapes which problems each approach solves effectively, what risks they introduce, and how you design systems that combine both philosophies appropriately. Most successful agent deployments in engineering don't choose one approach exclusively. They architect hybrid systems that use deterministic logic where predictability matters and autonomous reasoning, where flexibility provides value.

Deterministic Flow-Based Agents

Deterministic agents follow predefined decision trees, workflows, or rule sets. Given the same inputs, they always produce the same outputs by executing the same sequence of steps. This category includes traditional robotic process automation (RPA), scripted workflows, business process automation, and rule-based expert systems that dominated AI applications before the current machine learning era.

Consider classic engineering automation: a design rule checker that validates CAD models against geometric constraints. The logic is explicit and deterministic. If the wall thickness is less than the minimum specification, flag error. If hole diameter is not in the standard set, flag warning. If the draft angle is less than the required value, flag manufacturability concern. The checker follows its rules exhaustively and predictably. Given the same CAD model twice, it produces identical results.

This determinism offers significant advantages for engineering applications. Behavior is completely predictable and you know exactly what the system will do in any situation you've programmed it for. Results are reproducible across runs, which matters for validation, verification, and regulated environments that require audit trails. Debugging is straightforward because you can trace through the explicit logic to find where unexpected behavior originates. Certification and compliance are feasible because the complete decision logic can be documented, reviewed, and approved. Resource consumption is bounded because you control exactly what operations execute and in what sequence. These characteristics make deterministic automation the foundation of reliable, high-stakes engineering systems.

The limitations are equally clear. Deterministic agents cannot handle situations that are not explicitly programmed. Every possible condition, every edge case, every exception must be anticipated and coded. This creates brittle systems that fail when encountering novelty and engineering work involves substantial novelty. Maintaining these systems becomes burdensome as rule sets grow, with hundreds or thousands of if-then-else branches that interact in complex ways. Changes require programming effort; you cannot simply explain new requirements in natural language. The systems lack contextual understanding, applying rules mechanically without grasping whether those rules make sense in a particular situation. They also provide no natural language interface. Interaction requires structured inputs, buttons, forms, or API calls rather than conversation.

Non-Deterministic Autonomous Agents

LLM-powered autonomous agents operate fundamentally differently. They reason through problems using language models trained on vast corpora, generating responses probabilistically rather than deterministically (Figure 2.3). Given the same prompt twice, they might produce different responses not randomly, but because they're sampling from distributions of possible continuations, applying reasoning that isn't reducible to explicit rules.

Consider an autonomous agent asked to "review this bracket design for potential issues before we send it to manufacturing." The agent doesn't follow a predetermined checklist. Instead, it examines geometry, retrieves relevant context about similar past designs, reasons about what manufacturing processes this geometry implies, identifies potential concerns based on patterns it has learned, and explains its findings in natural language. The reasoning emerges from the LLM's learned representations, not from explicitly programmed logic.

This autonomy provides complementary advantages. The agent handles novel situations by reasoning from principles and patterns rather than requiring every case to be explicitly programmed. It understands natural language, enabling engineers to interact through conversation rather than formal interfaces. It provides contextual reasoning, considering not just whether rules are satisfied but whether the design makes sense given broader project context. It learns from examples by accumulating organizational knowledge in its memory and improving its responses based on feedback. In addition, it can explain its reasoning in ways humans understand, describing not just what it found but why it matters.

The trade-offs are equally significant. Behavior is less predictable. You cannot guarantee the exact sequence of checks the agent will perform or the precise phrasing of its response. Reproducibility is approximate rather than exact. Running the same request twice yields similar but not identical results. Debugging is harder because the reasoning happens inside large neural networks that resist easy interpretation. Certification and compliance face challenges when regulators ask "what exactly will your system do?" and the honest answer is "it depends on the situation." Resource consumption is variable and potentially unbounded. A complex request might trigger many LLM calls and tool invocations. In addition, the agent can hallucinate, generating confident-sounding outputs that are factually wrong.

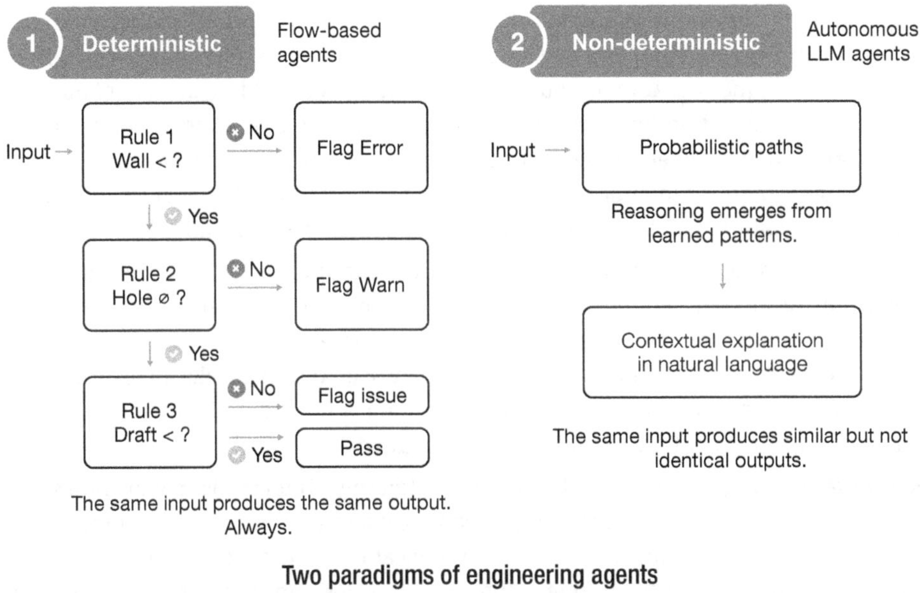

Figure 2.3 The two fundamental paradigms of engineering agents contrasted: deterministic flow-based agents that always produce the same output from the same input, and non-deterministic LLM agents that reason probabilistically and generate contextual natural language explanations (© Iryna Novoseletska)

When to Use Each Approach

The decision between deterministic and autonomous approaches should be driven by task characteristics rather than technology preferences. Several dimensions determine which approach fits better. Novelty and variability strongly favor autonomous agents. If every instance of a task is substantially similar, deterministic workflows work well. If each instance requires different approaches based on context, autonomous agents handle that variability more gracefully. A design rule check that validates the same ten geometric constraints on every model is deterministic territory. A design review that must identify whatever issues matter for this particular design in this particular context benefits from autonomous reasoning.

Criticality and risk tolerance create pressure toward determinism. High-stakes decisions where errors have severe consequences such as safety certifications, regulatory compliance verifications, or financial approvals typically demand the predictability and auditability that deterministic systems provide. Lower-stakes decisions where errors can be caught and corrected downstream can accept the autonomy-reliability trade-off differently. An agent that automatically runs and archives nightly simulation jobs can be more autonomous than one that approves designs for production release.

Explainability requirements matter differently for the two approaches. Deterministic systems can provide complete execution traces, showing exactly which rules fired and in what sequence. Autonomous systems provide natural language explanations that are more intuitive but less formally complete. When regulators require proof that every part was checked against every applicable standard, determinism wins. When engineers need to understand why a design might have thermal issues, autonomous explanation may be more useful even though it's less formally rigorous.

Development and maintenance costs favor different approaches at different scales. Deterministic automation requires upfront programming effort but minimal ongoing inference costs. Autonomous agents require less programming but consume LLM resources for every interaction. For high-frequency, well-defined tasks, investing in deterministic automation pays off. For lower-frequency tasks with high variability, autonomous agents avoid the programming investment.

Response time requirements will constrain autonomy. Deterministic workflows will execute predictably quickly because you control exactly what happens. Autonomous agents might need multiple LLM calls, tool invocations, and reasoning cycles that introduce variable latency. Real-time responses favor determinism; tasks that can wait seconds or minutes for thoughtful analysis can leverage autonomy.

Hybrid Approaches: The Best of Both

Most effective engineering agent systems employ hybrid architectures that combine deterministic and autonomous components strategically. Several patterns have emerged from practical deployments. The deterministic orchestrator pattern uses rule-based logic to decide which tasks to execute and in what sequence, while autonomous agents perform the tasks themselves. The workflow is predictable because you know the stages a design will go through, and how each stage executes and adapts to the specific design. A product development workflow might deterministically require concept generation, preliminary analysis, cost estimation, and design review, but you might use autonomous agents to perform each phase with flexibility appropriate to that particular product.

The autonomous router pattern inverts this: An LLM-based agent analyzes incoming requests and routes them to appropriate deterministic workflows. The routing decision requires contextual understanding that autonomous agents provide well, but execution follows deterministic paths that provide reliability. When an engineer asks for "help reducing the cost of this assembly," an autonomous agent interprets the request, examines the design, and routes to specific deterministic workflows, as perhaps a standard fastener substitution routine, a DFM analysis tool, or a material optimization script.

The fallback hierarchy pattern attempts autonomous processing first but falls back to deterministic logic for critical decisions. An autonomous agent might explore design alternatives creatively, but final validation against safety requirements follows deterministic checking. This preserves innovation where it adds value while protecting against autonomous errors in critical paths.

The guard rail pattern embeds deterministic checks around autonomous agents, verifying that agent outputs satisfy mandatory constraints before allowing them to proceed. The agent has freedom to reason and recommend within boundaries, but deterministic validators prevent violations of hard requirements. An agent optimizing a design might explore various geometries autonomously, but deterministic checks verify that wall thicknesses remain above minimums, that fastener spacing meets standards, and that materials come from approved lists.

The confidence-based switching pattern lets autonomous agents handle situations where they're confident and escalates to deterministic fallbacks (or human review) when confidence is low. The agent assesses its own certainty, perhaps based on how similar the current situation is to training examples, and switches modes appropriately. Routine situations get autonomous handling for efficiency. Edge cases get more rigorous as deterministic processing or human review.

Implementation Considerations

Building hybrid systems requires careful interface design between deterministic and autonomous components. Data formats must be compatible as deterministic systems expect structured data with specific schemas, while autonomous agents work naturally with unstructured text and can adapt to format variations. Reconciling these expectations requires translation layers that structure autonomous outputs for deterministic consumption and enrich deterministic data with context for autonomous interpretation.

Error handling semantics differs. Deterministic systems fail explicitly when encountering unexpected situations. Autonomous systems might attempt to handle the unexpected, sometimes successfully but sometimes producing subtle errors that deterministic systems would have flagged as explicit failures. Hybrid systems need clear policies about when to fail fast versus attempting autonomous recovery.

Logging and observability must serve both paradigms. Deterministic execution logs show which rules were fired and what data they processed. Autonomous agent logs capture natural language reasoning chains and tool invocations. Both are necessary for understanding system behavior, but they require different analysis approaches. Organizations need unified observability platforms that make sense of both execution traces and reasoning logs.

Testing strategies must address both deterministic and autonomous components. Deterministic logic can be tested exhaustively for coverage of decision branches. Autonomous agents require different testing approaches such as validation against representative examples, adversarial testing with edge cases, and statistical sampling to characterize behavior distributions. Test suites for hybrid systems need both approaches.

Change management processes differ as well. Updating deterministic logic requires code changes, testing, and deployment. Improving autonomous agents might involve prompt refinement, context enrichment, or model updates changes that don't always require traditional code deployment but still need governance and rollback capabilities.

Looking Forward

The engineering agent landscape is evolving toward sophisticated hybrid architectures that match control paradigms to task characteristics. Pure determinism provides reliability but brittleness. Pure autonomy provides flexibility but unpredictability. The systems delivering sustained value in production combine both, using deterministic logic for well-understood, high-stakes operations while leveraging autonomous agents for contextual reasoning and novel problem-solving.

For engineering leaders evaluating agent strategies, the key questions aren't "should we use deterministic or autonomous agents?" but rather "which aspects of our workflows benefit from deterministic guarantees and which benefit from autonomous flexibility?" The answer varies by industry, risk tolerance, regulatory environment, and specific use cases. Organizations succeeding with agents are those developing principled frameworks for making these decisions and architectures that compose deterministic and autonomous components cleanly.

The distinction between deterministic and autonomous agents will likely blur as technologies mature. Autonomous agents are becoming more reliable and auditable through techniques like constitutional AI and interpretability research. Deterministic systems are incorporating more adaptive behaviors through dynamic rule generation and learned heuristics. However, the fundamental trade-off—predictability versus flexibility, explicit logic versus learned patterns—will remain relevant for the foreseeable future. Understanding this trade-off positions you to architect agent systems that deliver the reliability engineering demands while capturing the flexibility that makes agentic AI transformative.

2.1.4 Types of Agents

Different agents require different levels of autonomy. Designing the appropriate level of autonomy for each agent is a key architectural decision in multi-agent systems. Insufficient autonomy results in complicated scripts. Excessive autonomy reduces control and predictability. The spectrum shown in Figure 2.4 ranges from simple reactive behavior to full collaborative partnership:

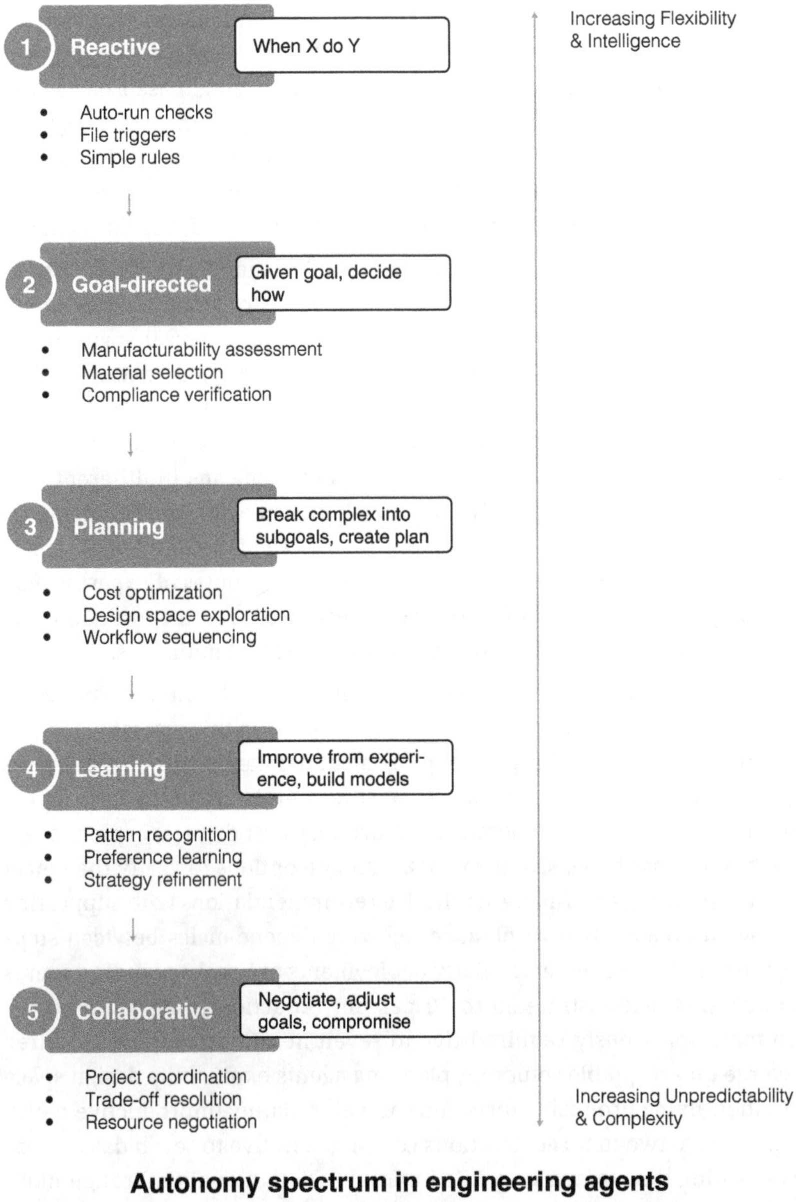

Figure 2.4 Engineering agents exist on a five-level autonomy spectrum, from simple reactive rules at one end to fully collaborative agents capable of negotiating goals and resolving trade-offs at the other—with increasing flexibility matched by increasing unpredictability (© Iryna Novoseletska).

At level 1, reactive agents respond to triggers with predefined actions: When X happens, do Y. An example is an agent that automatically runs a design rule check whenever a new CAD file is saved. This represents sophisticated automation that relieves engineers from remembering to perform routine checks and establishes infrastructure for agents to monitor engineering systems and take actions based on events. These reactive agents accelerate validation cycles by 40 to 60 percent, reducing what were previously twenty-minute manual checks performed inconsistently, to thirty-second automatic validations, performed on every save. Engineers catch errors immediately rather than discovering them during formal reviews hours or days later.

Level 2 agents are goal-directed and receive objectives rather than instructions. Instead of "run script A, then script B, then generate report C," the instruction becomes "check this design for manufacturability" and the agent decides how to achieve that goal based on the current situation. If the design is a sheet metal part, the agent checks bending radii, hole spacing, and flange clearances. If it's a machined part, the same high-level goal triggers different checks as tool access, undercut avoidance, and surface finish requirements. The agent understands what manufacturability means in different contexts and adapts its approach accordingly. Organizations deploying level 2 agents report reducing manufacturability assessment time from three hours of manual review by specialists to twenty minutes of agent analysis plus thirty minutes of expert validation. With that, they are freeing manufacturing engineers from routine evaluations to focus on complex process planning and continuous improvement initiatives.

Planning agents at level 3 can break complex goals into subgoals and determine the sequence of actions needed to achieve them. Asked to "optimize this assembly for cost while maintaining performance," a planning agent understands that this requires multiple steps executed in logical sequence. It must first understand the current design and baseline performance, then identify the primary cost drivers, explore alternative approaches to those expensive elements, simulate options to verify they meet performance requirements, and finally synthesize recommendations with supporting rationale. The agent creates its own plan, recognizing dependencies between steps and adjusting the plan if obstacles arise. Early deployments of Level 3 planning agents in design optimization demonstrate 50 to 70 percent reduction in iteration cycles. Where design teams previously required five to seven iterations over two to three weeks to converge on acceptable solutions, planning agents explore the design space systematically, identifying promising directions and eliminating unproductive paths, reducing the process to two to three iterations completed in five to seven days. These teams are accelerating time to market while improving design quality through more comprehensive exploration.

Learning agents at level 4 improve their performance over time based on experience. They identify patterns in which optimization strategies work best for certain types of designs. Topology optimization may be particularly effective for structural brackets but rarely improves cost for enclosures. They learn stakeholder preferences, recognizing that the manufacturing team consistently prefers design approaches that minimize setup changes, even at slight cost premiums. They build implicit models of how the system behaves, developing understanding of which designs will likely pass reviews, and which will require iteration. Each project improves performance on subsequent projects.

At level 5, collaborative agents can negotiate with other agents and humans, adjust their goals based on new information, and participate as team members in complex projects. They understand trade-offs across multiple objectives not just optimizing their own narrow domain but considering broader project success. They can advocate for certain solutions when they have strong technical rationale but can also compromise when other considerations outweigh their preferences. They recognize when their initial goals conflict with newly understood constraints and can propose alternative approaches that better balance all requirements.

Most practical multi-agent systems in engineering today operate at level 2 through level 4, with aspirations toward level 5 in specific domains. Different tasks require different levels of autonomy based on their complexity, stakes, and the degree of novelty involved. A design rule checker validating geometry against established standards might appropriately be level 1 or level 2. The rules are well-defined and the judgment is deterministic. A cost optimization agent working within a complex design space with multiple constraints might need level 3 with capabilities to plan and execute a multi-step exploration. A project coordination agent managing resources and schedules across teams might require level 5 and comes with capabilities to negotiate conflicts and adapt to changing priorities.

Why Context Matters

Autonomous agents require organizational context to make appropriate decisions. Consider an agent tasked with selecting materials for a component. Without context, it might optimize purely for cost and select the cheapest material that meets the specified mechanical requirements. With organizational context, it might know that

- the primary customer has banned certain suppliers for quality reasons,
- the manufacturing facility cannot process certain alloys,
- there is a strategic initiative to standardize on a smaller set of materials,
- the lead time for exotic materials would delay the project past an immovable deadline,
- a similar component failed in the field three years ago due to corrosion, and the company has a policy to over-specify corrosion resistance as a result.

This context is not in engineering textbooks or encoded in material databases, but it is essential for making appropriate decisions. An autonomous agent without this context operates with incomplete information.

Building effective multi-agent systems requires substantial investment in context capture and transfer. The underlying AI models and integration tools are widely available. What determines the effectiveness of a particular implementation is how well it captures and applies organization-specific knowledge.

Getting the Level Right

When designing agents for engineering workflows, several questions determine whether autonomy has been calibrated correctly for each task. These questions address risk, context, limitations, and feedback.

First, consider what decisions this agent can make safely on its own. Some decisions have limited consequences. If the agent gets it wrong, the results are minor and easily corrected. An agent that mis-categorizes a part for inventory purposes creates a small administrative issue. An agent that approves a design change affecting safety-critical components, could have serious consequences. Design agents with guardrails appropriate to the stakes. Low-stakes decisions can proceed autonomously with periodic human review. Medium-stakes decisions might require confirmation before execution. High-stakes decisions should always involve human judgment, with the agent serving as a recommender and analyst rather than a decision-maker.

Second, map out what information this agent needs to make good decisions. This context mapping exercise often reveals how much institutional knowledge remains undocumented. Some context might be readily available in databases and documents such as material properties, cost models, and design standards. Some context must be extracted from experts, through interviews and observation, as the judgment calls that distinguish good designs from adequate ones, or the unwritten rules about what customers actually require versus what they specify. Some context might need to be inferred from historical data through pattern analysis such as which design approaches tend to succeed for which types of products, and which suppliers reliably deliver quality versus which require extra scrutiny. The completeness and accuracy of this context mapping directly determine the quality of agent decisions.

Third, determine how this agent will know when it is out of its depth. Effective agents recognize situations they have not encountered before and escalate appropriately, rather than producing unreliable output. This capability epistemic humility is difficult to implement but essential for building trust. An agent that occasionally indicates "this situation is outside my experience; I recommend human review" is more valuable than one that always produces an answer regardless of uncertainty. Techniques include monitoring for inputs that deviate significantly from training data, tracking confidence levels in probabilistic reasoning, checking for internal contradictions in generated recommendations, and comparing the current situation to stored cases to quantify novelty.

Fourth, establish how this agent's decisions will be reviewed and corrected, especially in early deployment stages. Mechanisms are needed for humans to review agent decisions, provide feedback when they are wrong or suboptimal, and correct mistakes before they propagate. This feedback should flow back into improving agent performance and over time updating knowledge bases, refining decision criteria, adjusting confidence thresholds, and adding new cases to memory. The review process itself provides data about where agents struggle and where they excel and informs the continuous calibration of autonomy levels.

Autonomous agents should handle routine decisions that do not require senior expertise, allowing experienced engineers to focus on problems that require sophisticated judgment and creative problem-solving. They can only do this effectively if they understand enough context to know what "routine" means in the organization, and that definition of routine varies by product line, customer, development phase, and risk profile.

Liability and Accountability in Engineering Contexts

The deployment of autonomous agents in engineering raises fundamental questions about responsibility that organizations must address before operational issues force hasty decisions. When an agent approves a design that subsequently fails, when it recommends a material that proves unsuitable, or when it miscalculates a safety factor leading to product recall, who bears responsibility? The legal and organizational frameworks for these questions remain unsettled, but engineering leaders cannot wait for complete clarity before deploying agents. They must establish working frameworks that protect both, the organization and its stakeholders, while enabling the productivity gains that agents promise.

The liability question differs fundamentally from traditional engineering tool liability. When a finite element solver produces incorrect results due to a software bug, responsibility flows through established channels. The engineer who used the solver bears responsibility for validating results against expectations and engineering judgment. The software vendor may bear liability if the bug resulted from negligence or if the software was misrepresented. The organization that deployed the software bears responsibility for adequate training, appropriate use cases, and verification procedures. These liability frameworks evolved over decades and are well understood, even if occasionally disputed.

Agentic systems complicate this framework because agents make decisions rather than merely performing calculations. An FEA solver calculates stress distributions based on inputs the engineer provides. An agent might decide which mesh density to use, which boundary conditions to apply, whether the results are trustworthy, and whether the design meets requirements. Each of these decisions introduces a locus of potential failure and thus a question of responsibility.

The most straightforward framework treats agents as tools, no different in principle from any other engineering software. Under this view, the engineer who deploys the agent bears full responsibility for its outputs. The agent's recommendations must be validated, its logic must be understood, and its limitations must be respected. This framework has the advantage of clarity and consistency with existing practice. It places accountability where engineering judgment resides with human engineers who understand the stakes and possess the expertise to evaluate agent outputs critically.

However, this tool framework becomes strained when agents operate with substantial autonomy. If an agent makes thousands of routine decisions daily with only periodic human sampling, can the supervising engineer reasonably be held responsible for each one? If the agent's decision-making involves opaque neural network reasoning that cannot be fully inspected, how can engineers validate logic they cannot see? If the agent encounters a novel situation, which its designers never anticipated, and makes a decision no human explicitly approved, does treating it as a tool accurately reflect the agency it exercised?

An alternative framework treats certain agent actions as delegated authority rather than tool use. Under this view, an organization delegates specific decisions to agents much as it delegates decisions to junior engineers, with appropriate oversight and review mechanisms. The agent operates within a defined scope of authority, perhaps approving routine design changes below certain risk thresholds, selecting from pre-approved material options, or determining standard tolerance allocations. Within this scope, the agent exercises judgment. Outside this scope, it escalates to human decision-makers. Liability flows from how well the delegation was designed, how appropriately the scope was bounded, and whether adequate oversight mechanisms were in place.

This delegation framework aligns more naturally with how organizations actually deploy capable agents, but it introduces complexity. What constitutes appropriate scope? How is oversight adequacy determined? If an agent makes a thousand similar decisions and humans sample five percent for review, is that oversight sufficient? What if the sample happens to miss the one problematic decision? These questions lack universal answers and must be addressed in organizational context, considering risk tolerance, regulatory requirements, and stakeholder expectations.

Insurance and indemnification considerations add another dimension to liability questions. Professional liability insurance for engineering firms typically covers errors and omissions by licensed professionals and their employees. Whether this coverage extends to agent decisions remains an evolving question. Some insurers may view agents as tools covered under existing policies. Others may exclude agent-generated decisions unless humans review them. Still others may offer separate coverage for AI-augmented engineering at higher premiums, reflecting perceived increased risk or uncertainty. Organizations deploying agents must engage with their insurers early to understand coverage implications and potentially negotiate appropriate terms before liability events occur.

Regulatory and standards bodies are beginning to address these questions, though approaches vary by industry and jurisdiction. Aerospace regulators have historically required that all safety-critical decisions involve human judgment and signature authority. This creates natural limits on agent autonomy in aircraft: Design agents may recommend, analyze, and assist, but humans must approve. Medical device regulators similarly emphasize human oversight for safety-critical determinations. Automotive regulators grappling with autonomous vehicle questions are developing frameworks that may inform how engineering agents are regulated more broadly. They are establishing principles about transparency, auditability, and human override capability.

The distinction between agent-as-tool and agent-as-decision-maker often comes down to sign-off protocols. When an engineering deliverable requires a professional engineer's seal, that engineer accepts legal responsibility for the work's adequacy. If an agent contributed to that work, the signing engineer must be able to represent that they understand what the agent did, that the agent's contribution was appropriate, and that the result meets professional standards. This may require different levels of review depending on the agent's role. An agent that gathered and formatted information requires less scrutiny than one that made design decisions or performed safety-critical calculations.

Organizations deploying agents in safety-critical applications face the most stringent requirements and clearest constraints. An agent that influences the design of pressure vessels, medical implants, aircraft structures, or any product where failure risks life requires extraordinary caution. For these applications, several principles have emerged from early deployments and regulatory guidance. First, agents should remain at level 2 or level 3 autonomy maximum. They may be goal-directed or planning, but not learning in ways that could drift from established safe behaviors, and not collaborative to the point of negotiating safety requirements. Second, agent reasoning must be auditable, even if not fully transparent. While neural network internals may be opaque, the chain of evidence and reasoning that led to conclusions must be reconstructable. Third, human oversight must be mandatory for safety-critical determinations, not optional or sampling-based. Every decision that could affect safety must involve human review and approval. Fourth, validation must be extensive and ongoing agents must be tested against known cases, their performance must be monitored in operation, and any degradation or unexpected behavior must trigger review and potential restriction of authority.

These constraints limit how much productivity gain agents can deliver in safety-critical contexts, but they reflect the reality that society demands extraordinarily high reliability for products where failure risks life. Organizations in these domains report that, even within these constraints, agents still create value. They contribute through information synthesis, preliminary analysis, documentation automation, and decision support. What they do not take over is autonomous, safety-critical decision-making.

The practical approach for most engineering organizations involves establishing clear policies that address several key questions before deploying agents widely. First, categorize decisions by risk level: What are low-stakes decisions where agent autonomy is acceptable? What are medium-stakes decisions where agent recommendations require human confirmation? And what are high-stakes decisions where agents assist but humans decide? Second, define sign-off requirements: Which deliverables require professional engineer review and seal, and how must agent contributions be documented and validated? Third, establish audit trail requirements: What must be logged about agent reasoning and decisions to enable later review if questions arise? Fourth, create escalation criteria. Under what conditions must agents stop and request human judgment rather than proceeding autonomously? Fifth, determine validation procedures: How will agents be tested before deployment, how will their performance be monitored in operation, and what triggers will require revalidation? Sixth, work with legal counsel and insurers to understand liability implications, coverage questions, and any contractual or policy adjustments needed. Seventh, communicate with relevant regulatory bodies if your products or services are regulated, seeking guidance on acceptable agent use and any approval requirements.

The accountability questions extend beyond liability to organizational culture and professional responsibility. Engineers have professional and ethical obligations to protect public safety and welfare. When agents perform work that engineers would traditionally do, those obligations don't disappear, they evolve. Engineers must ensure they understand agent capabilities and limitations, that they validate agent outputs appropriately, that they don't abdicate judgment to systems that lack the ethical framework human professionals bring, and that they maintain the competence needed to evaluate agent work critically.

This raises workforce development questions. If agents handle routine calculations and standard analyses, how do junior engineers develop the expertise to evaluate those outputs? If agents automate tasks that were learning experiences, how do engineers develop judgment? Organizations deploying agents must consciously design development paths that preserve skill building, even as automation changes what tasks humans perform. The senior engineer who can evaluate an agent's structural analysis developed that expertise by performing thousands of analyses personally. The next generation needs different, but equally rigorous development, to achieve equivalent expertise.

The long-term trajectory points toward frameworks that treat agent capability and authority as continua rather than binary categories. Low-autonomy agents operating on low-stakes decisions with extensive logging may require minimal special treatment beyond normal tool validation. High-autonomy agents operating on consequential decisions will require governance frameworks approaching those for human professionals: defined scopes of practice, ongoing competence evaluation, professional oversight, and clear accountability mechanisms. Organizations will likely develop internal classification systems for agents, much as they have job levels for engineers, with authority and oversight calibrated to agent capability and decision stakes.

What remains clear is that deploying agents without addressing liability and accountability is organizationally reckless. The questions are complex and answers are evolving, but uncertainty is not permission to ignore them. Engineering leaders must establish working frameworks now, accept that those frameworks will mature as experience accumulates and regulations develop, and recognize that accountability for agent decisions ultimately flows back to the organization and the humans who deployed those agents. The goal is not to achieve perfect certainty about liability before proceeding. Such certainty will not arrive. The goal is to proceed thoughtfully with appropriate safeguards, clear policies, and ongoing attention to these questions as operational experience reveals what works and what requires adjustment.

2.1.5 Multi-Agent Systems

While individual agents provide value, many engineering workflows require multiple specialized agents working together. This section explores how agents coordinate, communicate, and are architected into cohesive systems.

The Coordination Problem

Autonomy is powerful, but autonomy alone isn't enough. Real engineering work requires multiple perspectives, multiple skills, and multiple tools. A single agent, no matter how sophisticated, can't hold all the knowledge needed for complex engineering projects. This is where multi-agent systems (MAS) become interesting. Instead of building one super-agent that tries to do everything, you build a team of specialized agents that work together. One agent understands CAD geometry. Another understands manufacturing processes. Another knows your cost models. Another tracks project schedules. Together, they can tackle problems that would be impossible for any single agent.

However, here's the challenge: How do you get multiple autonomous entities to work together effectively? If each agent is making its own decisions based on its own goals and information, how do you prevent conflicts, duplicated work, or outright contradictions? This is the coordination problem, and it's been studied extensively in both computer science and organizational theory. We have well-established patterns that work. However, implementing them well requires careful design.

Four Coordination Patterns

The first pattern, hierarchical coordination, represents the simplest and most familiar approach (Figure 2.5). One agent acts as coordinator, delegating tasks to specialist agents and synthesizing their results. This mirrors traditional management structures and carries intuitive appeal for organizations with established hierarchies. Consider a design review agent that receives a new design and breaks the review into functional components. It delegates geometry validation to the geometry agent, manufacturability assessment to the manufacturing agent, cost estimation to the cost agent, and standards compliance to the standards agent. Each specialist performs its focused task and reports results back to the coordinator, which compiles everything into a unified assessment.

This pattern offers clear advantages. Lines of responsibility are unambiguous. You always know which agent made which decision. The coordination logic is easy to understand and debug because information flows through well-defined channels. The pattern maps naturally to organizational structures, making it easier for engineering teams to reason about agent behavior. However, hierarchical coordination also has notable weaknesses. The coordinator becomes a potential bottleneck as all communication flows through it, limiting the throughput. The pattern handles unexpected situations poorly because specialists can't adapt independently. They must wait for coordinator direction. Specialists also can't easily communicate with each other, preventing the kind of direct peer collaboration that often proves valuable in engineering problem-solving.

Market-based coordination offers greater flexibility through decentralized task allocation (Figure 2.5). In this pattern, tasks are announced to a pool of capable agents, which bid based on their capabilities and current availability. The best bid wins the work. When a new engineering change request arrives, for instance, the system broadcasts the requirements. Various agents evaluate their fit. Perhaps the thermal agent has relevant expertise but heavy current load, the structural agent has capacity but less direct experience, and the multi-physics agent offers both strong capability and availability. Through the bidding process, work naturally flows to where it can be handled most effectively.

This pattern provides dynamic load balancing, automatically distributing work based on real-time capacity and capability. It's resilient to agent failures because work simply gets bid to other agents. It encourages agents to specialize in areas where they can consistently win bids. Yet market-based coordination introduces overhead in the bidding process itself. Agents must evaluate opportunities, formulate bids, and participate in selection. This behavior can be less predictable than hierarchical coordination, which some organizations find uncomfortable. Success requires carefully designed bidding rules that properly value different dimensions like quality, speed, cost, and current load.

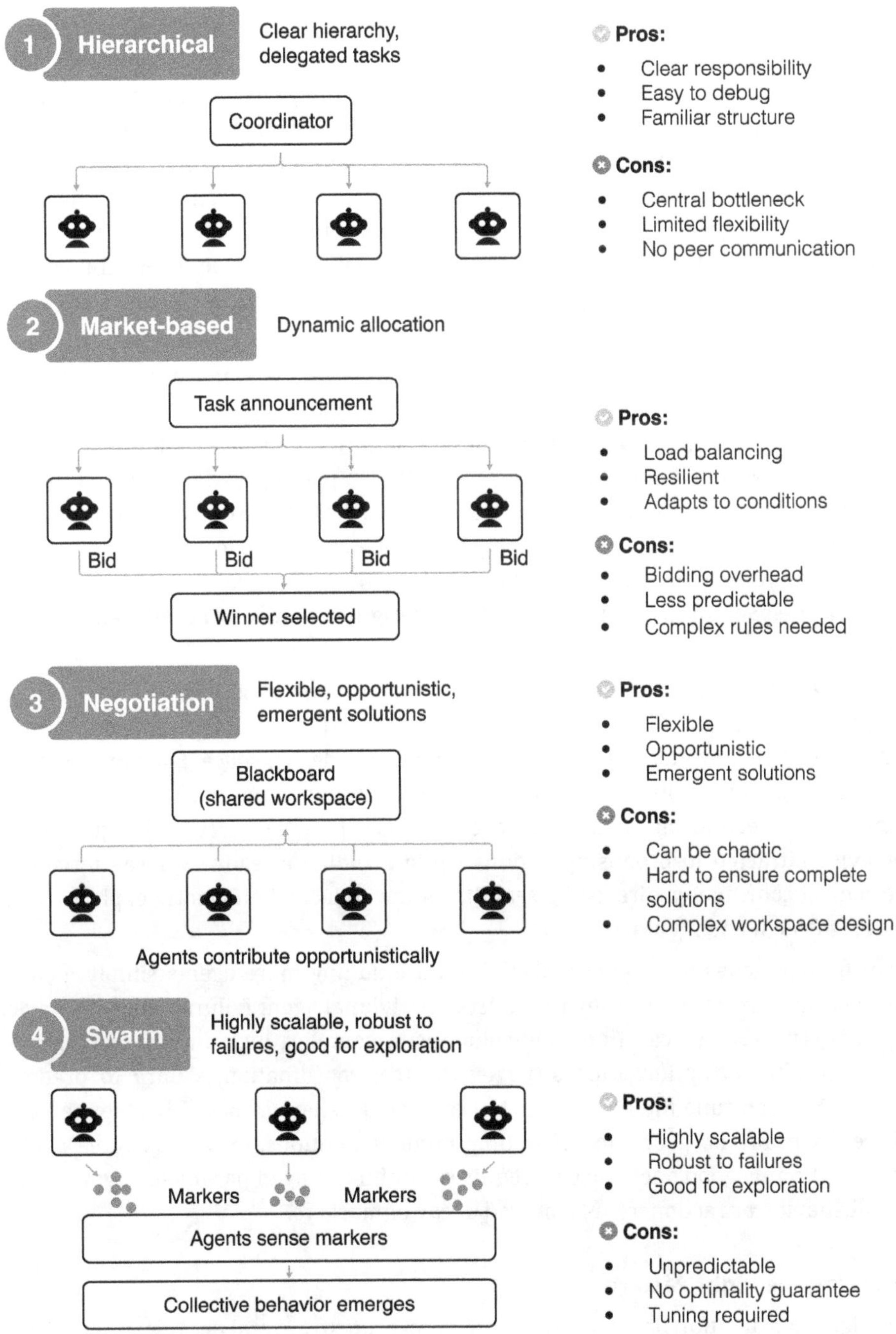

Figure 2.5 Four architectural patterns for coordinating multiple agents—hierarchical, market-based, negotiation via shared blackboard, and swarm—each with distinct trade-offs across predictability, scalability, flexibility, and ease of debugging (© Iryna Novoseletska)

Blackboard systems take a different approach, establishing a shared workspace where agents post problems and partial solutions (Figure 2.5). Each agent monitors the blackboard and contributes when it sees something it can help with, enabling truly opportunistic collaboration. Imagine a complex multi-objective optimization problem posted to the blackboard. The geometry agent notices opportunities to simplify the design and posts modified geometry. The simulation agent sees the new geometry and recognizes it as amenable to a particular analysis method, runs that analysis, and posts results. The cost agent sees the simulation results and contributes cost implications. Gradually, through these independent contributions, a complete solution accumulates on the blackboard.

This pattern shines in its flexibility and its ability to leverage agents opportunistically without predefined workflows. Agents don't need to know about each other's existence. They just need to understand the blackboard's structure. Solutions emerge from collective contribution rather than coordinated planning, which works well for problems with unclear solution paths. However, blackboard systems can become chaotic if not carefully managed. Ensuring completeness is challenging. How do you know when you have a sufficient solution rather than just a partial one? The blackboard workspace itself requires thoughtful design to balance expressiveness with structure.

Swarm coordination, inspired by biological systems like ant colonies and bee hives, uses simple local rules followed by many agents to produce complex emergent behavior (Figure 2.5). Consider multiple agents exploring a design space. Each explores locally, leaving markers in the shared space indicating what it has tried and how promising each direction appears. Other agents sense these markers and adjust their behavior attracted to promising regions while avoiding already-explored territory. No central coordinator directs the search, yet the collective efficiently explores vast spaces through emergent patterns.

Swarm approaches are highly scalable because adding more agents simply means more parallel exploration. They're robust to individual agent failures since no single agent is critical. They can find good solutions in complex, high-dimensional spaces where traditional optimization struggles. Swarm coordination is hard to predict, though. You can tune the local rules, but emergent behavior may still surprise you. There's typically no guarantee of finding optimal solutions, only reasonable confidence of finding good ones. Success requires careful tuning of parameters, governing local behavior, attraction, repulsion, and decay of markers.

Choosing the Right Pattern

The right coordination pattern depends on your context. Several organizational characteristics should guide your choice, and assessment of these factors will prevent implementation problems. Consider first how structured your engineering processes are. Organizations with well-defined review gates, formal approval workflows, and stage-gate development processes find hierarchical coordination maps naturally to their existing operations. The coordinator agent simply orchestrates steps that human project managers already coordinate manually. Conversely, if your engineering work is exploratory and creative, characterized by emergent requirements and evolving approaches, looser patterns like blackboard or swarm coordination might work better. These patterns accommodate the discovery-driven nature of the work without forcing it into predefined sequences.

The degree of task specialization matters significantly. When each agent has a very specific job that others can't perform, perhaps one agent wraps a proprietary simulation tool while another accesses a unique database, market-based or hierarchical patterns make sense because task allocation is relatively clear-cut. You know which agents can handle which work. However, when agents have overlapping capabilities, like multiple agents capable of geometry analysis or cost estimation, each with slightly different approaches, blackboard or swarm patterns can be more efficient. These patterns let the most appropriate agent contribute based on the specific problem characteristics rather than predefined assignments.

Explainability requirements significantly constrain your options. Regulated industries or safety-critical applications often require complete audit trails showing exactly who made what decision based on which information. Hierarchical patterns provide this clarity naturally as you can trace every decision through the coordination hierarchy. Market-based patterns also maintain reasonable transparency through the bidding process. Swarm patterns, by contrast, can be much harder to explain because behavior emerges from collective dynamics rather than traceable individual decisions. When regulators ask "why did your system make this choice," having to answer "it emerged from collective exploration" is rarely satisfying.

Your organizational tolerance for unpredictability plays a crucial role. Some engineering cultures demand predictable, repeatable processes where the same inputs reliably produce similar outputs. These organizations often work in regulated spaces, manufacture safety-critical products, or simply value consistency highly. For them, deterministic patterns like hierarchical coordination are essential. Other organizations value discovering novel solutions, even at the cost of some unpredictability. They're willing to accept variability in how problems get solved if it means occasionally finding breakthrough approaches. For these cultures, swarm or blackboard patterns can unlock creativity that more rigid patterns would suppress.

Most real systems ultimately use combinations of patterns, recognizing that different aspects of engineering work call for different coordination approaches. High-level project coordination might be hierarchical. A master project agent delegates to functional specialty agents covering mechanical design, electrical design, manufacturing engineering, and so forth. Within each functional area, though, agents might use blackboard patterns for collaborative problem-solving, allowing specialists to contribute opportunistically. For design space exploration, you might employ swarm coordination, searching vast parameter spaces efficiently. For resource allocation across competing priorities, market-based coordination might provide the fairest and most efficient approach. The key is matching pattern to purpose rather than forcing every interaction through the same coordination mechanism.

Where Humans Fit In

No discussion of cooperation would be complete without addressing how humans fit in. In most engineering applications today, agents cooperate with each other and with humans in a complex dance of authority and capability. The human remains the ultimate authority, but the nature of human involvement changes fundamentally from traditional automation.

Instead of performing every task, the human now sets goals and constraints that guide agent behavior, approves high-stakes decisions where the consequences matter too much for autonomous action, resolves conflicts between agents when their objectives clash or their analyses contradict, provides feedback to improve agent performance over time through corrections and explanations, and handles exceptions that fall outside agent capabilities or training. This list might sound similar to a manager's role, and that's not accidental. Humans are increasingly managing a team of agents rather than operating tools.

This shift from doing to directing, from executing to supervising, represents a significant change. Engineers accustomed to direct tool manipulation must learn new skills. They need to specify goals clearly enough that agents can pursue them independently but not so narrowly that they eliminate agent flexibility. They must review agent work efficiently, sampling and verifying rather than checking every detail. They need to diagnose problems when agents make mistakes, understanding whether the issue lies in inadequate context, insufficient capabilities, poor goal specification, or genuine edge cases requiring human judgment.

Organizations implementing multi-agent systems must invest in preparing their people for these new roles as much as they do in implementing the technology. Training programs, updated processes, new performance metrics, and cultural acceptance of human-agent collaboration, all matter as much as the agent architecture itself. For engineering leaders introducing agents, a practical first step is identifying engineers who already delegate effectively to junior team members. They'll adapt most readily to directing agents since they're already skilled at specifying goals, reviewing outputs, and providing constructive feedback rather than simply doing the work themselves.

Why This Matters

Communication enables agent coordination and collaboration. Agents that cannot communicate effectively cannot accomplish shared tasks, regardless of their individual capabilities. Communication in multi-agent systems encompasses four critical dimensions. First, what information is shared. The data formats, ontologies, and schemas that structure knowledge exchange between agents. Second, how information is transmitted. The protocols, channels, and APIs provide the mechanisms for data flow. Third, when information flows, whether communication is synchronous or asynchronous, whether agents push information proactively or pull it on demand. Fourth, why agents share information, goals, intentions, and context that give meaning to the data being exchanged. Communication failures represent one of the most common failure modes in multi-agent systems.

Keeping Context Intact

Communication requires preserving context along with data transmission. When a human engineer sends an email to a colleague, they include context naturally. "I ran the simulation with the new mesh. Results look concerning, but it might be ok because I used the summer cooling assumptions instead of the winter ones. Can you take a look?" The recipient understands not just the data (simulation results) but the context (why it might be misleading) and the request (review with awareness of the assumption).

When agents communicate, this context preservation must be designed explicitly. An agent that simply passes simulation results to another agent loses critical information. An agent that passes results along with assumptions, confidence levels, and known limitations enables better downstream decisions. Large language models can process and generate natural language, which is inherently context rich. Instead of passing structured data with separate metadata fields, agents can communicate in messages that naturally include context: "The stress analysis shows peak values of 342 MPa at the fillet radius. This is within the yield strength of 380 MPa, but the margin is tighter than we typically target. Note that I assumed room temperature if the service environment is elevated temperature, the yield strength will be lower, and this design may be at risk."

Five Communication Patterns

The request-response pattern represents the simplest communication model (Figure 2.6). One agent asks a question, another answers synchronously, with the requesting agent waiting for response before continuing. Consider the assembly agent needing to know if a component fits within an envelope. It asks the geometry agent a direct question: "Does component X with orientation Y fit within bounding box Z?" The geometry agent checks and responds with specifics: "Yes, with 3.2 mm clearance on the +X side and 1.1 mm on the -Z side." This pattern works for simple queries with clear answers, time-sensitive decisions where the requester must have information before proceeding, and situations where back-and-forth conversation adds value.

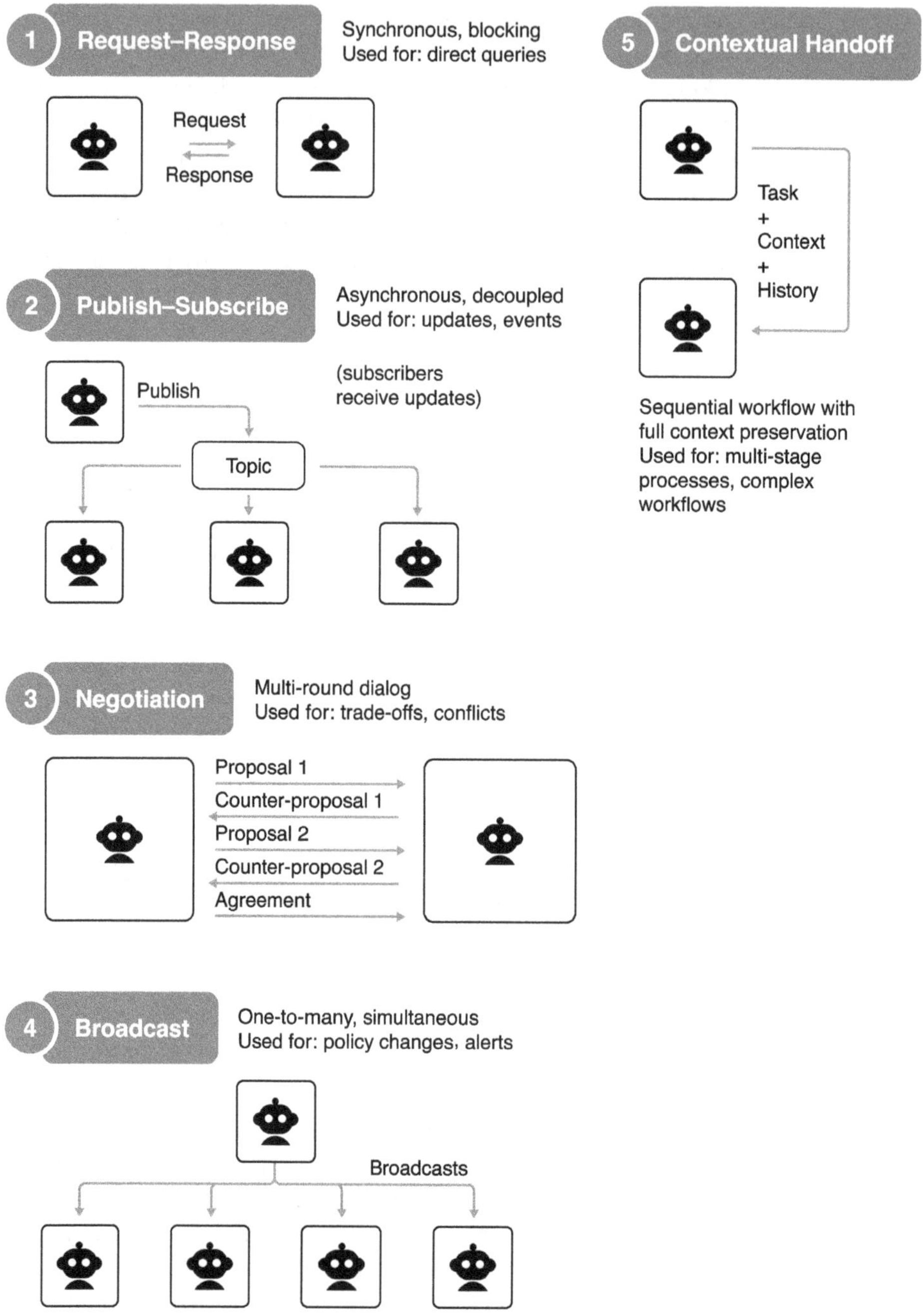

Figure 2.6 The five communication patterns available between agents in a multi-agent system: request-response for direct queries, publish-subscribe for decoupled event updates, negotiation for trade-off resolution, broadcast for policy changes, and contextual handoff for preserving state across sequential workflow stages (© Iryna Novoseletska)

Publish-subscribe patterns enable looser coupling and better scalability for information dissemination (Figure 2.6). Agents publish information to topics rather than sending it to specific recipients, and other agents subscribe to topics they care about. This happens asynchronously. Publishers don't wait for responses, and subscribers get updates whenever new information becomes available. The cost agent publishes updates to a "component-costs" topic whenever estimates change. The optimization agent subscribes to this topic and reacts when cost changes might affect its recommendations. The reporting agent also subscribes to include cost trends in dashboards. Neither the optimization agent nor the reporting agent needs to explicitly request updates. They simply receive them whenever relevant changes occur. This pattern supports disseminating updates to multiple interested parties, decoupling information producers from consumers, and enabling reactive behaviors without requiring producers to know all potential consumers.

Negotiation patterns support multi-round dialogs where agents exchange proposals and counter-proposals to reach agreement on contested issues (Figure 2.6). The performance agent might propose material X for maximum strength. The cost agent objects and proposes cheaper material Y instead. The performance agent counters with material Z, a compromise that's slightly less strong than X but significantly cheaper. The agents continue this exchange until they reach agreement or recognize that they need to escalate to human judgment. This pattern addresses resolving trade-offs where no single agent has authority, allocating shared resources across competing demands, and reaching consensus on complex decisions where multiple perspectives must be balanced.

Broadcast patterns serve system-wide announcements where one agent sends information to all other agents simultaneously (Figure 2.6). The project agent might announce a schedule change: "Customer has moved the delivery date forward by two weeks. All optimization efforts should now prioritize schedule over cost." Every agent receives this context update and adjusts its behavior accordingly. Broadcasts support policy changes that affect all agents with system-wide context updates that everyone needs to know, and emergency notifications requiring immediate attention across the system.

Contextual handoff represents perhaps the most sophisticated pattern (Figure 2.6). One agent completes part of a task and hands it off to another with full context about what's been done, why decisions were made, and what work remains. The concept agent might generate three design alternatives and hand off to the analysis agent with rich context: "I've created three options. Option A prioritizes performance with estimated cost of $X. Option B prioritizes cost with some performance sacrifice. Option C is a balance. The customer has expressed sensitivity to cost but also mentioned reliability concerns, which suggests option B might be risky. Please analyze all three but pay special attention to reliability metrics for option B." This comprehensive handoff ensures the analysis agent understands not just what to analyze but why each option exists, what customer context matters, and where to focus attention. The pattern applies to sequential workflows where context accumulates through stages, multi-stage processes where later stages depend on understanding earlier decisions, and tasks that require preserving the full reasoning chain from start to finish.

Shared Vocabulary

For agents to communicate effectively, they need shared understanding of what words mean. In formal terms, they need a shared ontology, a structured vocabulary of concepts and their relationships. In engineering domains, this is both easier and harder than in general conversation. It is easier because engineering has established terminology. Everyone knows what a "bolt" is, what "yield strength" means, or what "tolerance" refers to. It is harder because engineering also has enormous depth and specificity: the differences between various fastener standards, the nuances of different material models, and the subtleties of geometric dimensioning and tolerancing.

Building effective ontologies for multi-agent systems requires the following:

1. **starting with industry standards** where they exist (e.g., STEP for geometry, QIF for quality data)
2. **extending with domain-specific vocabulary**, the terms and concepts unique to your domain or company
3. **including relationships**, not just terms, knowing that a "rivet" is a type of "fastener" which is a type of "joining method"
4. **capturing context** about when different terms apply ("tensile strength" means something different for metals vs. polymers vs. composites)

The ontology that enables effective agent communication will include organizational terminology, categories, and problem-solving approaches. A generic ontology from a textbook will not capture how a specific organization actually works.

Natural Language Between Agents

Traditional multi-agent systems communicated in formal, structured languages XML messages, API calls, database transactions. These are precise and unambiguous, but they cannot capture context and nuance effectively. The integration of large language models has changed this. Agents can now communicate in natural language, which offers several advantages:

- **Richness:** Natural language can express subtlety, uncertainty, and context that structured formats struggle with. "I'm fairly confident this design will work, but there's an unusual loading case I couldn't fully analyze" conveys information that's hard to express in a structured message.

- **Flexibility:** Agents can discuss unexpected situations without needing pre-defined message types. When something novel happens, natural language provides a way to describe it.
- **Transparency:** Natural language communications are readable by humans, making it easier to audit, debug, and understand what agents are doing.
- **Context accumulation:** Conversations build context naturally. Each message is understood in light of what came before, enabling sophisticated multi-turn interactions.

However, natural language also introduces challenges:

- **Ambiguity:** The same words can mean different things in different contexts. Systems need mechanisms to resolve ambiguity.
- **Consistency:** Natural language is variable. The same information might be expressed in many different ways. Systems need to handle this variability.
- **Verification:** It's harder to verify that a natural language message meets a specification than to validate a structured message against a schema.

Effective systems use hybrid approaches: natural language for rich, contextual communication between agents and structured data for precise technical information that needs formal handling.

Why Architecture Matters

So far, we've discussed the properties of individual agents (autonomy) and how they work together (cooperation and communication). Now we zoom out to look at the overall structure of how you organize a collection of agents into a coherent system.

Architecture decisions have long-lasting consequences. They determine how easily you can add new capabilities, how the system handles failures, how it scales with increasing complexity, and how maintainable it will be over time. Choosing the wrong architecture doesn't mean failure. Systems can be refactored, but it does mean unnecessary friction and rework.

Three architectural patterns are particularly relevant for engineering applications: holonic, service-oriented, and LLM-orchestrated. Each has strengths and weaknesses, and understanding them helps you to make informed choices.

Holonic Architecture: Nested Hierarchies

The term "holonic" comes from Arthur Koestler's concept of a "holon": something that is simultaneously a whole in itself and a part of a larger whole. Your liver is a complete organ with its own function, but it's also part of your body. A manufacturing cell is a complete production unit, but it's also part of a factory.

In a holonic multi-agent system, agents are organized in nested hierarchies. Each agent manages its own domain while also participating in higher-level collectives. This mirrors how many engineering organizations and manufacturing systems are actually structured.

Example Structure

Each agent at each level is autonomous within its scope. The CAD agent makes its own decisions about how to model geometry. The mechanical design agent coordinates across CAD, simulation, and tolerancing without needing to understand the details of each. The product development agent coordinates across disciplines (Figure 2.7).

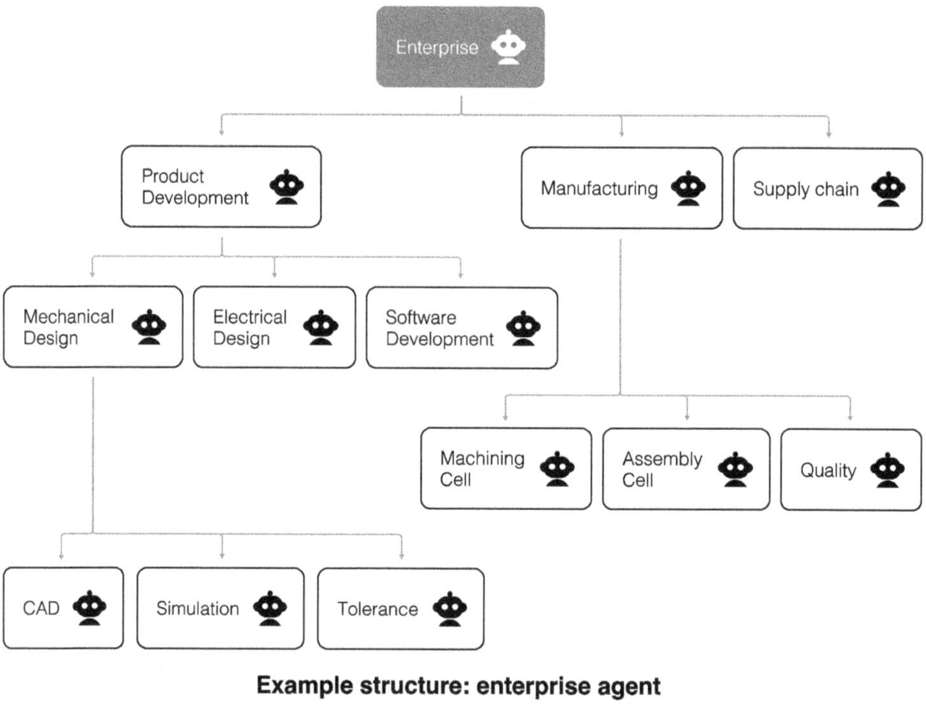

Figure 2.7 Holonic agent hierarchy (or simply referred to as multi agent systems) for a manufacturing enterprise. Agents at each level—from enterprise strategy down to individual engineering tools—operate autonomously within their scope while coordinating through their parent agents (© Iryna Novoseletska).

Holonic architectures offer several strengths. They provide natural mapping to organizational and system structures that engineering organizations already understand. Scope and responsibility are clear at each level, making it obvious which agent handles which decisions. The approach scales well because you can add new holons without redesigning the whole system. A new manufacturing process simply becomes a new agent under the manufacturing agent. Failure isolation improves reliability because problems in one branch don't necessarily propagate to others. If the assembly cell agent fails, the machining cell agent continues functioning.

However, holonic structures have notable weaknesses. They can become rigid if hierarchies don't match actual work patterns. Cross-branch communication can be cumbersome when agents need to collaborate across organizational boundaries. This pattern may struggle with highly collaborative, non-hierarchical work that doesn't fit neat hierarchies. This architecture works best for organizations with clear functional structures, systems that mirror physical hierarchies like factory-to-cell-to-station decomposition, and domains where scope and responsibility are well-defined from the outset.

Service-Oriented Architecture: Modular and API-Driven

Service-oriented architecture (SOA) treats each agent as a service with well-defined interfaces. Agents don't know or care about the internal workings of other agents, they only interact through published APIs. This creates loose coupling and high flexibility. A typical structure includes a geometry service providing geometric analysis and manipulation, a simulation service running and interpreting simulations, a cost service estimating and optimizing costs, a knowledge service storing and retrieving engineering knowledge, and a workflow service orchestrating multi-step processes. Any service can call any other service through its API. The workflow service might orchestrate a design review by calling geometry service for checks, simulation service for analysis, and cost service for estimates all in parallel if possible.

Service-oriented architectures deliver maximum flexibility in how agents interact. They make it easy to add, replace, or update individual services without affecting others. The patterns are well-understood from web services and microservices, and a good tool support exists for API management. These advantages make SOA appealing for large-scale systems with evolving requirements.

The weaknesses are equally significant. Service-oriented systems can become a "big ball of mud" without careful governance, every service potentially calling every other service creates complex dependency graphs. Every agent needs to know what services exist and how to call them, creating a discovery and coordination challenge. Context can be lost in service-to-service calls as information passes through multiple intermediate layers. Testing and debugging of distributed services prove challenging because failures can result from complex interactions between services.

This architecture excels when integrating with existing enterprise systems that are themselves likely service-oriented, in domains where capabilities map cleanly to well-defined services, and in organizations with strong API management practices and governance disciplines.

LLM-Orchestrated Architecture: Flexible and Adaptive

The newest architectural pattern leverages large language models as orchestrators that understand intent, manage context, and coordinate other agents dynamically. Instead of rigid hierarchies or pre-defined service calls, an LLM-based orchestrator determines what needs to happen based on the current situation.

A typical structure includes an orchestrator agent powered by an LLM that receives requests, determines approach, and coordinates specialists; tool agents serving as wrappers around specific tools like CAD systems, simulation engines, and databases; knowledge agents that access and interpret domain knowledge; and interface agents handling communication with humans and external systems.

A request like "Check if this design meets our reliability requirements" goes to the orchestrator. The orchestrator understands the request and determines that it needs to check several things. Material selection, stress levels, fatigue life, or environmental factors will identify which tool and knowledge agents can help, can coordinate their work, and can synthesize a response.

LLM-orchestrated architectures are highly flexible, capable of handling novel requests without reprogramming. Natural language interfaces make interaction intuitive for engineers who can describe what they need rather than specifying procedural steps. Context is maintained throughout complex interactions, enabling coherent multi-turn problem-solving. The system can learn and improve from experience as the LLM accumulates organizational knowledge.

The weaknesses are real and significant. These architectures are less predictable than structured alternatives because the LLM makes decisions dynamically rather than following predetermined logic. LLM costs can be significant at scale, especially complex workflows requiring many inference calls. The systems may struggle with highly precise or regulated processes where deterministic behavior and complete explainability are essential. Understanding why the LLM made particular coordination decisions can be challenging as well as complicating debugging and compliance.

This architecture excels in exploratory and creative work where rigid procedures would limit valuable flexibility, in situations with high variability and novelty where predefined workflows can't anticipate every scenario, in organizations that accept some unpredictability in exchange for adaptability, and in domains where natural language interaction creates value by bridging technical specialists and non-technical stakeholders.

This approach is perfect for creative work that needs flexibility rather than strict rules. It thrives in unpredictable situations where traditional plans fail. It's ideal for teams that value adaptability over perfect predictability and for projects where plain language helps tech experts and non-experts work together better.

Hybrid Architectures

In practice, most successful multi-agent systems use hybrid architectures that combine elements of all three patterns. A typical hybrid might employ holonic structure for overall organization, dividing the system into product development agents, manufacturing agents, and supply chain agents. Service-oriented interfaces handle integration with existing enterprise systems like PLM platforms and ERP systems, leveraging standard APIs and protocols. Within each holon, LLM orchestration provides flexible, context-aware coordination that adapts to specific situations without rigid procedural logic.

The key is to match the architecture to the work being done. Stable, well-defined processes benefit from structured approaches that provide predictability and auditability. Creative, exploratory work benefits from LLM flexibility that accommodates novel situations. Integration with existing systems benefits from standard service patterns that enterprise IT organizations understand and support.

Matching Architecture to Your Situation

The right architecture for your multi-agent system depends on your specific situation. Consider your organizational structure. Does your company operate in clear hierarchies or in fluid, project-based teams? Hierarchical organizations map naturally to holonic architectures, while project-based organizations may benefit from more flexible service-oriented or LLM-orchestrated approaches. Process maturity matters as well. If your engineering processes are well-defined and stable, structured architectures provide efficiency and predictability. If processes are evolving and variable, more adaptive architectures accommodate change without constant re-architecting. There is no universally "best" architecture. There is only the architecture that best fits your context. Understanding your context is the first step in building an effective system.

How you connect to other tools changes your design choices significantly. What software must the agents talk to? Are their digital links ready? Is their data formatted clearly? Systems that plug into a large company's main network need structured patterns, while standalone tools allow for more creative freedom. Your comfort with risk also limits your options: How much random behavior can you tolerate? Regulated fields or high-stakes jobs usually require systems that follow exact, repeatable rules. You also have to plan for growth. A setup that works for a few agents might fail if you try to manage hundreds at once. Finally, the need to show your work can rule out some designs. If you must prove why every choice was made for legal reasons, "black box" AI might be the wrong choice despite its other strengths.

Multi-Agent Systems

A single agent, no matter how sophisticated, has limitations. It might be powerful at natural language reasoning but lack specialized knowledge of thermal analysis. It might excel at geometry manipulation but know little about manufacturing processes. Just as engineering organizations employ specialists who collaborate, multi-agent systems employ multiple specialized agents that coordinate to accomplish complex tasks.

The architecture typically includes several types of agents. Task-specific agents specialize in particular domains. A manufacturing agent understands process capabilities and constraints. A cost agent knows estimation methods and has access to pricing databases. A simulation agent can set up and interpret analyses. Coordination agents orchestrate the work of specialists, receiving high-level requests, determining which specialists to involve, and synthesizing their contributions into coherent outputs. An interface agent handles communication with humans and external systems, translating between natural language, structured data, and system-specific formats.

What makes this a system rather than just a collection of separate tools is the communication and coordination between agents. They can exchange information, request help from each other, negotiate when their objectives conflict, and collectively accomplish tasks that none could handle alone. This coordination can follow different patterns depending on the task: hierarchical for structured workflows, market-based for dynamic resource allocation, and collaborative for exploration and problem-solving.

The key technical challenge in multi-agent systems is maintaining coherence to ensure that agents work toward aligned goals, despite their specialized perspectives. This requires shared understanding of concepts (ontologies), protocols for exchanging information, mechanisms for conflict resolution, and often a coordinating layer that maintains overall task context. Done well, multi-agent systems can tackle engineering problems with a level of sophistication that begins to approach the level of human engineering teams. Done poorly, they produce confusion as agents work at cross-purposes, or fail to share critical information.

For Engineering Leaders

Understanding these technical foundations enables better decision-making about agent adoption. When evaluating vendors or internal development efforts, you can ask informed questions: Which LLM powers the system, and what are its context limits? How are tools integrated, and what reliability guarantees exist? How is memory managed, and can agents learn from your organization's specific experience? What coordination patterns do the multi-agent systems use, and why?

You can also set appropriate expectations. LLMs are powerful but not infallible. They need verification, especially for quantitative engineering work. Agents can be remarkably autonomous but still require human oversight for high-stakes decisions. Multi-agent systems can coordinate sophisticated workflows but need a careful design to avoid confusion or conflicts.

Understanding what's possible, what's reliable, and what's still aspirational allows you to make informed decisions about how these technologies serve engineering goals.

Multi-Agent Systems Beyond Engineering: Evidence From Other Industries

While this book focuses on engineering applications, examining how other industries have successfully deployed multi-agent systems will provide valuable context for understanding their capabilities and maturation. Finance, healthcare, and supply chain management have all demonstrated measurable results from agent deployments, offering lessons that engineering organizations can apply.

The financial services sector has emerged as one of the most active adopters of multi-agent systems, driven by the need to process vast amounts of data, make rapid decisions, and maintain regulatory compliance. JPMorgan's COIN (contract intelligence) system demonstrates the efficiency gains possible, when agents handle routine, but cognitively demanding tasks. COIN parses legal documents to extract key data points, reducing what was previously a 360,000-hour annual task to seconds (Anglara 2025). The system doesn't replace legal expertise but automates the extraction and initial analysis that human lawyers would otherwise perform manually. Recent platforms like FinRobot and Fincon have introduced open-source frameworks, specifically designed for financial applications, enabling smaller institutions to deploy sophisticated agent capabilities (Moolchandani 2025).

Production deployments across financial services show substantial returns. According to a November 2025 IDC study, certain organizations were identified as "frontier firms," as they embedded AI agents across workflows successfully and reported returns on their AI investments roughly three times higher than slow adopters (Borden 2025). Separately, 77 percent of financial services executives reported an achieved positive ROI from generative AI initiatives within the first year (Brown 2025). These returns stem primarily from efficiency gains in back-office operations, document processing, compliance monitoring, and customer service automation. The highest concentration of these frontier firms operates in finance and technology sectors, where data availability and process standardization facilitate agent deployment (Pan et al. 2025).

Healthcare applications demonstrate multi-agent systems handling coordination challenges that parallel engineering's multi-disciplinary work. Leading institutions including Stanford Medicine, Johns Hopkins, and Mass General Brigham are exploring agent orchestrators for complex clinical tasks such as cancer care coordination

(Lungren 2025). Stanford Medicine processes 4000 tumor board patients annually, with clinicians already using AI-generated summaries in tumor board meetings. Multi-agent systems promise to streamline these workflows by reducing fragmentation and surfacing insights from trial eligibility criteria, treatment histories, and diagnostic results spread across multiple systems. Research published in Nature Digital Medicine in 2025 found that multi-agent conversational systems outperformed single models in diagnostic accuracy, achieving optimal performance with four doctor agents plus a supervisor agent based on GPT-4 (Chen et al. 2025). The global AI in healthcare market reflects this growing adoption. It is projected to grow from $14.6 billion in 2023 to $102.7 billion by 2028, a 47.6 percent compound annual growth rate (Bulwark Health 2025).

Supply chain management applications show agents handling the dynamic optimization problems that also characterize engineering design. Research published in December 2025 demonstrated that LLM-based multi-agent systems with consensus-seeking frameworks reduce bullwhip effects in inventory management. Outperforming both traditional restocking policies and centralized demand approaches (Jannelli et al. 2025). A European retailer using AI-powered supply chain intelligence identified their top 150 SKUs and revised allocations, immediately realized logistics savings of up to €2 million annually while achieving on-time-in-full delivery rates exceeding 90 percent ([x]cube LABS, 2025). Warehouse automation systems employing communicating agents to coordinate picking, packing, and transportation demonstrated increases in order fulfillment rates of 27 percent while reducing operational costs by 22 percent compared to traditional systems ([x]cube LABS 2025).

Perhaps most relevant for engineering leaders is data from the first large-scale systematic study of production AI agents. "Measuring Agents in Production," published in December 2025, surveyed 306 practitioners and conducted 20 in-depth case studies across 26 domains (Pan et al. 2025). The research found that 73 percent of practitioners deploy agents primarily to increase efficiency and decrease time spent on manual tasks. The same motivation drives the engineering agent adoption. Teams prioritize output quality over real-time responsiveness with 66 percent, which allows response times of minutes or longer. This suggests that batch-oriented engineering workflows, like design validation or analysis setup, align well with current agent capabilities. The study captured deployed systems, serving user bases from hundreds to millions of daily users, with highest deployment concentrations in finance, technology (including software development), and corporate services.

These cross-industry findings reveal several patterns relevant to engineering applications. First, successful deployments focus on well-defined tasks where success criteria are clearly documented such as analysis, data extraction or routine decision-making within established boundaries. Second, the highest returns come from automating cognitively demanding, but repetitive work that doesn't require unprecedented judgment. Third, multi-agent architectures outperform monolithic agents for complex workflows which require multiple types of expertise. Fourth, organizations achieve results by starting with focused pilots, measuring outcomes carefully, and expanding systematically rather than attempting comprehensive transformation immediately.

For CAD and simulation engineers, these industry examples offer practical perspective. If financial analysts trust agents to parse contracts and healthcare professionals rely on them for diagnostic support, the technical foundations will exist for agents to handle design rule checking, tolerance analysis, and simulation setup. The key difference isn't capability, it's context. Financial institutions invest heavily in capturing their specific compliance requirements, risk tolerances, and decision precedents. Healthcare systems encode clinical guidelines, treatment protocols, and institutional practices. Engineering organizations must similarly invest in capturing their design rules, manufacturing constraints, material specifications, and lessons learned.

> The technology works. The question is whether you'll invest in making it work for your specific engineering context.

When and Why Multiple Agents? Evidence From Practice

The question of when to deploy multiple specialized agents, rather than a single general-purpose agent, arises in every engineering organization as they start their agentic journey. The intuitive appeal of a single agent that "does everything" collides with accumulated evidence that specialized agents working together often outperform monolithic ones. Understanding when and why this is true requires examining both research findings and practical experience from engineering deployments.

The theoretical argument for specialization is straightforward. Human organizations don't assign all engineering work to generalists. They employ mechanical engineers, electrical engineers, manufacturing engineers, quality engineers, each with deep expertise in their domain. These specialists collaborate on projects, but the collaboration is between people with focused capabilities, not between jacks-of-all-trades. Multi-agent systems extend this specialization principle to software, recognizing that the capabilities needed for geometry manipulation differ from those needed for cost estimation, which differ from those needed for regulatory compliance verification.

Empirical evidence from AI research supports this intuition. Studies comparing single large agents to teams of specialized smaller agents consistently show that decomposition improves performance on complex tasks. When researchers at Google DeepMind evaluated different agent architectures for software development tasks, they found that systems with specialized agents for planning, coding, testing, and debugging outperformed single agents attempting to handle all phases, even when the single agent had access to more computational resources. The specialized agents could optimize their prompts and tools for narrow tasks, while the general agent had to maintain enough generality to handle everything, making it master of none.

Similar patterns emerge in agent benchmarks beyond software development. The AutoGPT experiment, an early attempt at a fully autonomous general-purpose agent, demonstrated both the potential and the limitations of monolithic approaches. AutoGPT could formulate plans and execute them across diverse tasks, but it frequently got lost in complexity, pursuing irrelevant tangents or getting stuck in loops. Subsequent architectures like BabyAGI and GPT-Engineer showed improvements by introducing specialization via having separate components for task planning versus execution, for high-level strategy versus low-level action. The trend in agent research has been consistently towards more specialization, not less.

For engineering applications specifically, the argument for multiple agents strengthens because engineering work inherently involves distinct types of expertise that don't naturally combine. Consider a design review workflow. Geometry validation requires understanding CAD data structures, geometric relationships, and feature recognition capabilities that have little to do with cost estimation, which requires knowledge of manufacturing processes, material pricing, and overhead allocation. Structural analysis requires setting up finite element models, interpreting stress distributions, and applying failure criteria. Regulatory compliance requires understanding applicable standards, mapping design features to requirements, and documenting verification. Manufacturing feasibility assessment requires knowledge of process capabilities, tooling constraints, and production economics.

A single agent attempting to handle all these aspects must either maintain shallow understanding across all domains and recognizing basic issues, but missing subtleties that specialists would catch, or it must be enormous and slow, carrying all the specialized knowledge for every domain, even when most is irrelevant to the current task. Specialized agents can maintain deep capability in narrow areas, invoking each other as needed but not paying the computational and cognitive cost of generality when specificity suffices.

Practical deployments in engineering organizations provide additional evidence. A major aerospace manufacturer experimenting with agent-assisted design validation, initially deployed a single large agent that could handle geometry checks, analysis interpretation, and documentation generation. The agent worked acceptably but struggled with edge cases in each domain. When the aerospace manufacturer restructured to use specialized agents as a geometry agent with deep CAD integration, an analysis agent trained on years of simulation results, and a documentation agent familiar with their specific templates and compliance requirements, the performance improved markedly. The geometry agent caught subtle modeling errors which the general agent missed. The analysis agent provided more sophisticated interpretation of simulation results. The documentation agent produced reports that better matched organizational standards.

The communication overhead between agents represents the primary cost of specialization. Each hand-off between agents introduces latency, requires context to be packaged and transmitted, and creates opportunities for miscommunication or lost information. A single agent that handles an entire workflow internally doesn't pay these costs. This overhead is real and matters in some situations, particularly for simple, linear workflows where specialization provides limited benefit. For complex workflows with substantial depth in multiple domains, however, the overhead is typically outweighed by the performance gains from specialization.

The decision framework for one versus many agents considers several factors. How you design your system depends heavily on how hard the work is and how many fields it covers. If you are dealing with basic tasks in just one area of expertise, a single agent is usually the best choice. However, as projects grow more difficult and start to cross into different engineering branches, multi-agent systems become the better option. This approach allows specialized agents to focus on their specific niche while working together on the bigger picture. The frequency of the task matters, because specialization requires upfront investment in building and integrating multiple agents, which only pays off if the task runs often enough to amortize that investment. The criticality of the decision influences the trade-off for high-stakes decisions. The improved performance from specialization may justify overhead and complexity, while for low-stakes routine tasks, simpler single-agent approaches may suffice.

The availability of existing specialized capabilities also affects the decision. If your organization has already developed agents for specific functions, say a well-tested cost estimation agent and a geometry validation agent, then building a new capability as a multi-agent system that leverages these existing agents is more practical than building a new monolithic agent from scratch. The incremental cost of adding another specialized agent to an existing ecosystem is lower than the initial cost of creating the first specialized agent, which encourages further specialization over time.

Failure modes differ between single and multi-agent approaches in ways that matter for engineering applications. A single agent that fails stops the entire workflow. A multi-agent system can exhibit partial failure. One specialized agent fails while others continue functioning. This can be either better or worse than monolithic failure depending on how the system handles it. If the system recognizes the partial failure and escalates appropriately, partial failure is preferable. You get results from the domains where agents succeeded and clear indication of where human intervention is needed. If the system doesn't recognize partial failure and proceeds with incomplete information, the outcome can be worse than outright failure because the problem may not be obvious.

The scalability characteristics also differ. Single agents scale vertically. You make them larger, give them more context, and train them on more data. This works until you hit fundamental limits of model size, context windows, or inference cost. Multi-agent systems scale horizontally. You add more specialized agents, each focused on a specific domain. This approach can scale further but introduces complexity in coordination and integration.

Looking at evidence from production deployments, patterns emerge about when multi-agent architectures deliver clear advantages. Design review and validation workflows benefit substantially from specialized agents for different validation aspects (geometry, analysis, cost, compliance, manufacturability). Each check requires different expertise, and specialized agents can maintain that expertise at greater depth than generalist agents. Optimization and design space exploration workflows benefit from separation between exploration strategy (handled by a coordinator agent that decides what to explore) and evaluation (handled by specialist agents that assess specific options). Knowledge retrieval and synthesis workflows benefit from specialized retrieval agents for different knowledge domains (past projects, technical standards, supplier capabilities) coordinated by a synthesis agent that combines findings.

Conversely, some workflows show little benefit from multi-agent approaches. Simple data transformation tasks converting between formats, extracting specific information from documents, generating standard reports typically perform adequately with single agents because the domain expertise required is limited. Interactive troubleshooting and debugging benefits from continuity that single agents provide more naturally than multi-agent handoffs, where context about the debugging process needs to be maintained and communicated repeatedly. Straightforward question-answering from well-structured knowledge bases works well with single retrieval agents because the task doesn't require multiple types of expertise.

The trend in engineering agent deployments is toward hybrid architectures that use single agents for focused tasks and multi-agent systems for complex workflows. This reflects a growing understanding that the question isn't "single agent or multiple" but rather "where does specialization add value and where does it add unnecessary overhead?" Organizations building agent capabilities are developing portfolios of specialized agents that can be composed in different ways for different workflows, with the composition itself sometimes handled by coordinator agents that decide which specialists to involve for each task.

The evidence suggests a clear principle: Specialization adds value when tasks require depth in multiple distinct domains, when those domains involve different types of expertise and tools, when the task complexity justifies the coordination overhead, and when the frequency or criticality of the task warrants the investment in building and maintaining multiple specialized agents. For engineering organizations, where work inherently spans multiple technical disciplines and where the stakes are often high enough to justify sophisticated solutions, multi-agent architectures frequently prove superior to monolithic approaches, not as a universal truth, but as a pattern that holds across a wide range of important use cases.

2.1.6 Summary

This section established the foundational understanding of agentic AI systems for engineering applications.

We began by examining **what makes software agentic**, exploring how large language models transform from text generators into action-taking systems through tool integration, memory, and structured reasoning. The five essential components: brain (LLM), hands (tools), memory (context storage), senses (input processing), and voice (output generation) work together in continuous cycles of perception, reasoning, and action (Section 2.1.2). The agent equation (LLM + Tools + Context) clarifies that agent quality depends multiplicatively on all three factors, with organizational context providing competitive differentiation.

The distinction between **deterministic and autonomous agents** reveals a fundamental design choice (Section 2.1.3). Deterministic flow-based agents provide predictability, auditability, and reliability for well-defined tasks. Autonomous LLM-powered agents offer flexibility, contextual reasoning, and natural language interaction for novel situations. Most effective systems employ hybrid architectures that strategically combine both approaches, using determinism where reliability matters and autonomy where flexibility provides value.

Types of agents span a spectrum of autonomy levels (Section 2.1.4). Level 1 reactive agents respond to triggers with predefined actions. Level 2 goal-directed agents decide how to achieve objectives based on context. Level 3 planning agents break complex goals into subgoals and create execution strategies. Level 4 learning agents improve from experience. Level 5 collaborative agents negotiate and adjust goals as team members. To make an agent effective, its level of freedom must match the specific requirements of the task. You have to consider how high the stakes are, whether the agent has enough information to act, and if the problem is something entirely new. Getting this balance right is what determines if the system succeeds or fails.

Multi-agent systems enable capabilities beyond individual agents through specialization and coordination (Section 2.1.5). Cooperation patterns like hierarchical, market-based, blackboard, and swarm suit different engineering workflows in different ways. Communication between agents must preserve context through appropriate protocols and shared vocabularies. System architectures (holonic, service-oriented, LLM-orchestrated, etc.) structure how agents organize and interact, with hybrid approaches matching specific architecture to specific workflow characteristics. Evidence from production deployments shows that specialized agents working together and outperforming monolithic agents for complex multi-disciplinary tasks.

The common thread throughout these concepts is the primacy of context. Technical components become increasingly commoditized. LLMs are available to everyone, and tool integration follows standard patterns. What differentiates effective agents from generic ones is the organizational knowledge they encode: manufacturing constraints, design heritage, customer requirements, lessons learned, and stakeholder preferences. This context cannot be purchased; it must be deliberately captured, structured, and maintained.

With these foundations established, the next section shifts to implementation: the practical components, frameworks, integration strategies, and deployment patterns that transform conceptual understanding into working systems.

2.2 Building Agentic Systems

The last section established the theoretical foundations of what agents are, how they cooperate, how they communicate, and how systems can be architected. This chapter shifts focus to implementation: the practical components, frameworks, integration strategies, and deployment patterns that transform conceptual understanding into working systems.

The challenge facing engineering organizations isn't whether agentic AI works. The technology has matured sufficiently. The challenge is building systems that work reliably within your specific engineering environment, connecting to your CAD tools, understanding your design standards, accessing your organizational knowledge, and delivering value consistently rather than occasionally. This requires moving beyond demos and prototypes to production-grade implementations.

This section addresses the practical questions that engineering leaders and technical teams face when implementing agentic systems. What actually goes inside an agent? Which frameworks and models should you choose, and what trade-offs do different options entail? How do you connect agents to existing engineering infrastructure such as CAD systems, simulation engines, PLM platforms, databases, and other tools, where engineering work happens? How do you blend rule-based automation with AI flexibility to get reliability where you need it and adaptability where you want it? What actually works in production today versus what remains aspirational?

We'll examine implementation through concrete components and real constraints. When vendors promise their agentic platform will "seamlessly integrate with your engineering systems," you'll understand that integration actually requires APIs, data formats, authentication, error handling, and the organizational knowledge that makes generic tools useful for specific engineering contexts. When they tout "advanced reasoning capabilities," you'll know which reasoning patterns matter for engineering work and which are marketing. When they claim "production-ready deployment," you'll recognize the gap between running in a demo environment and operating reliably in yours.

The goal is practical preparation. By the end of this chapter, you'll understand not just what agentic systems can do conceptually, but what building them requires concretely. You'll recognize which vendor claims are credible and which are aspirational. You'll know which components you can adopt off-the-shelf and which require organizational investment. You'll be equipped to evaluate whether your team should build, buy, or partner and what each choice demands.

2.2.1 From Concepts to Components

With the foundational concepts established, what LLMs are, how they become agents, what makes systems "multi-agent," we can now examine the practical building blocks. The remainder of this chapter shifts from conceptual understanding to implementation details. We'll dissect what's actually inside an agent, exploring the five core components that every system needs, regardless of architectural choices or vendor platforms. We'll examine how to select and evaluate the frameworks and models that best fit engineering applications. We'll address the critical challenge of connecting agents to the CAD systems, simulation tools, PLM platforms, and other infrastructure where engineering work actually happens. We'll explore the hybrid approach that combines rule-based automation with AI flexibility, and we'll discuss what actually works in production deployments versus what remains experimental.

Throughout these sections, the focus remains practical. What capabilities should you look for? What questions should you ask vendors? What trade-offs will you face? What investments will you need to make? The goal is to equip you to make informed decisions distinguishing between agent systems that deliver sustained value and those that merely demonstrate well.

2.2.2 Choosing Frameworks and Models

Model Selection for Engineering Agents

Before examining frameworks, engineering leaders must understand how to select appropriate language models for different agent roles. The proliferation of models from compact mini models to sophisticated reasoning systems to multimodal variants creates both opportunity and confusion. Matching model capabilities to task requirements optimizes both performance and cost.

This model selection framework guides both initial architecture decisions and ongoing optimization. Most production systems evolve toward hybrid architectures where model selection becomes dynamic. Agents choose which model to invoke based on task characteristics, with expensive models reserved for situations that genuinely require their capabilities. The cost differential between models is substantial enough that thoughtful selection can reduce inference costs by an order of magnitude while maintaining or improving performance.

Current Options

You don't need to build agent infrastructure from scratch. A growing ecosystem of frameworks provides foundations for agent development, handling the common infrastructure that every agent system needs while leaving you free to focus on what makes your application unique. Frameworks vary significantly in their capabilities, maturity levels, and fit for engineering applications. Selecting an inappropriate framework creates friction that compounds over time. You find yourself fighting the framework rather than building on it or discovering critical limitations only after significant investment.

The evaluation of frameworks for engineering applications differs from evaluation for general-purpose chatbots or content generation. Engineering agents need deep integration with specialized tools, robust handling of long-running processes, and careful attention to reliability and auditability. A framework that excels at building customer service chatbots may lack the capabilities that engineering workflows demand. The right framework choice accelerates deployment significantly (Figure 2.8).

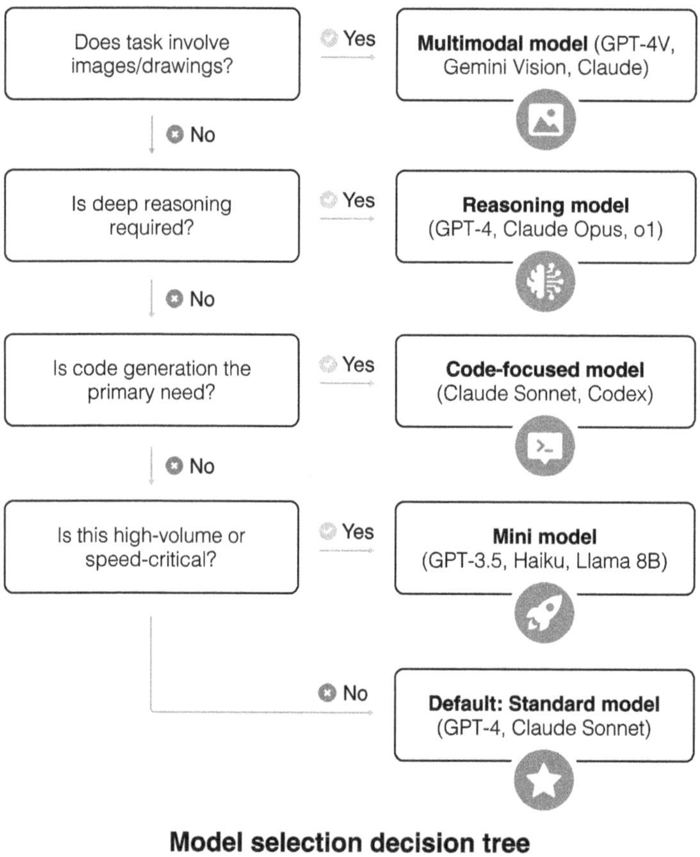

Figure 2.8 A decision tree for selecting the right LLM for a given agent task, routing through criteria such as image involvement, reasoning depth, code generation needs, and throughput requirements to recommend multimodal, reasoning, code-focused, mini, or standard models (© Iryna Novoseletska)

Organizations that select frameworks, matching their technical requirements and organizational capabilities, report agent deployments for progressing from concept to production in eight to twelve weeks rather than the six to nine months typical of custom-built solutions. Frameworks that provide pre-built connectors for common engineering tools such as PLM systems, major CAD platforms or simulation engines can reduce integration effort by 60 to 70 percent, allowing teams to focus development resources on encoding organizational context and refining agent behaviors rather than building infrastructure.

Tool Integration

The most critical capability for engineering agent frameworks is tool integration which is the ability to connect agents to the CAD systems, simulation engines, databases, and enterprise applications where engineering work actually happens. Without effective tool integration, agents remain conversational interfaces that can discuss engineering but can't perform engineering tasks.

When evaluating how a framework handles tool definition, consider whether the approach is primarily code-heavy or declarative. Code-heavy frameworks offer maximum flexibility. You can wrap any API, implement any logic, handle any edge case but they require significant development effort for each new tool. Declarative approaches let you describe tools through configuration files or visual interfaces, making them faster to create but potentially limited when your engineering tools have complex, stateful interactions that don't fit neatly into simple request-response patterns. The most practical frameworks for engineering applications support both approaches: declarative definitions for straightforward API wrappers where you're simply exposing existing functionality, and programmatic definitions when you need custom logic to translate between how agents think about problems and how your engineering tools expect to receive instructions.

Equally important is how the framework manages tools once they're defined. Tool capabilities evolve as underlying systems are upgraded or as you refine the interface based on experience. The framework should support versioning, so you can update tools without breaking agents that depend on previous behavior. Access control matters when different agents should have different capabilities. Perhaps some agents can read simulation results, but only specialized agents can launch new simulations. Error handling determines how gracefully agents respond when tools fail, return unexpected results, or time out during long-running operations. Frameworks with robust error handling patterns save substantial debugging effort compared to those that simply propagate exceptions.

Tool discovery addresses whether agents can learn about available tools dynamically or whether every tool must be explicitly configured for each agent. Dynamic discovery enables more flexible architectures where new capabilities become available to agents automatically, but it also introduces complexity in ensuring agents don't attempt to use tools they shouldn't access or don't understand. For engineering applications, a middle ground often works best: core tools that agents always know about, combined with discovery mechanisms for specialized capabilities that become relevant in specific contexts.

The ability to compose tools into higher-level workflows distinguishes sophisticated frameworks from basic ones. Engineering tasks often require sequences of tool invocations: extracting geometry from CAD, running simulation, comparing results to requirements and generating reports. Frameworks that support workflow composition let you define these sequences as reusable patterns rather than encoding them in agent prompts every time. Some frameworks go further, enabling agents to construct their own tool chains dynamically based on the task at hand. This capability is powerful but requires careful design to ensure agents don't create workflows that violate constraints or consume excessive resources.

Enterprise Integration

Engineering organizations have established tool chains, security requirements, and governance processes. The framework must facilitate integration with this existing infrastructure rather than requiring that everything adapt to the framework's assumptions. Connectivity to enterprise APIs is required. REST, GraphQL, gRPC or whatever protocols your systems use, the framework should support them. More subtle is how the framework handles the authentication, rate limiting, and error patterns that enterprise APIs typically require. A framework that assumes simple, unauthenticated API calls will struggle in environments with OAuth tokens, API keys with rotation policies, and circuit breakers that activate under load.

Database access is required for agents that need to query structured data. Many frameworks provide connectors for common databases, but engineering applications often use specialized databases such as time-series databases for sensor data, graph databases for relationship modeling, and domain-specific databases for materials or components. Evaluate whether the framework's database support extends to your specific needs or whether you'll be building custom connectors.

File handling is particularly important for engineering. Engineering data lives in files: CAD models, simulation inputs, analysis reports, or specifications. The framework should support reading and writing various file formats, with particular attention to engineering-specific formats that general-purpose frameworks often ignore. Consider whether the framework handles large files gracefully, whether it supports streaming for files too large to load entirely into memory, and whether it provides abstractions for working with file-based data.

Enterprise governance requirements such as authentication, authorization and audit logging are mandatory in most engineering organizations. The framework should work within your IT governance, not require exceptions to it. Can agents authenticate with your identity provider? Can their actions be logged into your audit systems? Can access controls limit what different agents can do? Frameworks designed primarily for consumer applications often treat governance as an afterthought. For engineering applications, it must be foundational.

Observability

When agents make mistakes and they will, you need to understand what happened. When agents perform well, you need to understand why, so you can build on that success. Observability encompasses the logging, tracing, debugging, and monitoring capabilities that make agent behavior comprehensible to human operators.

Comprehensive logging of agent reasoning, tool calls, and decisions provide the foundation for understanding agent behavior. Raw logs can be overwhelming, though. Frameworks should provide structured logging that makes it easy to filter, search, and analyze. The level of detail matters: Too little logging and problems are impossible to diagnose. Too many important signals are buried in noise. Frameworks should provide configurable logging levels so you can capture detailed traces during development and debugging while running with lighter logging in production.

Tracing follows chains of events across multiple agents and tool calls. When a design review produces unexpected results, you need to trace backward through the coordinating agent's decision-making, through each specialist agent's analysis, through each tool invocation, to identify where things went wrong. Distributed tracing to correlate events across multiple agents with unique trace identifiers is essential for debugging multi-agent systems.

Debugging tools let you step through agent reasoning, inspect state at various points, and reproduce issues reliably. Some frameworks provide interactive debugging environments where you can pause agent execution, examine context, and continue with modifications. Others provide replay capabilities that let you re-run previous interactions with identical inputs. These capabilities accelerate diagnosis when problems occur.

Metrics and monitoring can support with oversight on ongoing operational mechanisms. How many agent interactions are occurring? What's the latency distribution? What fraction of tool calls succeeded versus failed? What resources are agents consuming? Frameworks that integrate with standard monitoring infrastructure such as Prometheus, Grafana and cloud monitoring services enable operational practices that engineering organizations already understand.

Safety and Control

Agents operating in engineering systems can cause real problems if they malfunction. A runaway agent that launches unlimited simulations could consume computational resources needed for production work. An agent that modifies CAD files without appropriate checks could corrupt design data. An agent that approves designs without proper review could allow defective products to reach customers. Safety and control mechanisms prevent these scenarios.

Human-in-the-loop mechanisms enable agents to request human approval for significant decisions. The framework should make it easy to define which actions require approval, to present approval requests clearly to human operators, and to incorporate human decisions into agent workflows. The approval mechanism should handle timeouts gracefully. What happens if the human doesn't respond? And ideally, it should be designed to support delegation when the designated approver is unavailable.

Rollback and undo capabilities allow reversing agent actions when mistakes are discovered. This requires actions to be recorded in sufficient detail to enable reversal and requires the underlying systems to support undo operations. Not all actions can be undone. You can't unsend an email or undo a part that's already been manufactured but where reversal is possible, the framework should support it.

Rate limiting and quotas prevent agents from consuming excessive resources. Limits might apply to LLM calls (which have direct costs), to tool invocations (which might consume computational resources or API quotas), or to actions per time period (which prevents runaway loops). The framework should support configurable limits with clear behavior. When limits are reached, graceful degradation is better than hard failure.

Access control determine the tools each agent can use and what data it can access. The principle of least privilege applies. Agents should have access only to what they need for their designated purpose. A cost estimation agent doesn't need write access to CAD files. A design review agent doesn't need access to HR data. The framework should support fine-grained access control that can be configured per agent.

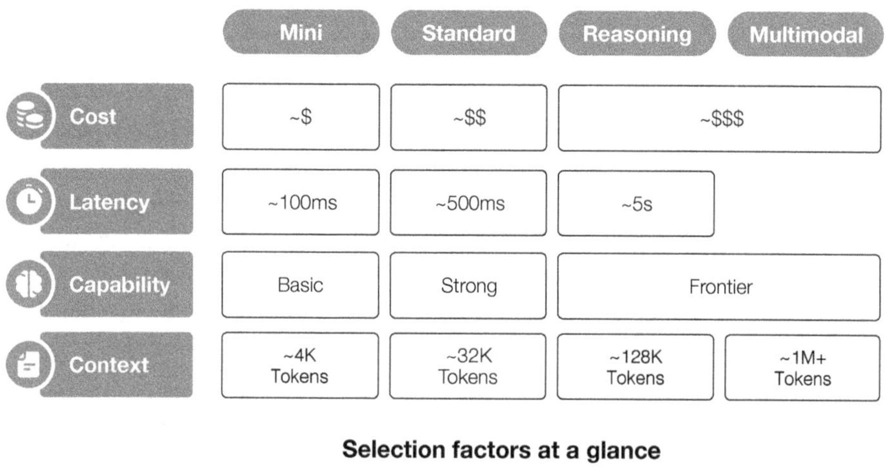

Figure 2.9 A comparative matrix of four model tiers—with examples of mini, standard, reasoning, and multimodal—evaluated across cost, latency, capability, and context window size to guide engineers in selecting the right model for each agent task (© Iryna Novoseletska)

Testing frameworks enable safe experimentation before agents are deployed with real authority. Unit tests verify that individual agent components behave correctly. Integration tests verify that agents work correctly with actual tools and data. Simulation environments provide sandboxes where agents can operate without affecting production systems. The framework should support these testing approaches, or at least not impede them.

Options Today

The framework landscape for agent development is evolving rapidly, and any specific recommendations would be outdated quickly. Instead, it's useful to understand the categories of options you'll encounter. General-purpose agent frameworks like LangChain, LlamaIndex, and AutoGen provide building blocks that can be assembled into agent systems. They offer flexibility and active communities but require significant customization for engineering applications. Development effort is needed to build the engineering-specific capabilities these frameworks don't provide.

LLM orchestration platforms provide managed services for LLM calls, prompt templates, and basic tool use. Often cloud-based, they simplify development at the cost of flexibility and control. They may be appropriate for simpler agent applications but often lack the customization depth that engineering workflows require.

Low-code agent builders let non-developers create agents through configuration and visual interfaces. They offer fast initial development but typically hit limitations when requirements become complex. For engineering applications with specialized integrations and nuanced logic, these limitations are often reached quickly.

Industry-specific platforms designed for manufacturing and engineering are emerging, some with pre-built integrations for common engineering tools. These may provide faster implementation if their capabilities align with your needs, but they may also constrain your architecture to patterns their designers anticipated.

Model Evolution and System Stability

Engineering leaders face a peculiar challenge when deploying agent systems: the foundation large language models are improving at unprecedented rates while simultaneously introducing volatility that complicates operational stability. New models emerge every few months with substantially better capabilities, different behavioral characteristics, and sometimes incompatible interfaces. Building stable engineering systems on this shifting foundation requires thoughtful strategies that balance the benefits of model improvements against the risks of instability.

The pace of model evolution creates both opportunity and challenge. GPT-4 released in March 2023 represented a massive leap over GPT-3.5. Claude 3 Opus in March 2024 brought new capabilities in analysis and reasoning. OpenAI's o1-preview in September 2024 introduced extended reasoning that changes how agents should be prompted and used. Each generation brings meaningful improvements such as better reasoning, larger context windows, more reliable tool use and reduced hallucination rates. Organizations that can quickly adopt these improvements gain competitive advantages through more capable agents.

However, these improvements come with behavioral changes that can destabilize production systems. A prompt that worked reliably with one model version may produce different outputs, sometimes better, sometimes worse, with the next version. Tool calling interfaces evolve, requiring code changes to maintain compatibility. Cost structures change, potentially making previously economical approaches prohibitively expensive. Even subtle shifts in model behavior—e.g. changes in verbosity, formatting preferences, or reasoning patterns—can cascade through multi-agent systems in unexpected ways.

The fundamental tension is between stability and capability. Engineering systems in production demand predictability. The same inputs should produce consistent outputs, or at least outputs whose variation is understood and acceptable. However, model improvements often introduce inconsistencies precisely because they handle situations differently, sometimes in ways the previous model couldn't. An agent system tuned for GPT-4's characteristics may perform sub-optimally or even fail when switched to a newer model, even though that newer model is objectively more capable in general.

Several strategies help organizations navigate this tension. The first is abstraction: introducing layers between your agent logic and the specific model implementation that isolate most of your system from model-specific details. Rather than calling OpenAI's API directly throughout your codebase, create an abstraction that presents a consistent interface regardless of which underlying model you're using. This abstraction handles differences in prompting patterns, tool calling formats, and response parsing. When you need to switch models, changes are concentrated in the abstraction layer rather than scattered throughout your application.

The second strategy is versioning and gradual migration. Treat model changes like you would treat any significant infrastructure change with testing, staged rollouts, and fallback options. When a new model becomes available, deploy it initially to a test environment where you can evaluate its behavior on representative tasks. Run comprehensive tests that capture not just correctness but also subtle quality differences. Is the new model more or less verbose? Does it require different prompt structures for comparable results? How do its latency and cost profile compare? Only after this evaluation should you begin migrating production workloads, and even then, do so gradually. Perhaps you migrate low-risk tasks first, monitoring carefully for issues before expanding to critical workflows.

The third strategy is to maintain model flexibility through feature flags and configuration. Your system should be able to use different models for different tasks or even A/B test models against each other in production. This flexibility serves multiple purposes: It lets you optimize cost by using cheaper models where they suffice while reserving expensive models for tasks that genuinely need their capabilities; it provides insurance against model degradation or unexpected issues by letting you quickly roll back to a known-good model; and it enables empirical comparison, so you can make data-driven decisions about when model upgrades improve your specific use cases versus when they introduce regressions.

The fourth strategy is prompt engineering discipline that reduces model-specific brittleness. Prompts that rely on language-based shortcuts are fragile across model changes. Prompts that clearly specify desired behavior provide examples and explicitly state constraints tend to be more robust. Invest in prompt testing infrastructure that lets you quickly evaluate whether a prompt still works as intended when the underlying model changes. Maintain a prompt library with version history so you can understand how prompts evolved and potentially roll back when upgrades cause issues.

The fifth strategy is monitoring and alerting that detects behavioral changes automatically. Don't wait for users to report that agents are behaving differently. Instrument your systems to detect deviations from expected patterns. Track metrics like response lengths, tool usage frequency, decision distributions, latency, and cost. When these metrics shift significantly, investigate whether model changes are responsible. This monitoring provides early warning of issues and quantitative evidence of whether model upgrades improve or degrade your specific workloads.

The cost management implications of model evolution deserve explicit attention. Early in the agent adoption curve, organizations often optimize for capability, using the most powerful models available with generous context windows and verbose outputs. As deployments scale and monthly bills grow from hundreds to thousands to tens of thousands of dollars, cost optimization becomes imperative. Model evolution helps here. Newer models often provide better capability per dollar, and the emergence of specialized models (vision, code, reasoning) lets you pay only for capabilities you actually need for each task. However, these optimizations require deliberate effort and flexibility to shift workloads between models based on evolving cost-benefit trade-offs.

The strategic question is how much to invest in futureproofing versus accepting that agent systems will require ongoing maintenance to adapt to model evolution. Complete future proof is impossible. You cannot know what capabilities or interface changes next year's models will bring. However, thoughtful architecture that embraces abstraction, maintains model flexibility, and treats model selection as a configuration choice rather than a hard-coded decision positions your organization to adapt more easily as the landscape evolves.

The longer-term perspective recognizes that model evolution is inevitable and probably perpetual. Large language models are not approaching a plateau. Research continues advancing capabilities, and commercial incentives drive ongoing improvement. Organizations building agent systems must plan for this reality rather than hoping for stability that won't arrive. This doesn't mean constant disruption, mature abstractions and good engineering practices can provide operational stability, even atop a changing foundation. It does mean though, that the agent platforms and frameworks you select should explicitly support model evolution, and your development practices should treat model updates as routine events requiring testing and validation rather than exceptional circumstances requiring crisis response.

The question isn't whether to upgrade models but when and how. New capabilities are too valuable to ignore. An agent that can reason more deeply, handle larger contexts, or make fewer errors simply delivers genuine business value. The challenge is capturing these benefits while maintaining the stability that production engineering systems require. Organizations that develop systematic approaches to model evaluation, staged migration, and behavioral monitoring will adapt more successfully than those treating each model change as a one-off event which requires custom handling.

The paradox of building on rapidly improving foundations is that the improvement itself creates work. In most engineering domains, better components simplify the overall system. Take for example a more reliable sensor which leads to requiring less error handling, or a stronger material that leads to reduction in safety factors. With LLMs, better models create new opportunities but also new decisions. Should we redesign to leverage new capabilities? Can we simplify prompts that worked around previous limitations? Should we migrate workloads to cheaper models that now meet our needs? These questions recur with each model generation, turning model selection from a one-time decision into an ongoing optimization problem.

Engineering leaders should approach model evolution with the mindset that informed infrastructure management plans for change: abstract where practical, monitored constantly, and migrated deliberately. The organizations that succeed with agent systems will be those that treat model evolution as a managed process rather than a disruptive surprise, building the flexibility and discipline that lets them harness improvements without sacrificing stability.

2.2.3 Connection to Engineering Systems

The Integration Challenge

Agents only become valuable when they connect to real engineering systems. This is where theory meets practice and where many agent projects stumble.

Engineering organizations typically have a complex landscape of systems:

- CAD (computer-aided design) systems for geometry
- CAE (computer-aided engineering) systems for simulation

- PLM (product lifecycle management) systems for data management
- ERP (enterprise resource planning) systems for cost and business processes
- custom databases and applications for specific functions

These systems were rarely designed with AI integration in mind. They have proprietary APIs (if any), complex data models, and their own security and governance requirements. Connecting agents to these systems is engineering work, not just configuration. However, this integration work delivers substantial efficiency gains. Organizations that have successfully integrated agents with their engineering tool ecosystems report that routine data extraction tasks such as gathering design specifications from PLM, pulling simulation results, collecting cost estimates, and compiling compliance documentation that previously consumed two to four hours of engineering time per design review now execute in five to ten minutes of agent operation. This automation doesn't just save time, it enables more frequent design validation and catching issues earlier when they're less expensive to fix. Teams report 30 to 40 percent reductions in late-stage design changes because agent-enabled continuous validation identifies problems during design development rather than at formal review gates.

Required Layers

A platform purpose-built for engineering agents requires several architectural layers working in concert, each addressing specific requirements that generic AI platforms don't adequately serve.

The Integration Foundation Layer

At the foundation sits deep integration with engineering tools and infrastructure. This extends beyond API connectivity to semantic understanding of engineering artifacts. The platform must comprehend that a CAD assembly isn't merely a file but a hierarchical structure with parts, constraints, mates, and design intent. It must understand that a simulation setup represents engineering decisions about mesh density, boundary conditions, and physics models. It must recognize that a PLM item exists in a web of relationships, used by these assemblies, manufactured by these processes, sourced from these suppliers, and subjected to these change orders.

This foundation layer provides connectors that preserve engineering semantics. When an agent retrieves a design from PLM, it gets not just geometry but the full context what requirements drove this design, what alternatives were considered, what analyses validated it, what manufacturing concerns shaped it. When an agent requests a simulation, the platform understands the trade-offs between fidelity and turnaround time, can recommend appropriate solver settings based on the problem type, and interprets results with awareness of simulation assumptions and limitations.

The integration foundation also handles the reality that engineering tools weren't designed for programmatic access by AI agents. CAD APIs might be synchronous and blocking when agents need asynchronous operation. Simulation solvers might require complex job submission through batch systems. PLM platforms might have data models so intricate that naive queries produce nonsensical results. The foundation layer abstracts these complexities, presenting agents with interfaces that match their operational model while handling the implementation details of actual engineering tools.

The Compute Orchestration Layer

Engineering agents need to orchestrate substantial computational resources, and this orchestration has requirements distinct from typical cloud workload management. The platform must support the heterogeneous compute of local workstations for interactive work, departmental servers for routine analysis, cloud bursting for design space exploration, and HPC clusters for high-fidelity simulation. It must handle licensing constraints as many engineering tools use floating licenses with limited concurrent seats, and the platform must allocate these resources intelligently across competing agent needs.

The compute layer also manages workflows that span widely varying timescales. An agent might need instant feedback from a simple calculation, results in minutes from a coarse analysis, and hours or days for detailed simulation. The platform must support asynchronous patterns where agents submit long-running jobs, continue with other work, and respond appropriately when results arrive. It must handle failures gracefully, e.g. solver crashes, job preemptions, or resource timeouts, without requiring agents to implement complex retry logic.

Cost management enters the picture as well. Cloud compute for engineering workloads can become expensive quickly. The platform should track costs, enforce budgets, recommend cost-effective resource allocation, and help agents make appropriate fidelity trade-offs. A design space exploration involving ten thousand FEA runs has dramatically different cost implications than a single validation analysis, and agents should have visibility into these economics.

The Knowledge Management Layer

Engineering decisions require access to organizational knowledge accumulated over years or decades. This knowledge doesn't fit the typical retrieval-augmented generation (RAG) pattern of searching documents and injecting text into prompts. Engineering knowledge is structured, temporal, and deeply interconnected.

The knowledge management layer maintains several distinct but related knowledge structures. Design knowledge captures what has been built past projects, components, assemblies, and their outcomes. Process knowledge captures how work is done with standard procedures, best practices, and lessons learned. Constraint knowledge captures limitation requirements, manufacturing capabilities, supplier qualifications, regulatory requirements, and corporate policies. Relationship knowledge captures connections which design served similar functions, which suppliers provide which materials, and which engineers have expertise in which domains.

This knowledge has temporal dimensions. Knowing that a component design exists is insufficient. You need to know whether it's current or obsolete, whether it's approved for new designs or only for service parts, whether it has a history of field failures or has performed flawlessly. The platform must enable agents to reason about knowledge in time, understanding not just the current state but the evolution and trajectory.

The knowledge layer also handles the challenge of tacit knowledge expertise that resides in engineers' heads but has never been formally documented. The platform captures this knowledge when an expert reviews and corrects an agent's decision. That correction becomes knowledge. When an agent encounters a novel situation requiring human judgment, human reasoning becomes accessible to future agents facing similar situations.

The Governance and Control Layer

Engineering governance is a fundamental requirement driven by liability, regulation, and organizational prudence. The platform's governance layer enforces policies consistently across all agent operations.

Authentication and authorization must respect engineering organizational structures. Different roles have different authorities. A senior engineer might authorize design changes that a junior engineer can only propose. Different data has different sensitivity levels. Some cost information might be widely accessible while detailed supplier pricing might be restricted to procurement. Agents must operate within these constraints, just as human engineers do.

Audit and traceability provide complete records of agent decisions and actions. When an agent approves a design for manufacturing, the platform captures what data the agent examined, what rules it evaluated, what AI reasoning it applied, what confidence level it assessed, and what human oversight was involved. Years later, if questions arise about that decision, complete provenance is available. This supports both compliance requirements and organizational learning. Understanding why agents make certain decisions helps improve their performance and reveals gaps in their knowledge or reasoning.

Access control extends beyond simple read/write permissions to encompass operational authorities. Which agents can submit manufacturing orders? Which agents can approve engineering changes? Which agents can commit to customer deliveries? These authorities must be managed centrally, not scattered across individual agent implementations, especially when organizational structure changes, for example an engineer gets promoted, a team reorganizes, or a supplier gets de-qualified. Those changes propagate automatically to agent authorities.

The governance layer also manages agent lifecycle. New agents undergo approval before deployment. Running agents are monitored for performance and correctness. Agents that consistently make poor decisions get flagged for review or retirement. This lifecycle management maintains quality as the agent ecosystem evolves.

The User Interface Layer

Different engineering roles require fundamentally different interactions with agents, and the platform must provide role-appropriate interfaces rather than forcing everyone through the same generic chat window. Creators, engineers who build and configure agents, need workflow editors that let them define agent behaviors, specify tool access, configure knowledge sources, and set governance policies. They need visibility into how agents perform and the ability to refine agent logic based on actual usage. The platform provides abstractions that let engineering subject matter experts create agents without becoming AI developers, while still allowing AI specialists to build sophisticated custom capabilities when needed.

Experts, who oversee agent operations, need monitoring dashboards which show agent activity, decision quality, and anomalies which require attention. They need interfaces for reviewing agent decisions when governance requires human-in-the-loop approval. They need tools for providing feedback that improves agent performance. The platform makes expert oversight efficient rather than burdensome surfacing and decisions visible that genuinely need human judgment while letting routine operations proceed autonomously.

Consumers who use agents to accomplish engineering work need interfaces that feel natural within their existing workflows. An engineer working in CAD shouldn't have to leave that environment to get agent assistance; the agent should be available in context. An engineer reviewing a design shouldn't have to manually copy data into a chat interface; the agent should already have access to what's being reviewed. The platform meets users where they work rather than forcing them to adapt to the platform's preferred interaction model.

IT administrators need control panels for the entire platform to monitor resource consumption, to manage integrations, to enforce security policies, and to troubleshoot issues. They need visibility across the full stack, from LLM usage to tool integration to governance enforcement. The platform treats IT administration as a first-class user persona with dedicated interfaces and capabilities.

The Context Layer

Raw integration alone is insufficient. A context layer must transform data into meaningful information. Basic integration returns data. Effective integration returns data enriched with the context that makes it interpretable and actionable.

Consider a query to your PLM system for similar past designs. Basic integration returns a list of part numbers and descriptions—technically correct but of limited utility. Effective integration provides much richer information: the reasoning for why these particular designs are considered (similar to the current situation, how successful they were in practice), including whether they experienced quality issues or customer complaints, who worked on them and thus has expertise you could consult about design decisions and lessons learned, what insights were captured in design reviews or retrospectives about what went well and what should be done differently, and how they differ from the current situation in ways that might affect whether past approaches would work again.

This context layer embodies organizational knowledge that distinguishes experienced engineering organizations from novices. Building it requires systematic effort across several dimensions. Raw data must be augmented with metadata and relationships, tagging designs with the problems they solve, the requirements they meet, the manufacturing processes they employ, and the performance they achieved. Knowledge graphs must capture connections between engineering artifacts, namely, which components are used in which assemblies, which suppliers provide which materials, which engineers have expertise in which domains, which design patterns succeeded or failed in which contexts.

Institutional knowledge that traditionally lives only in engineers' heads must be documented in searchable form. This is perhaps the most challenging aspect because it requires capturing tacit knowledge such as the "we tried that approach on the X project, and it didn't work because ..." Insights that inform experienced engineers' judgment but rarely get written down. The context layer must include feedback loops that capture lessons learned from agent operations themselves. When an agent's recommendation is followed and succeeds, that success becomes part of future context. When a recommendation is rejected or fails, understanding why enriches future decision-making.

The context layer fundamentally distinguishes functional integrations from superficial ones. Without it, agents can access data but cannot interpret its significance. They become sophisticated search engines that find information but don't understand it. With robust context layers, agents provide responses, informed by organizational experience and priorities, drawing on decades of accumulated wisdom rather than merely querying current databases. This transformation from data access to context-aware intelligence represents the difference between agents that impress in demonstrations and agents that deliver sustained value in production.

2.2.4 The Bridge: Rules, AI, and Agents

Rule-Based Automation Today

Engineering automation has traditionally been rule-based, and for good reasons. Rules are how we codify engineering knowledge as minimum wall thickness requirements, stress safety factors, geometric dimensioning and tolerancing standards, or manufacturing process capabilities. If the wall thickness is less than 3 millimeters in this material for this loading condition, flag an error. If the material is steel grade 1045, use this cost factor and these material properties. If the assembly sequence would require inserting a part through an opening smaller than the part itself, reject it as impossible.

This approach has served engineering well for decades. Rule-based automation is fundamentally predictable. The same input always produces the same output, which matters when designing products where lives depend on reliability. It's completely explainable. You can trace exactly why a decision was made, following the logic chain from inputs through rules to conclusions. This transparency satisfies auditors, supports regulatory compliance, and builds engineering confidence. Rule-based systems are also fast. No expensive neural network inference, just straightforward logic evaluation that runs in microseconds even on modest hardware. Rules encode expert knowledge in a form that can be shared, reviewed, improved, and maintained by teams of engineers who understand the domain.

The mechanical engineering field has utilized rule-based automation extensively. Design rule checkers validate that parts meet manufacturing constraints, that bend radii don't exceed press brake capabilities, that hole sizes match available tooling, and that tolerances are achievable with the intended processes. Finite element analysis often includes rule-based mesh quality checks to ensure elements don't have excessive aspect ratios or skewness that would compromise results. Assembly validation uses rules to detect interferences, verify fastener accessibility, and ensure adequate clearance for thermal expansion. Configuration management systems apply rules to maintain product consistency, ensuring that when a component changes, all affected assemblies are flagged for review.

Industrial engineering relies heavily on rules. Production scheduling systems use priority rules as shortest processing time, earliest due date, or critical ratio to sequence jobs through manufacturing resources. Quality control applies statistical process control rules to detect when production drifts out of specification. Inventory management systems use reorder point rules and economic order quantity formulas. Safety systems apply rigid rules about lockout-tagout procedures, machine guarding requirements, and hazardous material handling.

Where Rules Work

Rules work well when certain conditions hold. The underlying pattern must be consistent and well-understood (we know that yield strength decreases with temperature), following predictable relationships, such as that certain geometric features create stress concentrations and that specific material combinations cause galvanic corrosion. The number of relevant variables must be manageable (a rule checking for minimum wall thickness might consider material, loading condition, and manufacturing process), perhaps ten factors total. The relationship between inputs and outputs should be relatively straightforward, even if there are many rules, each individual rule's logic should be clear.

Rules also work when the environment is stable. The physics of materials doesn't change. Standard manufacturing processes have well-characterized capabilities. Regulatory requirements update slowly with advance notice. In this stability, rules capture institutional knowledge and make it consistently accessible. The engineer who discovered that particular combination of features tends to cause cracking doesn't need to be consulted every time because now their insight is encoded in a rule that flags that pattern automatically.

Rules work when completeness is achievable. You can enumerate all the important cases. You can write rules that cover them. When an experienced engineer reviews a design, they're mentally running through checklists. Have all fasteners been specified? Are materials compatible? Is assembly feasible? These checklists can be transformed into automated rules. For well-understood product families and established processes, this completeness is realistic.

Where Rules Fail

However, rules fail when engineering requires something they fundamentally cannot provide: context-sensitive judgment. This failure manifests in several distinct ways, each revealing a different limitation of purely rule-based approaches. The first failure mode is the edge case explosion. Real engineering situations have vast combinatorial complexity. You might write a rule: "For sheet metal parts, minimum bend radius is 1.5 times material thickness." Simple enough, but then the exceptions begin accumulating: unless the material is spring steel, where work hardening near bends requires 3 times thickness (except for materials over 6 mm thick, where spring back dominates and you need 2.5 times thickness); unless you're using a press brake with precision tooling and computer-controlled back gauge, in which case 1.2 times thickness is achievable; unless the part has multiple bends in different directions, creating residual stress interactions that require additional margin; unless it's a low volume part where the tooling investment for tighter radii isn't justified; unless, unless, unless ...

Each exception generates more rules. The rule base grows from dozens to hundreds to thousands. Maintaining this becomes increasingly difficult when manufacturing capabilities improve or new materials arrive. Which of the thousand rules need updating? When rules interact in complex ways, unexpected emergent behavior appears. An engineer encounters a situation where three rules give contradictory guidance, and there's no meta-rule for resolving the conflict. The system becomes brittle, technically correct in the cases it was designed for, but unusable when reality presents something slightly different.

The second failure mode is the inability to understand intent and context. Consider a design guideline: "Minimize the number of unique parts to reduce inventory complexity." This is sound advice. A rule-based system might flag any design that introduces a new part number when a similar existing part could be reused. However, the rule doesn't understand that sometimes introducing a new part is the right answer. Perhaps the existing part is specified for a product line that's being phased out, and the design effort to reuse it will be wasted. Perhaps the similar part is sourced from a supplier the company is trying to reduce dependence on for strategic reasons. Perhaps the new part consolidates three existing parts, actually reducing inventory even though it adds one part number.

A human engineer considers this broader context naturally. They know the product roadmap, understand supplier relationships, and recognize strategic initiatives. Rule-based systems don't. They only know the facts explicitly provided. You could theoretically encode all this context into rules, but the context changes constantly. Product roadmaps shift. Supplier relationships are evolving. Strategic priorities get reprioritized. The rule base would need continuous updating to reflect current context, and someone would need to ensure that updating happened. In practice, rule-based systems end up working with stale context, generating recommendations that were correct last year but aren't anymore.

The third failure mode is the inability to adapt flexibly to novel situations. Engineering inherently involves encountering situations you haven't seen before: new customer requirements, new materials, new manufacturing technologies, or new combinations of existing elements. Rules handle novelty poorly because they only encode what someone previously thought to encode. When confronted with something outside their rule coverage, rule-based systems typically either reject it conservatively ("this doesn't match any known-good pattern, so flag it as suspicious") or fail silently (the situation doesn't match any rule, so no check is performed).

Consider a design using a relatively new additive manufacturing process. The rule base was developed for traditional subtractive manufacturing such as machining, casting, or forming. It checks draft angles on cast features, tool access for machined features, and bend radii for formed features. For additively manufactured parts, these rules are irrelevant, though. The new process has completely different constraints as support structure requirements, minimum feature sizes, surface finish limitations from layer buildup, and residual stress from thermal cycling. A rule-based system doesn't recognize that its entire framework of checks no longer applies. It might reject a perfectly valid additive design because it violates conventional manufacturing rules, or worse, approve a problematic additive design because its issues aren't covered by the existing rule set.

Why Rules Can't Think Like Engineers

The fundamental limitation of rule-based automation is that it cannot mirror how humans actually make engineering decisions. We like to think that we follow procedures and checklists, and to some extent we do. However, experienced engineers rely heavily on pattern recognition, analogical reasoning, and intuitive judgment built from years of seeing what works and what doesn't.

When an experienced mechanical engineer looks at a design, they don't consciously execute thousands of rules. They look at the overall form and think "this reminds me of the bracket we designed for the X project, which had problems with fatigue at the mounting points." That recollection triggered by visual similarity and functional analogy, not by matching a rule pattern, focuses attention on critical areas. The engineer then applies deeper analysis where experience suggests it matters most, rather than mechanically checking everything with equal attention.

This pattern-matching happens fluidly across multiple dimensions simultaneously. The engineer considers geometry, materials, loading, manufacturing, cost, schedule, supplier capabilities, customer requirements, and company strategy in an integrated way. These factors don't get evaluated sequentially by independent rules that then somehow get combined. They inform each other continuously. The realization that a design will be expensive influences that performance requirements feel essential versus negotiable. The knowledge that the customer is price-sensitive versus performance-driven changes which aspects of the design deserve the most attention.

Capturing this integrated, context-aware, pattern-driven decision-making in rules is extraordinarily difficult, perhaps impossible in the general case. You can create rules for specific decisions "if stress exceeds 80 percent of yield, flag for review" but you can't create a practical rule-based encoding of everything a senior engineer knows. The knowledge is too distributed, too contextual, too pattern-based, too dependent on nuance and judgment.

Moreover, human engineering work involves creativity and adaptation that rules can't replicate. When a design approach isn't working, engineers don't just optimize parameters within the existing approach. They reconceive the problem entirely. They borrow solutions from other domains. They invent new combinations of existing techniques. This creative problem-solving requires stepping outside the framework of existing rules, not just applying them more thoroughly.

Generative AI: Strengths and Limits

On the opposite end of the spectrum sits generative AI: large language models that can handle novel situations, reason about ambiguous problems, and produce creative outputs. Generative AI brings flexibility, handling situations never explicitly programmed. It demonstrates creativity, generating novel solutions by combining concepts in unexpected ways. It manages contextual understanding, considering complex nuance and situational factors. It communicates naturally in language that engineers understand without special training.

Yet generative AI brings its own severe limitations for engineering applications. It's fundamentally unpredictable. The same input might produce different outputs, and you can't always predict what output will emerge. This unpredictability is problematic in engineering, where reproducibility often matters. It's also computationally expensive. Neural network inference costs significantly more than rule evaluation, which matters when you're processing thousands of designs or running checks continuously. Perhaps most critically, generative AI lacks the reliability guarantees that engineering often requires. It might occasionally miss obvious problems, hallucinate capabilities that don't exist, or confidently assert incorrect information.

Neither extreme pure rules nor pure generative AI serves engineering well. Pure rule-based systems can't handle the novelty, nuance, and context that characterize real engineering work. Pure generative AI lacks the reliability, explainability, and consistency that engineering work demands.

The Bridge

Multi-agent systems occupy the middle ground between pure rule-based automation and pure generative AI. Different tasks within any engineering workflow have different characteristics and match the appropriate approach to each task. It produces results that neither approach could achieve alone.

Rule-based approaches excel at well-defined checks with clear criteria, at high-volume routine validations where speed matters, at safety-critical decisions that require guaranteed behavior, and at situations where explainability is legally required. When you know exactly what to check and can specify the criteria unambiguously, rules execute faster, more consistently, and more transparently than any AI system.

Generative AI excels in complementary situations: interpreting ambiguous requirements that can't be reduced to simple rules, reasoning about novel situations that don't match established patterns, generating creative options that rules could never enumerate, communicating in natural language that humans find intuitive, and understanding context and nuance that formal specifications don't capture. When the problem is open-ended, when judgment is required, when the situation is new, AI reasoning provides capabilities rules can't match.

Agents provide the orchestration that makes these approaches work together. They recognize which approach is appropriate for each situation, invoke rules when those rules apply, escalate to AI reasoning when rules don't cover the case, combine results from both approaches into coherent outputs, and maintain context across the full workflow. This orchestration is itself intelligent. Agents don't simply follow a script but make contextual decisions about how to handle each situation they encounter.

Knowing When to Use What

A key capability of effective agents is knowing when to use rule-based logic versus when to invoke AI reasoning versus when to escalate to humans. This meta-level decision, choosing how to approach each situation, is itself a form of intelligence that can be designed carefully and refined through experience.

The default should favor rules when the situation matches patterns where rules were designed for, when the decision is routine and low stakes, when speed is critical, and when audit trails are required. Rules are the fast path, the efficient path, and the predictable path. When they apply cleanly, use them.

Escalation to AI reasoning is appropriate when no rules apply to the situation, when the situation has unusual characteristics that rules don't cover, when natural language understanding is needed to interpret requirements or communicate findings, and when creative problem-solving is required to generate options or work around obstacles. AI brings capabilities that rules lack, but at a cost in speed and predictability. Use AI when those capabilities are needed.

Escalation to humans is appropriate when the stakes are high enough that autonomous decision-making is inappropriate, when AI confidence is low enough that its reasoning shouldn't be trusted without verification, when policy exceptions are needed that go beyond what agents are authorized to decide, and when learning opportunities exist that should be captured for future improvement. Humans provide judgment that neither rules nor AI can replicate, and oversight that responsible engineering requires.

This escalation hierarchy should not be static. As experience with the multi-agent system accumulates, patterns emerge. AI reasoning may consistently add value for certain types of designs such as those with novel geometries, unusual material combinations, or innovative features. The threshold for AI involvement on those designs can be lowered. AI may frequently struggle with certain situations: highly regulated components, heritage designs with extensive history, or customer-specific requirements. In such cases, escalation to humans for those situations should be mandated. The hierarchy should evolve based on evidence of what works.

Building This in Practice

Building this hybrid approach in practice requires systematic attention to several activities that transform conceptual architecture into operational reality. Begin by inventorying existing rule-based automation. What design rule checkers already exist? What validation scripts run as part of workflows? What approval workflows encode business rules? These are assets representing accumulated engineering knowledge. They should be preserved and leveraged, not discarded and rebuilt. The goal is to augment rules with AI capabilities, not to replace working systems with experimental ones.

The next step is wrapping existing rule-based systems as tools that agents can invoke. This is largely a technical integration task, but it requires thoughtful interface design. The agent should be able to invoke the design rule checker, receive results in a structured format it can reason about, and understand enough about what the checker does to interpret results intelligently. The wrapper should handle errors gracefully, report not just pass/fail but the details that inform downstream reasoning and provide metadata about what was checked and with what confidence.

With rules wrapped as tools, identify the gaps: the situations where rules fall short and humans currently intervene. These gaps are candidates for AI augmentation. Rules may check individual tolerances, but humans must assess whether the tolerance stack-up is appropriate. Rules may verify material properties, but humans must judge whether the material is suitable for the specific application context. Rules may flag deviations from standards, but humans must determine which deviations are acceptable and which require design changes. Each gap represents an opportunity for AI reasoning to add value.

Design escalation paths that specify clear criteria for when to use rules, when to invoke AI, and when to involve humans. These criteria should be configurable and adjustable based on experience without requiring code changes. Parameters might include stakes thresholds (decisions above this cost or risk level require human approval), confidence thresholds (AI assessments below this confidence level require human verification), and novelty thresholds (situations with similarity below this level to known patterns require AI analysis rather than rule-only processing).

Build feedback loops that track where AI adds value versus where it struggles. When AI analysis catches an issue that rules are missed, record that success. When AI analysis raises a false alarm that human review is dismissed, record that failure. When humans override AI recommendations, capture the reasoning. This data enables continuous improvement of the balance between approaches of adjusting thresholds, refining AI prompts, and identifying new rules to encode lessons learned.

Throughout all of this, maintain explainability. For any decision the system produces, it should be possible to explain what rules were evaluated and what they found, what AI reasoning was applied and what it concluded, why this particular path was chosen among the alternatives, and what confidence level attaches to the conclusion. This explainability serves multiple purposes: It builds trust with users who can understand how decisions are made, it supports debugging when decisions are wrong, it satisfies audit requirements in regulated environments, and it enables the learning loops that improve the system over time.

Regulatory Compliance and Certifiable Autonomy

The enthusiasm around autonomous AI agents collides with an inconvenient reality in regulated industries: Regulatory frameworks were built around human judgment and deterministic processes, creating fundamental barriers to fully autonomous systems in contexts where certification matters. Understanding these constraints prevents organizations from pursuing agent architectures that cannot achieve regulatory acceptance, regardless of their technical capabilities.

The idea of autonomy levels is a helpful way to understand legal and safety limits. In our five-level system, ranging from simple reactions to full collaboration, industries like aerospace, medicine, and car safety usually set a hard limit. They rarely allow systems to go beyond level 3 or level 4. This isn't just a technical choice, it's about how safety laws are written. Current certification processes are designed to test predictable rules, and most regulators simply don't have a way to verify or approve a system that has complete level 5 independence.

Level 5 autonomy agents that negotiate, adjust their own goals, compromise on requirements, and operate as genuine collaborative partners, are fundamentally non-certifiable under current regulatory paradigms in safety-critical domains. Certification requires demonstrating that a system will behave in specific, predictable ways under defined conditions. An agent that adjusts its own goals based on context operates outside this framework. When an aerospace regulator asks "what will your system do if it encounters condition X?," the required answer is deterministic and complete, not "it depends on how the agent interprets the situation and what goals it prioritizes at that moment."

This is not merely regulatory conservatism or lack of understanding of AI capabilities. It reflects fundamental challenges in validating systems whose behavior emerges from complex interactions rather than following predetermined logic. How do you test an agent that can adjust its objectives? The test space becomes unbounded. How do you prove safety when the agent might redefine what "safe" means in novel contexts? The verification problem becomes intractable.

Level 4 learning agents face similar but slightly less absolute constraints. An agent that improves its performance over time through experience learning from operational data, presents certification challenges because its behavior changes after certification. The certified configuration is the initial one, but the operational configuration evolves. Regulators have no framework for certifying systems with deliberate post-certification behavioral evolution, even when that evolution aims at improved performance.

Some regulated domains are exploring constrained approaches to learning systems, such as freezing learning after initial deployment, limiting learning to specific parameters while keeping decision logic fixed, or requiring recertification whenever learning produces sufficiently large behavioral changes. These approaches may eventually enable level 4 capabilities in regulated contexts, but they remain largely experimental. For engineering leaders planning agent deployments in regulated products today, assuming level 4 learning systems can be certified, is premature.

This leaves level 2 and level 3 as the practical ceiling for certified agent systems in most regulated industries currently. Level 2 goal-directed agents that decide how to achieve specified objectives following predefined logic can be certified because their decision space, while flexible, remains bounded and analyzable. Level 3 planning agents that decompose complex tasks into sequences of simpler ones can similarly be certified if the planning logic follows deterministic rules and the action space is constrained.

The key distinction is between agents that operate within certified boundaries and agents that define their own boundaries. An agent that selects from alternatives approved designs, following documented logic, can be certified. An agent that generates novel alternatives using learned patterns cannot, at least not under current frameworks. An agent that plans a sequence of validated operations to achieve a defined goal can be certified. An agent that formulates its own goals, based on contextual interpretation, cannot.

Quality management system compatibility adds another layer of constraint. Industries like aerospace, medical devices, and automotive operate under formal QMS frameworks such as AS9100, ISO 13485, IATF 16949, and similar standards. These systems require documented procedures, defined authorities, traceable decisions, and demonstrable control over processes affecting product quality and safety. Agentic systems must integrate with these requirements, not circumvent them.

This integration requirement affects agent architecture in several specific ways. First, agent decision logic must be documentable in ways QMS auditors can evaluate. This doesn't mean exposing neural network weights, but it does mean explaining in procedural terms what the agent does, what authorities it has, what constraints it observes, and how its decisions are verified. Second, agents must respect existing approval authorities. If a process requires engineering manager sign-off, an agent cannot autonomously make that decision, regardless of its analytical capabilities. The agent can prepare the analysis, identify the relevant decision, even recommend an outcome, but the human authority must retain the approval action.

Third, changes to agent behavior must follow change control procedures. Updating an agent's knowledge base, refining its decision criteria, or expanding its authorities are controlled changes requiring documented review and approval, just as modifying a design procedure or manufacturing process would be. This constrains how rapidly agent capabilities can evolve in operational environments. Fourth, nonconformances and corrective actions must extend to agent operations. When an agent makes an error or operates outside its intended bounds, this triggers the same investigation and corrective action processes that would apply to human errors. The organization must determine the root cause, implement corrective actions, and potentially revise the agent design or constraints.

Audit trail requirements in regulated environments demand comprehensive logging that goes beyond general best practice for software systems. Every agent decision affecting product realization must create a record, showing what data the agent accessed, what logic it applied, what outcome it reached, what confidence or uncertainty it assessed, and what human review or approval occurred. This record must persist as long as product records must be maintained—for aerospace or medical devices, potentially for decades. The logging overhead can be substantial, and agent architectures must accommodate it from the outset rather than adding it as an afterthought.

These audit requirements also affect agent performance. An agent that must write detailed logs for every decision executes more slowly than one that doesn't. In domains where real-time or near-real-time response matters, this overhead must be accounted in the system design. Some organizations address this through hierarchical logging. Use lightweight logging for routine operations, with detailed logging triggered only for significant decisions or when outcomes fall outside normal ranges.

The practical consequence of these constraints is that certified systems typically remain maximal at level 2 or level 3 autonomy. Within those levels, substantial value can still be delivered. Level 2 agents can handle goal-directed tasks like selecting appropriate simulation parameters based on analysis type, choosing materials from approved lists based on requirements, validating designs against established criteria, or generating documentation following template structures. Level 3 agents can orchestrate multi-step workflows like design space exploration within bounded parameter ranges, tolerance allocation following organizational standards, cost optimization through approved methods, or manufacturing process planning using qualified processes.

What certified systems cannot do, under current regulatory frameworks, is operate with the open-ended autonomy that level 4 and level 5 imply. They cannot learn new behaviors during operational use without recertification. They cannot adjust their objectives or negotiate requirements. They cannot generate genuinely novel solutions that fall outside validated solution spaces. These limitations are not temporary technical hurdles that better AI will overcome. They are fundamental constraints imposed by regulatory requirements for safety and predictability.

Organizations in regulated industries must design agent systems around these constraints from the beginning. Attempting to achieve higher autonomy levels and hoping to convince regulators later is a strategy of wasted resources. The viable approach is building sophisticated capability within level 2 and level 3 autonomy, demonstrating value there, and participating in industry-regulatory dialogs about how frameworks might evolve to accommodate more advanced capabilities safely.

Documentation for regulatory review requires careful consideration when agents are involved. The documentation must explain what the agent does in terms regulators can evaluate against their requirements. This typically means providing multiple views of the system: a functional description explaining the agent's purpose and authorities in engineering terms, a technical description explaining the agent's architecture and decision logic at a level sufficient for technical evaluation, and verification documentation demonstrating how the agent's performance was validated, what testing was performed, what acceptance criteria were applied, and how ongoing monitoring ensures continued correct performance.

The verification documentation deserves particular attention because validating agentic systems challenges traditional approaches. Deterministic software can be verified through input-output testing covering the decision space. Agentic systems with LLM components produce variable outputs from the same inputs, making traditional verification insufficient. Organizations, navigating certification, have developed several complementary approaches.

One approach is bounding verification, where you demonstrate that agent outputs always fall within acceptable ranges even if the specific output varies. For example, an agent selecting simulation parameters might produce different valid parameter sets for the same problem, but verification demonstrates all selections meet adequacy criteria. Another approach uses statistical validation, characterizing agent performance across representative samples rather than attempting exhaustive testing. You demonstrate that the agent achieves required accuracy, precision, and reliability metrics across realistic problem distributions.

A third approach employs multiple agent strategies for critical decisions, where independent agents analyze the same situation using different methods, and agreement between them provides confidence. Disagreement triggers human review. This redundancy has cost and performance implications but can satisfy safety requirements. Finally, deterministic bounds around agents ensure that critical requirements cannot be violated regardless of agent behavior, with agent reasoning operating within hard limits enforced by conventional logic. These verification approaches must be established during development and documented for regulatory submission. Attempting to retrofit verification onto completed agent systems is difficult and may be impossible if the architecture doesn't support the required evidence generation.

The regulatory landscape for AI in engineering is evolving, with aerospace regulators releasing position papers, medical device regulators issuing guidance, and automotive authorities developing frameworks for AI safety. However, evolution happens slowly in safety-critical regulation, and the direction is toward more structured requirements for AI validation, not relaxation of safety standards. Engineering leaders should track these developments but should not assume near-term relaxation of autonomy constraints for certified systems.

The strategic implication is clear: For products requiring regulatory certification, agent system design must account for autonomy constraints from initial architecture. Level 2 and level 3 capabilities, thoughtfully implemented, can deliver substantial value while remaining certifiable. Level 4 and level 5 capabilities, however impressive technically, remain incompatible with current certification frameworks in most regulated domains. Organizations pursuing agent deployment in certified products should design for constrained autonomy, comprehensive audit trails, QMS integration, and verification approaches acceptable to their regulators. Those that are designing for higher autonomy levels expecting regulatory acceptance, are likely to set themselves up for expensive redesign or outright project failure when certification proves unattainable.

Investing in Context

Context is the essential ingredient that transforms generic AI capabilities into useful engineering tools. Context doesn't appear magically, though. Capturing and encoding it requires deliberate effort that organizations often underestimate. The work of capturing context begins with the people who carry it. Structured interviews with experienced engineers, not casual conversations, but deliberate knowledge extraction sessions surface the tacit rules and judgment patterns that experts apply unconsciously. An engineer who has reviewed hundreds of designs can often articulate, when asked carefully, what patterns trigger their concern and what combinations they've learned to trust. The questions matter: not "how do you review designs?" which invites generic answers, but "tell me about a recent design that concerned you and what specifically triggered that concern" which surfaces concrete examples that reveal implicit criteria. This extraction is painstaking work, requiring skilled interviewers who can probe beyond surface answers, but it yields knowledge that no database contains.

Historical data offers a complementary source of context. Your past projects encode decisions in their outcomes like the designs that succeeded and the ones that required revision, the cost estimates that proved accurate and those that missed badly, the suppliers who delivered reliably and those who caused problems. Analyzing this history reveals implicit knowledge: which design approaches consistently work for which applications, which tolerance strategies survive manufacturing variation, and which analysis methods produce trustworthy results. The decisions themselves are recorded in PLM systems and project archives. The challenge is extracting the patterns they embody. This may require data science capabilities that engineering organizations don't traditionally possess, but the investment pays off in context that agents can leverage.

Going forward, the most valuable investment is capturing rationale alongside decisions. When an engineer approves a design, rejects a material choice, or accepts a manufacturing process, the recording of why they made that choice builds a growing knowledge base. Over months and years, these accumulated rationales become a corpus of organizational judgment that agents can learn from. The discipline of documenting rationale also improves human decision-making, articulating reasons, forces clarity that intuitive judgment sometimes lacks, and recorded rationales will enable later review when outcomes don't match expectations.

Creating feedback loops ensures that agent experience improves context over time. When agents make decisions that turn out well, capturing that success reinforces effective patterns. When agents make mistakes, capture the failure and its root cause to enable correction. When humans override agent recommendations, capturing the reasoning behind the override reveals gaps in agent understanding. These feedback loops require infrastructure to collect, store, and act on feedback, and they require organizational discipline to actually provide feedback rather than just accepting or rejecting agent outputs without explanation.

Investment in ontology, the structured vocabulary of concepts and relationships that agents use to reason makes context shareable and maintainable. When everyone agrees on what terms mean, how concepts relate, and what categories exist in your domain, the context captured by one person can be used by agents serving another. When ontology is informal or inconsistent, context remains fragmented and difficult to leverage. This work involves debating definitions, reconciling different mental models, and documenting agreements that seem obvious until you try to write them down. It provides the foundation that makes accumulated context systematically useful rather than ad hoc collections of notes that only their authors can interpret.

This context investment does not make impressive demos, but it determines whether a multi-agent system delivers sustained value. Organizations that skip this work end up with agents that produce generic outputs. Organizations that invest in context, capture build systems that reflect their specific engineering knowledge and practices.

Managing Expectations

Accurate assessment of what agents can and cannot do today prevents the disappointment that kills promising initiatives and builds the trust that enables sustained investment. Overselling generates excitement that fades into backlash when reality doesn't match promises. Underselling fails to capture opportunities that enable genuine capabilities. The goal is to have accurate expectations that guide appropriate application.

Today's agents can handle well-defined tasks with clear success criteria tasks where you can specify what good looks like and verify whether the agent achieved it. They can access and synthesize information from multiple sources, gathering data that would take humans hours to collect and combining it into coherent summaries. They can automate routine decisions within established boundaries, handling the repetitive judgment calls that consume engineering time, without requiring senior expertise. They can accelerate work that would otherwise be manual, reducing hours to minutes for tasks like documentation, data extraction, and standard analysis setup. In addition, they can learn from feedback and improve over time, becoming more valuable as they accumulate experience with your specific context.

Today's agents cannot reliably replace expert judgment on novel, high-stakes problems—the unprecedented situations where senior engineers earn their value. They cannot operate reliably with zero human oversight. Unexpected situations arise, edge cases appear, and agents occasionally make errors that humans must catch. They cannot guarantee correct answers in all situations. Even high-accuracy systems occasionally fail, and engineering contexts often include consequences which are severe enough that occasional failure is unacceptable without verification. They cannot handle situations dramatically different from patterns they've encountered. Generalization has limits, and genuinely novel situations may produce confident but wrong outputs. And they cannot yet explain their reasoning with complete transparency. While explanations can be requested and are often useful, the actual reasoning process of large language models remains partially opaque.

These limitations describe the state of practical deployment today. Organizations that deploy agents within these limitations achieve genuine value. Organizations that expect agents to transcend these limitations encounter frustration and failure that poison future efforts.

2.2.5 The Implementation Strategy

The Platform Question

As organizations deploy agents, a fundamental question emerges: Should you assemble capabilities from generic AI services and frameworks, or implement a platform specifically architected for engineering workflows? This is an architectural and organizational decision rather than purely a technological choice.

The distinction becomes apparent when examining agent operation at scale across engineering organizations. Generic AI tools assume a relatively simple model: Users interact with AI through chat interfaces, the AI calls APIs, and results return. This approach functions adequately for document processing or communication tasks but proves inadequate for engineering applications.

Why Engineering Is Different

Engineering workflows have characteristics that distinguish them from typical business applications in ways that affect agent platform requirements. These differences clarify why platform architecture matters. First, consider toolchain complexity. A marketing team might use a CRM, email system, and analytics platform—three or four integrated systems in total. An engineering organization routinely works across CAD systems, multiple simulation packages (FEA, CFD, thermal, electromagnetics), PLM platforms, costing tools, manufacturing planning systems, supply chain databases, and custom analysis applications. Each has its own data models, APIs (if any), authentication schemes, and operational characteristics. An agent platform for engineering must integrate with all of them through genuine understanding of engineering semantics rather than shallow API wrappers.

Second, governance requirements differ fundamentally. When a business AI agent makes a suboptimal recommendation, someone reviews and corrects it. When an engineering agent approves a geometry change that introduces a stress concentration, the consequences include potential safety failures and liability exposure. Engineering decisions require comprehensive governance, tracking who authorized what decision, based on which data, following what process, with what human oversight. This governance must be foundational to the platform architecture rather than added afterward.

Third, knowledge architecture requirements are distinct. Business knowledge tends to be relatively shallow and broad, such as customer preferences, market trends, or operational procedures. Engineering knowledge is extraordinarily deep and interconnected. Understanding why a particular material was selected for a component requires knowing the requirements that drove the choice, the manufacturing processes available, the supply chain constraints active at that time, the failure modes of similar designs in past products, and the evolving regulatory landscape. This knowledge forms a dense, temporal graph that must be navigated, not just retrieved.

Fourth, computational resource patterns differ dramatically. Business AI agents consume relatively modest compute: LLM inference, database queries, and light processing. Engineering agents orchestrate substantial computational workloads as finite element analyses that run for hours on HPC clusters, design space explorations that spawn thousands of parametric variants, and optimization loops that iterate between geometry, analysis, and costing. The platform must treat compute orchestration as a first-class concern.

Finally, organizational structure matters. Engineering organizations have clear hierarchies and specializations. Design engineers, analysis specialists, manufacturing engineers, program managers, and quality personnel have different responsibilities, different authorities, and different information needs. A platform must reflect these distinctions, providing appropriate capabilities and interfaces for each role rather than treating everyone as interchangeable users.

Strategic Considerations

The platform architecture question relates to the central theme of this book: Context provides practical value. A well-designed platform provides infrastructure for capturing, encoding, and deploying your organization's engineering knowledge at scale.

Generic AI tools provide chatbots that know general engineering principles. A purpose-built platform provides agents that know your engineering principles, your manufacturing realities, your customer requirements, and your lessons learned. The difference isn't the underlying AI models. Those are increasingly commoditized. The difference is the infrastructure—for encoding your context and making it accessible to agents throughout your organization.

Engineering leaders should evaluate agent platforms primarily on how well the platform architecture supports encoding and scaling organizational context. IT leaders should evaluate platforms on governance, security, integration depth, and operational manageability at scale. AI practitioners should evaluate platforms on flexibility, extensibility, and alignment with emerging best practices.

Organizations that implement engineering agents effectively recognize the platform question as strategic, not tactical. They invest in architecture that matches their organizational needs, whether that means building their own or selecting platforms that align with their requirements. They avoid adopting generic AI tools as a substitute for an agent strategy.

The platforms and tools continue improving. However, no platform can substitute for the work of capturing your organization's context and encoding it for agents. The architecture you choose should facilitate this work. It should support your organization's development of context-aware engineering agents, not create technical debt.

Throughout, one theme has been constant: Context provides practical value.

The technology of multi-agent systems continues maturing. The frameworks are improving. LLMs are becoming more capable. The integration patterns are being established. Within a few years, much of what's cutting-edge today will be commodity infrastructure.

What won't be commoditized is your organizational knowledge. The understanding of your customers, your processes, your capabilities, your lessons learned. This must be captured, structured, and deployed. This is what agents need to learn. Organizations that implement multi-agent systems effectively will be those that capture their context and encode it in their systems. They will be those that understand when to use rules, when to use AI, and when to keep humans in the loop.

The tools are available to everyone. The context is organization specific. The question is: What will you teach your agents?

2.2.6 Summary

This chapter translated conceptual understanding into practical implementation guidance for engineering agent systems.

The section **Choosing Frameworks and Models** (Section 2.2.2) addressed the practical selection of infrastructure for agent development. Model selection matches capabilities to task requirements: multimodal models for drawings and images, reasoning models for complex trade-off analysis, fast mini-models for high-volume simple tasks, code-focused models for automation scripting, and reliable large models for orchestration. Hybrid architectures that combine model types, according to task characteristics, optimize both: performance and cost. Framework selection must evaluate tool integration depth, memory architecture sophistication, coordination pattern support, enterprise integration capabilities, observability provisions, and safety mechanisms. The framework landscape evolves rapidly but fundamental requirements remain stable.

The section **Connection to Engineering Systems** (Section 2.2.3) examined the critical challenge of integrating agents with existing CAD tools, simulation engines, PLM platforms, and enterprise infrastructure. Connection patterns span direct API integration, file-based exchange, database access, and screen automation as last resort. Authentication, error handling, and transaction management require careful design. Engineering-specific considerations include handling large files, preserving design intent, managing long-running analyses, and maintaining data lineage. The quality of these integrations often determines whether agents deliver sustained value or remain impressive demos.

The section **The Bridge: Rules, AI, and Agents** (Section 2.2.4) revealed that effective systems combine rule-based automation with AI flexibility. Pure rules provide reliability but brittleness. Pure AI provides flexibility but unpredictability. Hybrid approaches use rules for validation boundaries, AI for creative exploration, and agents to orchestrate both. Patterns include AI-generated rules subject to human approval, rule-based guardrails around AI recommendations, and context-aware rule selection by agents. This middle ground delivers the reliability engineering demands while capturing the adaptability that makes agents valuable.

What Actually Works in production environments versus what remains experimental matters critically for implementation planning. Proven applications include design rule checking with natural language queries, automated documentation generation from CAD and simulation, conversational interfaces to engineering knowledge bases, routine simulation setup and post-processing, and guided design exploration within bounded spaces. Emerging capabilities show promise including autonomous multi-objective optimization, cross-disciplinary coordination, and failure mode prediction. Fully autonomous designs from requirements, unsupervised manufacturing planning, and general-purpose engineering problem solving are still experimental. Understanding this maturity spectrum prevents both over-conservative rejection of ready capabilities and premature deployment of unproven ones.

The section **Implementation Strategy** (Section 2.2.5) presents a fundamental strategic choice. Point solutions address specific workflows with focused functionality, faster initial deployment, and lower upfront investment. Platforms provide comprehensive infrastructure, unified interfaces, and long-term flexibility at the cost of complexity and integration effort. The decision depends on organizational factors: Point solutions favor limited scope pilots and specialized high-value workflows, while platforms suit organizations ready for comprehensive transformation with IT resources to support integration. Many organizations adopt a deliberate progression: piloting with point solutions, validating value, then consolidating to platforms as agent adoption matures.

Throughout these implementation topics, several themes recur. Context remains differentiating. Generic agents provide generic value while agents enriched with organizational knowledge provide competitive advantage. Integration quality determines practical utility: Agents, disconnected from engineering tools, remain conversational curiosities. Hybrid approaches outperform pure approaches, combining deterministic and autonomous components, rules and AI, with specialized and general models. Human involvement evolves but remains essential. Agents augment expertise rather than replace judgment.

With these implementation patterns established, organizations can move from understanding what agents are and how they work to actually building and deploying them effectively. The following chapters examine specific applications and provide concrete examples of these principles in practice.

3 From Theory to Practice—Agentic Engineering in the Real World

This chapter marks the transition from principles to practice. The following sections are grounded in hands-on experience from real projects across different types of engineering organizations, including suppliers, OEMs, and engineering service providers. The examples, patterns, and lessons presented here did not emerge from theory or isolated demonstrations. They emerged from the practical challenge of connecting multi-agent systems (MAS) to real engineering tools, real processes, and real organizational constraints.

> There is no universal blueprint. Every organization differs in its products, workflows, data landscapes, and culture. What creates value in one context may fail in another. For this reason, the scenarios and approaches described in this chapter should not be read as prescriptions. They are reference points. They illustrate what has proven possible in practice, where value emerged, where friction appeared, and which assumptions broke down under real conditions.

Some of you will recognize their own challenges immediately. Others will need to translate the examples to fit their environment. This translation is not a weakness. It is a necessary part of adopting agent-based systems responsibly and sustainably.

The purpose of this chapter is therefore not to define a single "correct" way of using multi-agent systems. It is to make their practical implications tangible. It shows how agents interact with engineering workflows, where human involvement remains essential, and how value accumulates over time through learning and reuse.

3.1 Winning the RFQ Race: An Agentic Approach in Automotive Supply

Use case ideas are often similar across companies. However, when these ideas are examined in greater depth during process analysis, it quickly becomes clear that each organization must implement them differently. This is exactly the challenge we face in the practical chapters of this book. Our goal was to strike a meaningful balance between staying too abstract and becoming too specific, which could otherwise limit applicability.

In this part of the book, we therefore chose to be concrete in selected areas, particularly where we have gained experience through repeated implementation in our daily work and where the results have proven to deliver significant value.

How should "Winning the RFQ Race" be interpreted? Consider it as inspiration. Take the ideas that make sense for your products and processes and adapt them to your organization. Some of the aspects presented here can even be applied beyond the RFQ process, or outside the Tier business entirely.

With that in mind, we encourage you to experiment and think creatively. We believe that agents only perform at their best when they are carefully tailored to a company's specific challenges and processes, ensuring both reliability and quality in their outcomes.

3.1.1 Executive Snapshot

In the automotive supply chain, a tier supplier provides components or subsystems to an OEM (original equipment manufacturer). Most tier suppliers are highly specialized, which means they are focusing on a narrow product range that they deliver to several OEMs. This section centers on tier suppliers competing in commodity-driven markets. In these segments, suppliers frequently respond to RFQs (requests for quotation) against five or more competitors. The products are typically build-to-print parts or modular systems customized to each customer's specifications.

By 2025, these companies are facing a turning point. After declining revenues in 2024 and a prognosed stagnant or moderate recovery in 2025, leadership teams have realized that improvement won't come naturally (Berylls 2025). Many Western tier suppliers have reacted by diversifying—expanding into the Chinese customer market and entering adjacent industries.

But as always, new strategies bring new challenges.

The biggest of these is RFQ handling:

- **Speed expectations have exploded.** Customers now expect quotes up to ten times faster than before.
- **More work upfront, less certainty later.** The ratio of engineering effort before award to actual program volume has shifted unfavorably to raising bid costs and risks.
- **The complexity is increasing.** Diversification adds new variants, standards, currencies, and compliance regimes to every quote.

These factors have made the RFQ process a strategic bottleneck—a constraint that now directly affects competitiveness and profitability.

Section Focus

This section demonstrates how a multi-agent system (MAS) can transform RFQ processing to reduce cycle time, improve accuracy, and scale quoting capacity without adding headcount.

The MAS orchestrates a fully connected workflow:

- **Intake & triage:** It analyzes the RFQ package, classify scope, extract requirements, and assign the right process route.
- **Similarity search:** It identifies comparable past quotes, designs, and outcomes to ground cost and feasibility estimates.
- **CAD adaptation:** It automatically configures or adjusts CAD models and drawings to meet customer-specific constraints.
- **DFM & compliance:** It runs automated manufacturability and standards checks across regions and regulations.
- **Costing & planning:** It generates a transparent cost model (covering materials, tooling, logistics, and overheads).
- **Change impact:** It compares against prior baselines to evaluate risks, cost deltas, and margin effects.
- **Quote assembly:** It delivers a customer-ready commercial offer with accurate pricing, lead times, and terms.

The result: RFQ cycle times shrink from weeks to minutes, quote quality improves and win rates rise—even in the most competitive markets.

3.1.2 The RFQ Bottleneck: Why Speed Has Become the New Currency

In recent years, many tier suppliers have invested heavily in optimizing their RFQ processes. Dedicated quoting teams were established, data and communication channels were connected, and new digital tools were introduced. Yet the day-to-day reality looks quite different. Engineers still copy data manually between portals, emails, spreadsheets, and PLM systems. Quoting teams spend more time chasing information than evaluating feasibility. Costing often depends on tribal knowledge rather than reusable, validated models. In practice, each customer RFQ still feels like a first-time exercise, even when similar parts have been quoted dozens of times before.

For Western tier suppliers, the quantitative symptoms of this inefficiency are becoming increasingly painful. In the past, suppliers often had several weeks to prepare a quotation. Today, that window has collapsed, especially in the Chinese market, where RFQs must often be answered within 24 to 48 hours. Miss that deadline, and the opportunity is gone. This pressure is spreading quickly from east to west, and many tier suppliers already recognize that their existing processes cannot keep pace.

Another telling symptom is the persistently low win rate. In highly competitive markets, winning only a small fraction of quotes has long been the norm. This creates massive “blind effort”: engineering and commercial work that never turns into revenue. During economic slowdowns, the situation becomes even more critical: If overall RFQ volumes decline or project sizes shrink, maintaining revenue mathematically requires a higher win rate.

At the same time, sustainable business growth demands that revenue should double roughly every ten years while maintaining at least stable profitability. This fundamental principle adds another layer of urgency: Without major efficiency gains, the traditional quoting model simply cannot support the growth targets investors and boards expect. Meanwhile, Asian tier suppliers are catching up fast, closing technological gaps and competing head-to-head with Western companies. In such an environment, holding on to manual, fragmented quoting processes only makes the available slice of the pie smaller. Compared to these structural challenges, problems like human error, rough cost estimates, or limited expert capacity begin to look almost minor.

Ultimately, there is only one sustainable way out of this spiral: automation. Rule-based automation can already handle repetitive, well-structured tasks. However, the real challenge lies in the nature of RFQs themselves. They rarely arrive in a structured form. Instead, they come as a patchwork of CAD files, PDFs, spreadsheets, and emails–and that’s precisely where the ideal use case for a multi-agent system begins. A MAS can interpret unstructured data, coordinate specialized agents for CAD, costing, and compliance, and dynamically build the workflow needed to deliver fast, consistent, and data-driven quotes.

Throughout the next sections, we explore how such a multi-agent architecture works in practice and how distributed intelligence, embedded engineering logic, and adaptive data flows can turn today's RFQ bottleneck into a scalable competitive advantage.

3.1.3 The Anatomy of an RFQ: How Engineers Really Quote

Across the automotive supply chain, the way suppliers respond to customer RFQs varies widely. The surface process looks similar everywhere, yet the underlying logic changes depending on what the company sells. There are several archetypes in automotive supply, reflecting different product and engineering philosophies. Among them, two stand out as particularly suited for automation through multi-agent systems—simple single parts and modular systems. Both start from the same pain point. Each RFQ arrives as a massive information package, often exceeding one hundred pages and frequently including complex 3D geometry that must be interpreted before any meaningful evaluation can begin.

Simple Single Parts (Individual, Build-to-Print Components)

Each RFQ typically consists of two main elements. First, a 50–150-page specification document combining drawings, material data, standards, logistics terms, and contractual clauses. Second, a 3D CAD model, usually in STEP or a native CAD format, representing the part to be manufactured.

The first task for engineers is to extract the relevant content (Figure 3.1). They review the specification, isolating dimensional tolerances, surface finishes, materials, heat treatments, and quality clauses. This information is compared to previous RFQs to identify new requirements or changes in standards.

In parallel, the 3D geometry is opened to collect key part metrics such as envelope dimensions, wall thicknesses, draft angles, hole counts, and overall mass. These parameters support early manufacturability judgments and are used to estimate manufacturing time, material consumption, and tooling requirements. Some suppliers complement this with lightweight manufacturability checks or simplified finite element analyses to detect potential risks like thin-walled areas or stress concentrations.

Once the document and geometry analysis are complete, engineers proceed with an analog search. They query PLM or costing databases for similar parts. When a good analog exists, historical cost data and documented margins are reused as a baseline. When no analog can be found, a new estimate is built from first principles using the extracted geometry metrics to insert them into basic cost calculation tools.

The costing and review phase compiles material, process, tooling, and logistics costs, often blending data from ERP systems and spreadsheets. Sales and management then review margin, volume, and commercial risk before finalizing the quote for submission.

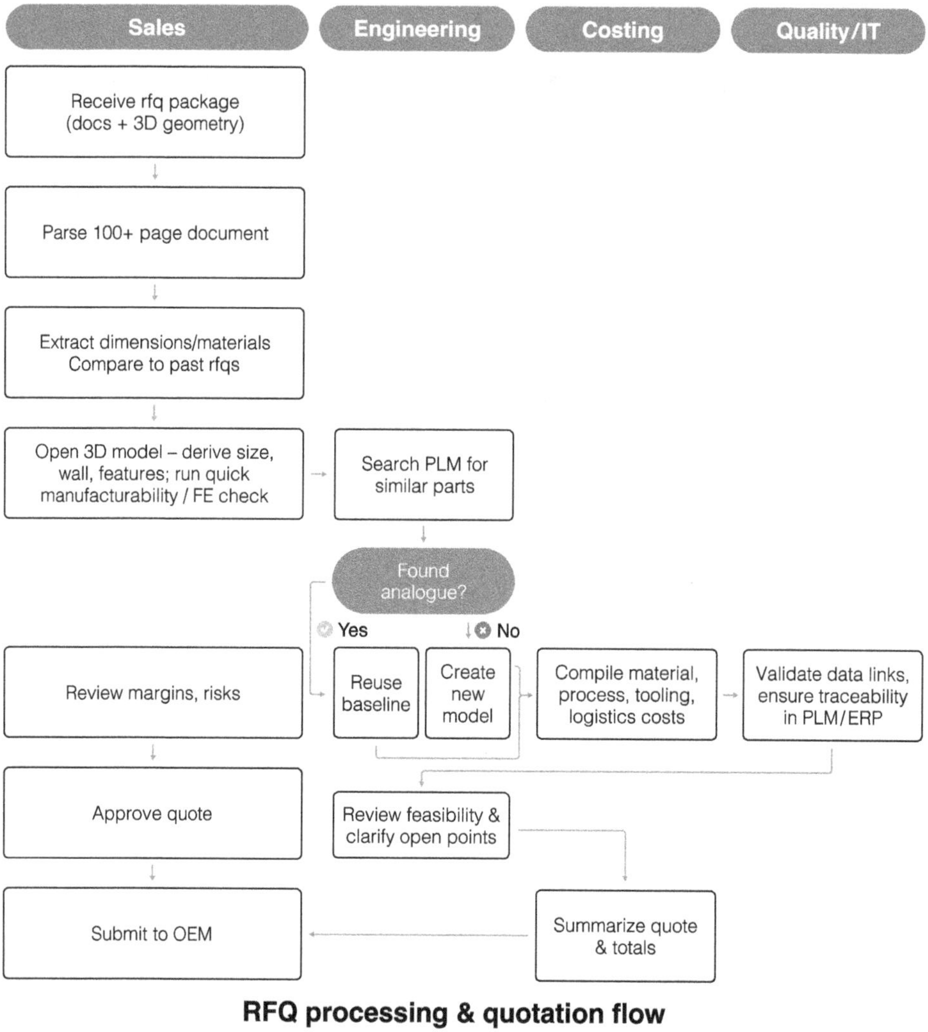

Figure 3.1 The cross-functional RFQ processing and quotation workflow spanning sales, engineering, costing, and quality/IT—from receiving the initial package and parsing documents through feasibility review, cost compilation, margin assessment, and final OEM submission (© Iryna Novoseletska)

Typical issues:

- Manual reading of documents and geometry files consumes several days.
- Similarity searches rely heavily on personal memory and visual comparison.
- Early FE checks are inconsistent and depend on individual experience.
- Data are fragmented across PLM, ERP, and Excel with no unified RFQ model.

Result: Even structured suppliers need five to ten working days per RFQ. Engineering involvement is high, reuse is limited, and quote accuracy varies significantly between projects.

Modular Systems (Assemblies Built from Standard Modules with Parametric CAD)

In modular systems, the RFQ describes a functional system rather than a single part. The specification focuses on performance and interface requirements instead of detailed geometry. Typical inputs could be load capacity, stiffness, vibration limits, temperature ranges, and mounting interfaces.

Engineers extract these parameters and check whether the requested configuration fits within existing catalog capabilities. Comparison with prior RFQs is essential to identify changes in performance or compliance requirements, such as a new vibration class or an updated EMC standard.

When the scope fits the catalog, engineers move to virtual validation. Using parametric CAD assemblies and simulation, they confirm strength, stiffness, modal behavior, and thermal performance. Minor adaptations such as modified brackets or housing geometries are tested to ensure they remain within permissible limits. The results form the technical basis for costing and quotation.

Next comes configuration and CAD preparation. For in-catalog variants, engineers adjust parameters, regenerate the model, and check for mechanical interferences. For out-of-catalog requests, they trigger engineering changes, extend template libraries, or design new sub-modules.

The costing and review step combines catalog price lists with estimates for modified parts. Simulation results are integrated into the cost and risk assessment, especially when tooling changes or material upgrades may be required. Quality and compliance teams prepare documentation packages aligned with regional requirements.

Typical issues:

- Extracting quantitative requirements from the RFQ is mostly manual.
- Detecting subtle context changes compared to prior RFQs depends on experience.

- Virtual validation often happens too late, sometimes after the quote is submitted.
- Optimization loops very often are not possible because of hard submission deadlines.

Result: Even with modular design and parametric rules, RFQ processing remains resource-intensive. Much of the engineering effort is spent interpreting documents, validating variants virtually, and synchronizing configuration data before the cost estimate can even begin.

Across both archetypes, RFQs share the same structure: a flood of data, a sequence of reasoning steps, and a predictable set of decisions. What differs is only the content, not the logic. This consistency allows us to formalize RFQ handling as an engineering process rather than an administrative burden.

In the following section, we translate that process into a multi-agent system and defining which agents take which roles, how they interact, and where humans stay in the loop.

3.1.4 From Coordination to Orchestration: The Target State of RFQ Processing

In the target state, the RFQ process is no longer a linear chain of tasks but a network of specialized agents that collaborate asynchronously. Each task, such as reading specifications, analyzing geometry, estimating cost, and validating compliance, is handled by a specialized LLM agent that collaborates with others through a shared data layer.

Instead of engineers moving information between documents, spreadsheets, and systems, the agents communicate continuously. They exchange structured data, trigger each other's actions, and keep the entire process synchronized.

The outcome is a quoting process that is characterized as follows

- **Fast:** Documents, CAD models, and historical data are processed in parallel, cutting lead time from days to hours.
- **Consistent:** Each agent follows standardized logics and verified rules, reducing variation between engineers and across sites.
- **Traceable:** Every decision, calculation, and assumption is automatically logged, creating a transparent digital audit trail.
- **Collaborative:** Engineers remain in control, reviewing and approving critical steps instead of chasing data or reformatting inputs.

In essence, the multi-agent system transforms RFQ processing from manual coordination to digital orchestration. It shifts the engineer's role from information handler to decision maker. It also establishes a foundation for continuous learning and scalable automation across the entire quoting process.

Figure 3.2 illustrates how a multi-agent system structures collaboration within an organization to support the RFQ process. Each agent operates through rule-based automation, enabling it to complete specific tasks within clearly defined constraints. It can remotely control engineering software and performs each task in a consistent, repeatable manner, ensuring reliability and traceability across projects. The MAS does not replace existing tools. It connects them. It ensures that CAx, costing, and quality share context in real time, so that decisions in one domain are immediately reflected in the others.

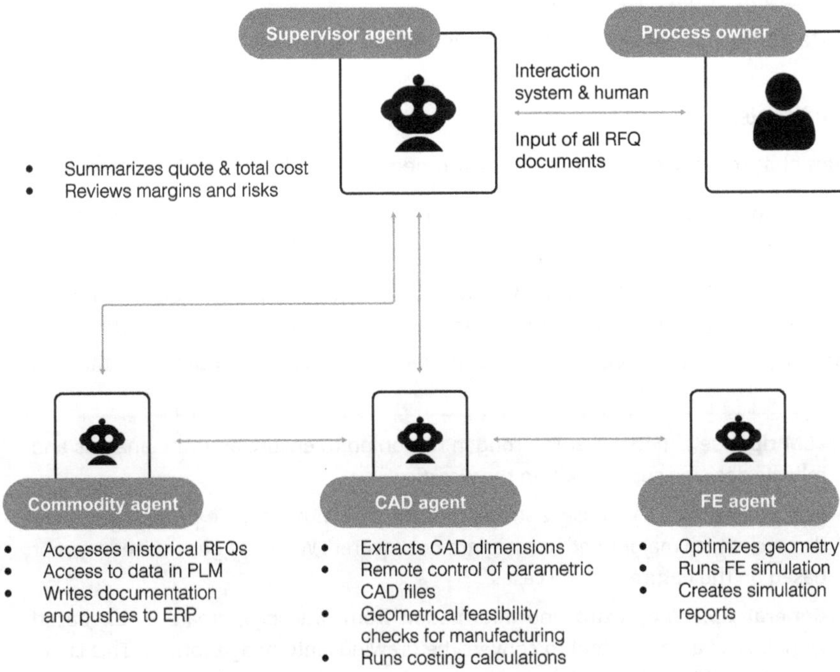

Figure 3.2 A three-agent RFQ automation system in which a supervisor coordinates a commodity agent, CAD agent, and FE agent to process incoming quote packages—handling document parsing, geometry analysis, costing, and simulation—before delivering a summarized quote to the process owner (© Iryna Novoseletska)

With the overall orchestration in place, the next section focuses on the individual agents. It explains their purpose, connected tools, and data interfaces that bring the system to life.

The Supervisor Agent: "Nice to meet you, lovely human."

This agent acts as the main orchestrator of the RFQ process and serves as the bridge between human decision-makers and all other agents. It manages the overall workflow, maintains data consistency, and consolidates the final results for review and approval.

Key functions:

- It accepts all incoming RFQ documents and initiates the quoting workflow.
- It triggers domain-specific agents such as CAD, FE, or commodity, depending on the input type and process stage.
- It merges intermediate results into a single, coherent summary.
- It presents consolidated insights, risks, and evaluated results to the process owner for validation and decision-making.

Input data from process owner: RFQ documents, 3D models, instruction via chat interface

Connected tools:

- human chat interface for communication between engineers and the system
- rule-based workflow that structures and sorts RFQ data, such as requirement documents, presentations with supplementary inputs, and drawings

The output is a unified RFQ summary that consolidates geometry metrics, FE results, and cost reports. It also includes a final quote overview with margin calculations and risk analysis, providing a clear basis for management review and decision-making.

LLM tip: Use a model that is strong in reasoning to ensure accurate analysis and reliable decision support within the workflow.

Prompting tip: As you use a strong model, start with a simple prompt and then discover which major or edge cases are not covered. Write the generalized prompt based on the nature of edge cases.

General tip: When extracting information from drawings, create a rule-based workflow as an agent tool to convert the drawings into image format. This is because a multi modal model can interpret images directly rather than extracting from PDF.

Special tip: Integrate human-in-the-loop capabilities through prompting. This approach reduces hallucination and ensures the system asks for clarification when information is missing or the next step is unclear.

The Commodity Agent: "I know your projects better than your team does."

The commodity agent is designed to maintain a comprehensive and up-to-date overview of historical data. It can access previous RFQ documents and compare them with new inquiries. By doing so, it identifies new elements or sections within the latest RFQ packages and flags them for special attention or user review.

In addition, the commodity agent can check out geometries from the PLM system and pass them on to the CAD agent for further processing. After analysis, it can check data back in, including both updated geometries and any quality or documentation files created during the process.

Key functions:

- connection to PLM and ERP systems for checking data in and out
- reading multi-page PDF documents and extracting relevant technical and commercial requirements
- reading drawings and identifying key information for downstream processes
- retrieval-augmented generation (RAG) to securely identify and handle critical building blocks within RFQ documents

Input data from other agents: RFQ documents; 3D data; process data and analysis results

Connected tools:

- rule-based automation to fill spreadsheet documents with structured data
- rule-based automation to check out data from PLM or ERP systems
- rule-based automation to check in updated data to PLM or ERP systems
- AI-enhanced, rule-based workflow to read and compare large RFQ documents efficiently
- rule-based workflow to search for similar parts in the existing parts database
- rule-based workflow to update the similarity database with new geometries

The outputs of this agent include feedback to the supervisor agent indicating whether the RFQ follows a standard pattern or contains specific elements that require manual review by the process owner. It also delivers completed compliance documents that are properly stored in the designated system.

In addition, the agent provides the technical requirements of the RFQ and 3D templates to the CAD agent, particularly relevant for modular system archetypes. It also shares historical metadata to support cost calculation and ensure data consistency across the workflow.

LLM tip: Use simpler base models to ensure computational efficiency and optimize LLM-related costs.

Prompting tip: Just as you navigate and teach a fellow engineer, prompt the agent to look at similar file/part search strategies. These are ways to search for and use multiple tools in necessary orders.

General tip: A commodity agent needs to know what the cases are for what you use your PLM systems for and how do you search for them. Observe how you find parts and capture the logic in.

Special tip: At the time of writing this book, many models still struggle to process extremely large documents. It is therefore recommended to convert such files into format .txt file within a rule-based workflow beforehand using packages like Docling, improving their readability and processing efficiency.

The CAD Agent: "I love what others hate—boring mouse clicks."

The CAD agent analyzes 3D geometry and extracts dimensions and attributes to running cost analysis. It also assists the FEA agent by identifying areas where boundary conditions will later be applied. In addition, the CAD agent can create new designs by steering a parametric CAD model, enabling automated geometry generation for variants or design updates. It performs manufacturability checks by comparing geometric features against predefined design guidelines and feasibility rules. While the overall architecture of the multi-agent system remains consistent across tier archetypes, this agent requires adjustments to match the specific needs of each archetype.

Key functions:

- It opens and interprets CAD models in STEP or native formats.
- It extracts key dimensions and color-coded surfaces, and calculates minimum bounding box, volumes, wall thicknesses, and feature counts.
- It runs geometrical feasibility and DFM checks by measuring local geometric characteristics.
- It controls parametric CAD templates to adapt or regenerate design variants (mainly for archetype modular systems).
- It executes cost calculations based on extracted geometry data and predefined rules.

Input data from other agents: 3D models, technical requirements from RFQ documents, PLM metadata, instructions via text

Connected tools:

- rule-based automation to remotely control a native CAD system (mainly for archetype modular systems)
- rule-based automation to open geometry with a CAD kernel, measure relevant dimensions, and extract key features

- rule-based automation to open geometry with a CAD kernel, measure local characteristics, and compare them against defined criteria
- rule-based automation to remotely control cost engineering software or Excel for cost calculation and reporting

The output includes the updated geometry for the FEA agent, with defined surfaces that enable the automatic application of boundary conditions. The CAD agent also provides manufacturability findings and a should-costing report to the supervisor agent. For modular system archetypes, it delivers the final geometry which might be included as a file in the final quotation.

LLM tip: Since LLM models do not process 3D CAD files natively, use a better tool calling model, which also has multi modal capabilities.

Prompting tip: How do you, as a CAD engineer, manipulate parts? Do you use parameters? Do you use visual outputs? Do you look at measurements? Capture this logic so that the CAD agent can also interpret and modify CAD accordingly.

General tip: Design your tools in such a way that there are detailed descriptions for each parameter. This is what the LLM is going to receive as input to control the CAD. Describing the CAD parameters as much as possible helps for a CAD agent.

Special tip: Make sure you have access to an automation platform with an integrated geometry kernel. It will save you a major headache, since automating CAD interactions is often the most time-consuming part of building the entire multi-agent system for automating the quotation process.

FEA Agent: "Stress-tested in seconds"

The FEA agent does exactly what its name suggests. It performs virtual validations of the design. Depending on the component or system, these can range from simple static analyses to complex dynamic simulations. The FEA agent is also capable of visualizing simulation results and deriving necessary design actions based on them.

Depending on the logic and setup of the multi-agent system, the FEA agent can further extend its role by autonomously performing design optimizations, refining geometry and parameters to meet defined performance targets.

Key functions:

- It builds or modifies simulation models based on requirements.
- It runs solvers and interprets results to evaluate structural or functional performance.
- It generates result reports, including visual representations and key findings.
- It uses and continuously trains AI models for result prediction.

- It executes optimization algorithms to improve design performance and efficiency.
- It provides recommendations for design changes based on simulation outcomes.

Input data from other agents: 3D models, load case requirements from RFQ documents or in-house guidelines, instructions via text

Connected tools:

- rule-based automation to connect components and integrate them into existing simulation models or build new models from scratch
- rule-based automation to trigger simulations in industry-standard FE solvers, either locally or on high-performance computing (HPC) systems
- rule-based automation to visualize simulation results, automatically cluster hotspots, set optimal viewing angles and zoom levels, and generate screenshots
- rule-based automation to predict simulation results using a reduced order model (ROM), while continuously updating the prediction model with every new simulation as an additional data point
- rule-based automation to simplify geometry models, for example by removing imprints, or to extend them with additional content such as weld seams
- rule-based automation to optimize geometry through parameter optimization or similar design-improvement techniques

From a holistic perspective, the FEA agent is far more powerful than it may first appear. One of its key strengths is that most of its work happens internally within the tool of the agent. As a result, its **output** remains relatively compact. The main delivery is the simulation result, potentially including optimized variants, provided in the form of a detailed report. When necessary, the FEA agent also issues recommendations for design adjustments to the CAD agent and guidance for the process owner.

LLM tip: Since interpreting simulation results requires the LLM to process images, it is recommended to use a strong multimodal model for this task. A model that also scores well on general reasoning, or a metric like GDPVal, could also be a great fit.

Prompting tip: The FEA agent has to decide a part's performance based on multiple perspectives and load cases. This is where the power of prompting can shine, as you don't necessarily link everything in an if-else condition, but rather generally writing your criterion.

General tip: In case your FEA agent needs to use multiple tools for different load cases, make sure they are in separate tool workflows so that process orchestration can be efficient.

Special tip: Since this is an FEA agent, make sure to also add interpretation guidelines that are specific to a certain component or material or boundary condition.

3.1.5 Measuring the Impact of Agents in RFQ Processing

At the time of writing this book, agent-based systems were still emerging technology. The experience we have gained in our daily work has therefore focused primarily on the development and implementation of such systems. Our current knowledge covers process analysis, the generation of multi-agent system architectures, quality testing, and roll-out planning.

What does this mean for evaluating the benefits? At this stage, our insights are strongest regarding leading indicators. We have been able to collect KPI data on RFQ cycle time, human effort, output quality, and user adoption rates. The lagging indicators, such as an increase in win rate or participation in a higher number of RFQs, can currently only be assessed hypothetically. The coming years will therefore be particularly exciting, as they will show whether these hypotheses prove to be true in practice.

The most important metric to examine first is the turnaround time of the entire quotation process. This metric directly influences several other strategically relevant benefits. So, let's take a closer look. Based on our experience, the typical time between RFQ receipt and quote submission for the types of RFQs described in this section ranges from one to six weeks. The typical engineering effort required lies between ten and forty working hours. This already shows that individual tasks often remain longer on an engineer's to-do list than the time actually spent working on them.

It is worth remembering that the multi-agent system we have described operates largely autonomously. In our projects, the system was able to generate a complete quotation proposal within 10 to 20 minutes, excluding FE simulation time. Simulation durations must therefore be added to these figures. Assuming the quoting process involves only short-running simulations, and that reduced order models are used for longer ones, a full quotation, including human pre- and post-processing, can be completed within two hours.

From our perspective, this estimate is conservative. In all our projects, the actual results were significantly faster. Even in a worst-case scenario, this represents a 98 percent reduction in total turnaround time, calculated as the ratio of two hours to five days of continuous work. Looking purely at human effort, the savings reach approximately 80 percent.

Of course, we also need to consider the financial perspective. The starting point varies significantly between companies, but based on our experience, we can define some general thresholds for when a cost neutral operation of the agentic system can be achieved purely through labor savings.

For the longer RFQs mentioned earlier, which typically take three to six weeks to complete, a small to mid double-digit number of RFQs per year should be processed to reach a positive return. For shorter RFQs, which require only a few hours of effort, the number should be well above one hundred per year.

Let's take a practical example. Assume a time saving of eight hours per RFQ and an average hourly rate of USD 80. This results in a saving of USD 640 per RFQ. With 250 RFQs per year, the total saving amounts to USD 160,000 annually.

Next, we need to look at the cost side. These costs depend heavily on the make-or-buy decision. So, before we calculate the potential ROI, let's explore the implications of that decision in more detail.

When setting up a multi-agent system, companies face an important make-or-buy decision. Two main approaches exist, each with distinct advantages and challenges:

1. Developing all tools and agents in-house (for example, using Python):

   Pros: no license costs for rule-based automation or agent creation; complete control over development and customization

   Cons: This requires deep expertise in API programming, high development effort and long project timelines before achieving a roll-out-ready system (based on our experience, approximately five times longer). Extensive knowledge of agent prompting is also required. In addition, maintenance costs rise whenever engineering tools are updated.

2. Using commercial automation platforms:

   Pros: Agent systems and tools can be built by subject matter experts from the RFQ process without advanced programming or prompting skills. Achieving a roll-out-ready system within six months is realistic.

   Cons: recurring license costs and a potential vendor lock-in risk

---

Depending on your internal processes, cost-effective open-source solutions can serve as a middle ground between these two options. We recommend paying close attention to the effort required to build the tools and ensuring that they can be made accessible to agents via a REST API or other protocols like A2A or MCP.

Let us now assume, for our return on investment (ROI) analysis, that we have decided to buy rather than build. Since we have the most in-depth experience with Synera, we will use this automation platform as our cost reference.

Based on our experience, the annual license costs for such a use case amount to approximately USD 150,000. In addition, there is a one-time cost of around USD 50,000 to set up the IT infrastructure and train the key users. Furthermore, one employee will be required for about six months (800 hours at USD 80 per hour), resulting in personnel costs of USD 64,000. For infrastructure operation and LLM usage, we can estimate an additional USD 10,000 per year.

This brings the total cost for the first year to approximately USD 274,000, and around USD 160,000 for each following year. If we compare these costs with the annual savings of USD 160,000 calculated earlier, it becomes clear that in this scenario, the savings roughly cover the operating costs.

Despite this, we still recommend implementation. Why? Because in a highly competitive market environment, win rates are typically low. According to a study by the Center for Automotive Research, the average win rate for suppliers in this category is around 25 percent (Morell et al. 2002).

Assuming that faster response times and the ability to handle more RFQs improve the win rate by just 2 to 5 percent, the financial benefits can quickly reach several million euros. Compared to this potential upside, the financial risk of not achieving a fully deployable agent system using an automation platform is very low.

The adoption rate of agent-based systems depends strongly on the quality of results and the transparency of the system. In our projects, we achieved adoption rates above 80 percent by applying the following measures:

The active involvement of end users in development is essential. The users of the agent system participated intensively in the creation process. Automation platforms provide a major advantage here, as they enable subject-matter experts without programming skills to contribute directly to building the system. This involvement creates trust.

Call to action: Involve future users early in the development phase. Only through participation can a meaningful adoption rate be achieved.

The visibility of intermediate agent steps increases transparency. Our projects were designed so that users could follow each intermediate step executed by the agents. This made it possible for them to understand and validate the results easily, which strengthened trust in the overall system.

Call to action: Ensure that such process traces are available. They are indispensable for building confidence and are equally valuable for prompt fine-tuning and troubleshooting during later project stages.

The alignment of automation with real process needs boosts user acceptance. The selected use cases focused primarily on activities where the sales team previously had to wait for other departments to complete their work. Tasks that required personal judgment, such as strategic pricing or negotiation adjustments, remained under human control. The result was a clear quotation proposal generated by the multi-agent system, which the salesperson could modify further. The ability to test several scenarios quickly also provided tangible decision support. These aspects together increased both efficiency and win probability, and to be honest, every salesperson appreciates a higher chance of success and the potential for an additional bonus.

The quality of the results is, of course, directly dependent on the quality of the automation. The assessment presented in this section is based on the assumption that the following conditions have been met:

1. Everything that can be clearly described by rules has been implemented through rule-based automation and is not handled by the LLM.
2. The multi-agent system has been built up incrementally, meaning it was first optimized for quality with only a few agents and then gradually expanded with additional agents.
3. The subject-matter experts responsible for the individual process steps have actively contributed to building and validating the system.
4. The results of the overall MAS have been verified and validated.

With these guardrails in place, the core quality factors are under control. Although LLMs introduce probabilistic reasoning, their outputs are systematically verified through rule-based automation, defined acceptance criteria, and human review, to ensure robust and continuously improving result quality.

✓ In our projects, test results showed that quality targets were met in at least 95 out of 100 cases. From our perspective, this is a satisfying outcome, because let's be honest: Even humans make mistakes in manual processes.

3.1.6 The 90-Day Plan: A Small Step for You, a Big Step for Your Organization

The main goal of the 90 days is to analyze the RFQ process, identify bottlenecks, draft the multi-agent system architecture on paper, make a build-vs.-buy decision, and develop an MVP to prove technical and organizational feasibility.

Phase 1: Understand and Frame (Days 1 – 30)

Goal: Build alignment on the problem, the current process, and the automation opportunity.

Key activities:

- Conduct short interviews and shadowing sessions to document how RFQs are handled today.
- Map the current process (status quo), identifying delays, rework, and decision bottlenecks.

- Create a user journey capturing all key roles (sales, RFQ manager, engineering, costing, plant managers, and additional roles).
- Summarize the problem statement and define measurable KPIs.
- Draft a high-level concept for how a multi-agent system could address the identified challenges.

Deliverables:

- one-page problem statement
- current-state process map and user journey
- preliminary impact hypotheses, such as expected cycle-time reduction or effort savings

Decision Gate A: executive agreement on the problem definition and intent to prototype an MAS solution

Phase 2: Design and Decide (Days 31 – 60)

Goal: Define the future system and make the build-vs.-buy decision.

Key activities:

- Design the agentic architecture, defining core agents, data flows, and system boundaries.
- Evaluate build-vs.-buy options for orchestration platforms and AI tooling.
- If buy: Shortlist one vendor and define a minimal integration concept.
- If build: Specify the internal framework, data connections, and hosting approach.
- Define the MVP scope, typically one supervisor agent and two functional agents (for example, Document + Geometry or Document + Costing).
- Align on success criteria and human-in-the-loop checkpoints.

Deliverables:

- architecture one-pager showing roles, tools, and interfaces
- build-vs.-buy decision memo with rationale
- MVP specification with success criteria covering speed, accuracy, and traceability.

Decision Gate B: approval to build the MVP and allocate engineering resources

Phase 3: Build the MVP (Days 61 – 90)

Goal: Build and demonstrate a working prototype that automates key steps in the RFQ process.

Key activities:

- Implement a supervisor agent for orchestration and logging.
- Develop two functional agents, for example, a document agent for RFQ parsing and a geometry agent for CAD analysis.
- Integrate with existing systems (PLM, ERP) in read-only mode to avoid operational risk.
- Run two to three pilot tests on representative RFQs.
- Document key findings and estimate the effort required for production readiness.
- Develop a business case quantifying expected ROI, scaling costs, and payback period.

Deliverables:

- working MVP demonstration
- summary of technical and organizational effort required to reach production quality
- business case and rollout recommendation

Decision Gate C: executive go/no-go decision for production investment

3.1.7 Guest Perspective: Implementing Multi-Agent Systems in RFQ Engineering

Eric Stähle

Why We Reached the Limits of Manual RFQ Processing

As a development engineer, I work in a department that focuses on new technologies that can benefit the company. When we first heard about multi-agent systems, we had just finished investigating our RFQ process. The conclusion was that it was too complicated and took too long. We knew that we had to do something, but we were not sure what and how.

When we began exploring RFQ automation, the core challenge was not tooling or expertise. It was scale. RFQ volumes and complexity have increased steadily over the years. We were processing several thousand RFQs annually, many requiring tight coordination across engineering, purchasing, costing, and sales. Each request triggered a chain of manual steps across departments, systems, spreadsheets, and individual workarounds.

At the same time, customer expectations were shifting. Faster turnaround times and early price indications were increasingly required, sometimes within hours. This exposed a clear mismatch. Our processes worked well at lower volumes, but they were not designed for speed, consistency, or scalability. Adding headcount would not solve the coordination problem. It would only increase complexity.

That realization led us to explore a multi-agent system approach.

Starting with a Focused, Scalable Automation Approach

We started deliberately small. The initial scope focused on built-to-print parts, where customers provide drawings, CAD models, and specifications. These RFQs represent a significant share of our volume and are well suited for structured automation.

Our goal was not to replace existing systems. PLM, CAD, ERP, and costing tools remained unchanged. The agentic system acts as a coordination layer on top, responsible for data flow, action triggering, and consistency.

At the center is a Supervisor Agent that orchestrates the overall process. It coordinates specialized agents for tasks such as document analysis, geometry processing, and costing. Each agent reflects an existing organizational role but operates digitally through defined rules and interfaces rather than emails and spreadsheets.

This delivered two immediate benefits. Manual data transfer errors were reduced, and RFQs moved faster because information flowed automatically without waiting for handovers. Existing workflows were preserved, which proved critical for acceptance.

The architecture was modular by design. While the initial scope was narrow, the system can be extended to additional product families, manufacturing technologies, or more complex assemblies. Experts can intervene at any point, adjust results, or handle exceptions. Flexibility was a non-negotiable requirement.

How the System Fits into Existing Engineering Work

The system was intentionally designed to complement, not disrupt, established engineering processes. Agents connect systems that were already in place and enforce consistency across them, without forcing teams to abandon familiar tools. This approach reduced friction during rollout and allowed teams to adopt the system incrementally. Engineers retained their processes while gaining automation support where it created the most value.

How Daily Engineering and RFQ Work Has Changed

The most noticeable change is not just speed, but how work feels. Engineers spend far less time reading RFQ documents, copying data, or reconciling inconsistencies. Instead, they review structured outputs, validate assumptions, and focus on technical decisions. As one engineer put it, he previously worked across spreadsheets, CAD tools, and emails in parallel. Now, he is opening a single RFQ workspace where all relevant information is already aligned. Sales managers gain earlier visibility. Feasibility signals and cost ranges are available much sooner, reducing late escalations.

Onboarding has also improved. New team members become productive faster because process logic and best practices are embedded in the system, rather than residing only in individual experience.

Early Impact and Measurable Improvements

Even during the test phase, the impact was measurable. RFQ lead times decreased within the initial scope. Rework was reduced, with fewer reopened RFQs and post-submission corrections. Quote quality became more consistent across teams.

We deliberately ran the automated and manual processes in parallel. This enabled direct comparison and continuous refinement. Engineers reviewed outputs, corrected deviations, and fed their feedback back into the system. This human-in-the-loop learning turned out to be a major strength.

Workload peaks also became more manageable. Routine tasks were absorbed by the system, leading to less overtime and a more balanced distribution of effort.

Where Automation Needed Human Judgment

One early misconception was that everything could be automated immediately. In practice, some steps require human judgment, especially when data quality is poor or requirements are ambiguous. Drawings and CAD models vary more widely in quality than expected.

The solution was not to force automation, but to design robust human-in-the-loop mechanisms. The system requests confirmation when inputs are unclear and escalates critical cases to engineers. Modularity was essential. Individual components could be adapted or replaced without destabilizing the overall system.

Preserving Engineering Ownership and Trust

We consistently position the multi-agent system as a decision support, not a decision replacement. Certain steps are always reviewed by a person. Engineers can override agent suggestions at any time, and all overrides are logged transparently. The engineer's role shifts from execution to evaluation. Control remains with humans at all critical decision points. This clarity is essential for trust and long-term adoption.

What This Experience Taught Us

Three lessons stand out. First, success depends on a precise understanding of the end-to-end process. Roles, responsibilities, inputs, and outputs must be clearly defined. This is an organizational exercise, not a technical one. It often reveals inefficiencies even before automation begins.

Second, automation breaks down at unclear interfaces. Redundancies, media breaks, and inconsistent data flows typically sit between functions and systems. Clear ownership, standardized data formats, and well-defined interfaces are prerequisites for reliable automation.

Third, agent systems must evolve continuously. Modular architecture, monitoring, and regular user feedback enable this. Equally important is enablement. Training and transparency ensure the system is understood as support, not a black box. Long-term success requires alignment between technology, organization, and people.

Looking Back and Moving Forward

Would we do it again? Yes, however it is crucial to understand that the core of an agentic automation are the tools that enable the agent to do the work. In those tools the company knowledge is codified. AI is not the magical ingredient that solves all your problems, but it really enables you to overcome the obstacles that arise in typical automation. What surprised us most was how quickly benefits extended beyond the initial scope. Once coordination improves, adjacent processes become easier to optimize. Another side effect was that we could take out parts of the multi-agent system and apply them to different problems.

For engineering leaders facing similar challenges, my advice is simple. Do not wait for the perfect solution. If RFQs are already overwhelming your organization, inaction is the biggest risk. Start small, learn fast, and build from there. The benefits tend to appear sooner and more broadly than expected.

3.2 Aerospace OEMs: The Weight of Legacy vs. the Pace of Innovation

Simulation-driven engineering in aerospace follows its own logic. Even when companies operate within the same market segment, the structure of their validation processes, load cases, safety factors, and internal approval paths can differ significantly. This practical section therefore adopts a neutral perspective. It outlines a representative scenario without assuming that all organizations operate in the same way.

The examples in this section focus on lightweight structural components, simulation-driven decision-making, and cross-functional engineering processes. Your organization may use different tools, data models, or validation steps. That is entirely expected. Treat this section as inspiration. Select what fits your products, adapt what does not, and extend the ideas where your processes demand deeper integration.

As with any agent-based automation, the highest value arises when the system is built around the organization's real constraints. This section is not intended as a rigid blueprint. Instead, it serves as a reference model to illustrate how multi-agent systems can enhance simulation and validation workflows at scale.

3.2.1 Executive Snapshot

In aerospace engineering, weight and safety targets influence almost every design decision. Even small components such as brackets, secondary structures, or additively manufactured fittings have a direct impact on payload, range, and mission capability. At the same time, they must comply with stringent certification rules and withstand a broad spectrum of load cases.

Across commercial aircraft programs and space platforms, these requirements create a validation process that is both technically complex and organizationally demanding. Multiple specialist teams contribute to each iteration, and every step depends on the accuracy and timing of the previous one.

The key characteristics of the current environment are as follows:

- Weight sensitivity ranges from moderate in commercial aviation to extreme in satellite and eVTOL applications.
- Safety margins must satisfy internal engineering rules and external authorities, often requiring multi-physics validation.
- Validation workflows rely on input from stress engineering, loads and dynamics, materials, finite element analysis, and manufacturing.
- Iterations proceed slowly because each team must wait for upstream results before continuing.

These interdependencies cause delays during meshing, solving, interpreting results, and applying design changes. Consequently, components often remain heavier than necessary because limited simulation bandwidth and long approval chains restrict deeper optimization.

The pressure is increasing:

- Emerging NewSpace companies are operating with faster innovation cycles and tightly integrated toolchains.
- Their speed exposes the limitations of long-established validation workflows.
- Established OEMs now face rising expectations for shorter development cycles and higher digital maturity.

Section Focus

This section shows how a multi-agent system (MAS) can coordinate simulation and validation activities to increase throughput, improve design quality, and accelerate engineering cycles without compromising safety. The MAS enables a connected simulation workflow that integrates variant creation, analysis, interpretation, and documentation into one coordinated process.

These are the core capabilities of the MAS:

- **Variant generation:** It creates and manages design alternatives based on geometry, parameters, or material choices.
- **FE preprocessing:** It prepares meshes, assigns materials, applies load cases, and validates model consistency before analysis.
- **Multi-physics execution:** It runs structural, thermal, and dynamic analyses across different solvers.
- **Result interpretation:** It extracts safety factors, identify critical regions, and compares results against certification thresholds.
- **Lightweighting loops:** It explores parameter spaces, optimizes mass, and evaluates design trade-offs automatically.
- **Documentation support:** It generates structured evidence and maintains traceability required for later audits.

The result: Validation costs decrease, fewer physical tests are required, weight performance improves, and development cycles shorten. This holds true even under the demanding safety and certification standards of aerospace engineering.

3.2.2 Where Time Disappears in Aerospace Engineering

Aerospace engineering operates under extreme constraints. Weight targets, safety margins, and certification rules influence nearly every design decision. Even small components such as brackets, secondary structures, or additively manufactured fittings require extensive validation. They must withstand dozens of load cases, perform reliably across multiple simulation environments, and meet strict documentation requirements. As programs grow in complexity and span wider mission envelopes, the validation workload per component increases accordingly.

Across commercial aircraft programs and space platforms, this creates workflows that are technically sophisticated yet organizationally fragile. Multiple specialist teams contribute to each iteration. Stress engineering, loads and dynamics, materials, FE analysis, and manufacturing all depend on upstream results before they can proceed. This serialized structure slows development, increases the risk of context loss, and pushes teams toward conservative design choices simply because deeper optimization would exceed available time and simulation capacity.

Despite steady improvements in CAE tools, the fundamental structure of simulation work has changed very little. Toolchains remain fragmented across preprocessing, solving, and post-processing. File formats and naming conventions vary from project to project. Essential knowledge often resides in the heads of senior engineers rather than in shared systems. As a result, iterations take longer than they should. Meshing waits for geometry updates. Solving waits for load case definitions. Interpretation slows down because documentation rules differ across programs. Components frequently remain heavier than necessary, and engineering cycles stretch beyond what the market is willing to accept.

The competitive landscape sharpens this challenge. NewSpace companies operate with faster simulation cycles and tightly integrated toolchains. Their ability to iterate quickly, explore broader design spaces, and reduce physical testing demonstrates what becomes possible when digital workflows are cohesive. Their pace exposes the limitations of long-established internal validation processes and raises expectations for the aerospace industry as a whole. Established OEMs must respond by increasing simulation throughput, shortening development cycles, and strengthening digital maturity while still meeting demanding certification requirements.

Many organizations attempt to close the gap with scripting, macros, or isolated rule engines. These tools provide local improvements but optimize only single steps in the chain. A meshing script accelerates preprocessing. A batch solver speeds up execution. A reporting macro reduces formatting work. However, the overall bottleneck persists because coordination still relies on manual handovers and context remains fragmented across systems and teams. Script based automation becomes brittle when geometries change. Rule engines struggle with unstructured information such as requirement documents or design intent. None of these approaches orchestrates the validation loop as a unified workflow.

A multi-agent system provides a structured way to address these gaps. It mirrors existing organizational roles by assigning responsibilities to specialized agents that act as digital counterparts to stress engineers, loads experts, materials specialists, or documentation owners. These agents collaborate through a shared data layer. This allows variant generation, preprocessing, solving, interpretation, and documentation to function as one coordinated process rather than a series of disconnected activities.

Rule-based automation captures fixed constraints, safety margins, and certification requirements. LLM-based agents support tasks that depend on context, interpretation, and engineering judgment. The intention is not to replace expertise. It is to shift repetitive setup and data handling away from humans so that engineers can focus on evaluating design decisions and ensuring compliance.

This coordinated structure forms the foundation for a more efficient and transparent automation workflow. It also sets the stage for the next section: a closer examination of how individual agents collaborate, which responsibilities they assume, and how they interact with existing engineering tools and data sources. The following sections introduce the agent architecture and show how the validation workflow can be decomposed into clear digital roles.

3.2.3 How Aerospace Engineering Moves from Concept to Proof

Product development typically follows a standardized process. While the exact implementation differs from company to company, the high-level principles remain largely the same. In the early phase, often referred to as the concept or pre-design phase, the primary goal is to lay the foundation for later development. During this stage, multiple concepts are usually created and evaluated against one another. The level of engineering detail is deliberately limited. Simplified geometries and reduced load cases are used to enable rapid comparison and early decision-making.

The subsequent design phase significantly increases the level of engineering detail. By this point, a concept decision has already been made, and the overall direction of development is fixed. The focus now shifts to refining the chosen concept so that virtual validation produces realistic and reliable results. This phase is characterized by iterative optimization loops aimed at bringing the design closer to series readiness.

In the following validation phase, selected results from virtual verification are confirmed through physical hardware testing. These tests provide critical feedback, and their outcomes often lead to targeted design improvements that are fed back into the product.

Finally, the industrialization phase concentrates on production systems and manufacturing readiness. Even at this stage, feedback from production can flow back into engineering and result in further product adjustments.

AI agents can be applied across all phases of the product development process. They are useful when holistic optimizations with as few iterations as possible are required during the design phase, and they are equally valuable in later stages when the impact of late-stage changes must be assessed quickly and reliably.

Nevertheless, our recommendation is to focus first on the concept phase. This phase brings together several characteristics that make it particularly well suited for the use of agent-based automation. Multiple design scenarios must be compared in a short time frame, often under conditions of incomplete information. Missing inputs are compensated through estimation and hypothesis building, based on company data, general engineering knowledge, and expert experience.

There is also a decisive structural factor. The concept phase typically follows an 80/20 approach. Early decisions define a large share of the final outcome, even though they are made with simplified models and assumptions. This has an important implication for automation. Effective solutions can be built with relatively low effort, because they do not need to capture every engineering detail from the start.

As a result, multi-agent systems can be implemented and brought into productive use much faster in this phase. They deliver meaningful decision support early, when leverage is highest, and create a solid foundation that can later be extended into more detailed phases of development.

Let us now take a closer look at the status quo of a typical engineering task. In the concept phase, the initial situation usually looks as follows:

- There is a clearly defined performance, cost, and weight target.
- Additional objectives may apply, such as CO_2 footprint, delivery lead time, or quality requirements.
- Company-specific constraints must also be considered, for example material availability, sourcing strategies, or company internal technology restrictions.

It quickly becomes apparent that engineering must balance a wide range of parameters in parallel. The core task of the engineer is therefore to develop and compare multiple concepts. These concepts may rely on different manufacturing technologies or material choices. They must meet the hard targets while ensuring that softer criteria are not neglected.

Based on this starting point, we will now outline the following process. It represents a typical approach found today at aerospace OEMs. To keep the complexity manageable, we will focus on a single component that still interacts with neighboring parts and influences the surrounding system. In our example, this component is a bracket (Figure 3.3). This setup provides a realistic yet contained context for analyzing how engineering decisions are made in the concept phase and where current processes begin to show their limitations.

The engineer's task is to design a bracket that connects an attached component to the primary structure of the overall system. The weight of the attached component defines the primary load case, and the bracket must be capable of carrying this load reliably. In addition, dynamic requirements, such as natural frequency targets, must also be taken into account.

Cost and weight targets are derived top-down by a planning engineer, starting from the system level and allocated to individual components. With these boundary conditions defined, the concept engineer begins by gathering additional information. Typical questions at this stage include which materials and manufacturing processes are feasible within the given constraints.

Based on this input, the engineer usually develops at least three alternative concepts, drawing on experience and best judgment. In our example, these concepts could include the following:

- a 3D-printed bracket, optimized for weight and geometric freedom
- a machined bracket, manufactured from solid stock with well-understood process constraints
- a cast bracket, optimized for higher volumes and material efficiency

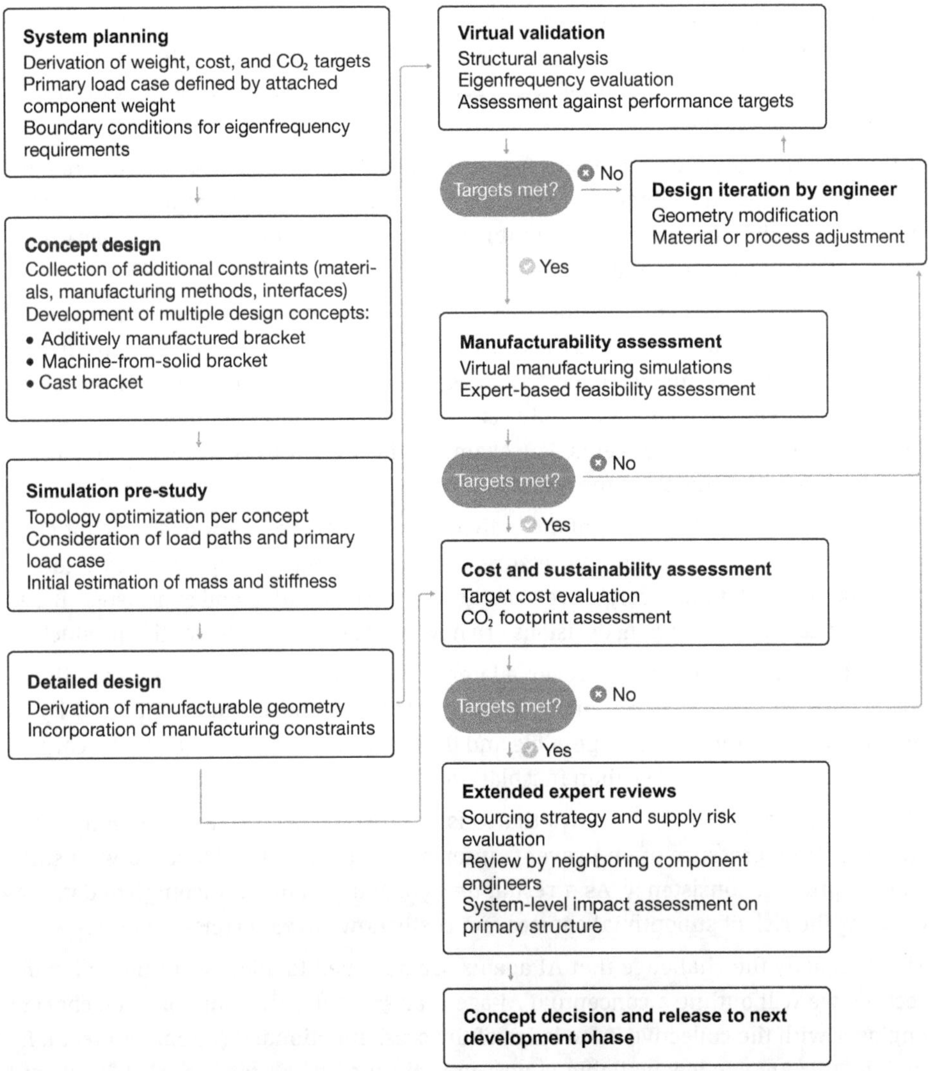

Figure 3.3 The end-to-end concept development workflow for aerospace structural components, spanning system planning through detailed design, virtual validation, manufacturability and cost assessment, and expert review before release to the next development phase (© Iryna Novoseletska)

For the selected concepts, an initial preliminary investigation is ideally carried out by the simulation department, using methods such as topology optimization. This step provides guidance for the later geometry by identifying principal load paths and structural efficiency potential.

The design engineer then takes this proposal and translates it into a manufacturable geometry. Manufacturing constraints are applied while preserving the structural intent defined by the simulation. Once the geometry is created, it is sent back to simulation for virtual validation.

If the design meets the defined performance targets, it moves on to further departments for additional evaluation. These assessments typically include manufacturability checks, which may be performed through additional simulations or expert judgment, followed by an evaluation of should-costs and the CO_2 footprint.

At each of these stages, it is possible that one or more targets are not met. In that case, the design must be adjusted, and the process starts again from an earlier step. Toward the end of the loop, further expert reviews are often required. These may include sourcing evaluations to assess supply risks or coordination with engineers responsible for neighboring components. For example, the weight of the bracket may influence the load distribution of the main structure.

After several weeks, the results of the individual concepts are finally available for comparison. Depending on schedule pressure, these results may be supported by rigorous quantitative validation or rely more heavily on expert judgment and experience. Based on the available information, decisions are now made that affect the entire product.

These decisions are difficult to reverse later in the process without significant financial investment. For that reason, it is essential that scenarios are supported by as much relevant information as possible and that decisions are evaluated in the context of the overall system rather than in isolation.

The reality today, however, shows that this is precisely where many organizations struggle. Time pressure often prevents information from being prepared with sufficient depth and consistency. As a result, decisions are made on incomplete data, increasing the risk of suboptimal choices and costly downstream consequences.

This is exactly the challenge that AI agents are designed to address. In the following section, we will outline a conceptual AI agent architecture that supports the concept engineer with the collective knowledge of the cross-functional development team. By making this knowledge available almost in real time, the system enables faster and more informed decisions and significantly reduces the risk of costly misinvestments early in the development process.

3.2.4 From Isolated Expertise to Coordinated Engineering in Future R&D

The process described in the previous section reflects how aerospace concept development is typically organized today. Each step is supported by highly specialized expertise and mature engineering tools. Yet, the overall workflow remains fragmented. Information moves slowly between disciplines, assumptions are reinterpreted multiple times, and iterations are often driven by availability rather than by long-term business priorities.

The core challenge is not a lack of simulation capability or engineering knowledge. It lies in how this knowledge is distributed across teams, tools, and phases of development. Design engineers, simulation specialists, manufacturing experts, and cost engineers each operate within their own context. Their contributions are essential, but they are rarely synchronized in a way that enables rapid and consistent comparison of alternatives at the system level.

As a result, concept decisions emerge from a sequence of partial evaluations. Geometry is prepared, simulated, reviewed, and revised largely in isolation. Manufacturing and cost considerations are often introduced later, when design freedom has already narrowed. Feedback loops exist, but they are slow and expensive, and they discourage broad exploration of the design space.

This structure stands in contrast to the nature of the concept phase itself. Engineers are expected to evaluate multiple scenarios in parallel, balance competing objectives, and make decisions under uncertainty. Doing this effectively requires continuous access to cross-functional knowledge and the ability to update assumptions quickly as new information becomes available.

A multi-agent system addresses this mismatch by making coordination a first-class element of the engineering process. Instead of treating simulation, cost assessment, manufacturability checks, and system impact analysis as separate activities, the system connects them through a shared context and a common orchestration logic. Each agent represents a specific domain perspective and contributes its assessment to a shared data layer.

This enables a state in which a single concept engineer gains live access to a multi-disciplinary digital coworker.

As a result, concept development is fundamentally transformed:

- Concept evaluations become available much faster, enabling earlier and more confident decisions.
- More than three concepts and follow-up scenarios can be assessed in parallel, rather than sequentially.
- Collaboration is enriched through human-in-the-loop mechanisms, allowing engineering judgment and experience to remain an integral part of decision-making.
- Cost-intensive misinvestments are avoided, because decisions are supported by broader and more consistent information.

The overall effect is a significant acceleration of the concept phase, leading to shorter time-to-market cycles. At the same time, risk is reduced and decisions are documented more clearly in their full system context. In this way, the approach lays the foundation for transforming the entire R&D process in the era of AI-driven agent systems.

Figure 3.4 illustrates how a multi-agent system for bracket development in the concept phase could be structured. As in previous practical sections, no CAx tools are replaced. Instead, they are connected to the multi-agent system and executed through the AI agents as part of the overall workflow. Figure 3.4 serves as a reference model, showing how existing engineering tools can be orchestrated by agents to support concept development without disrupting established toolchains.

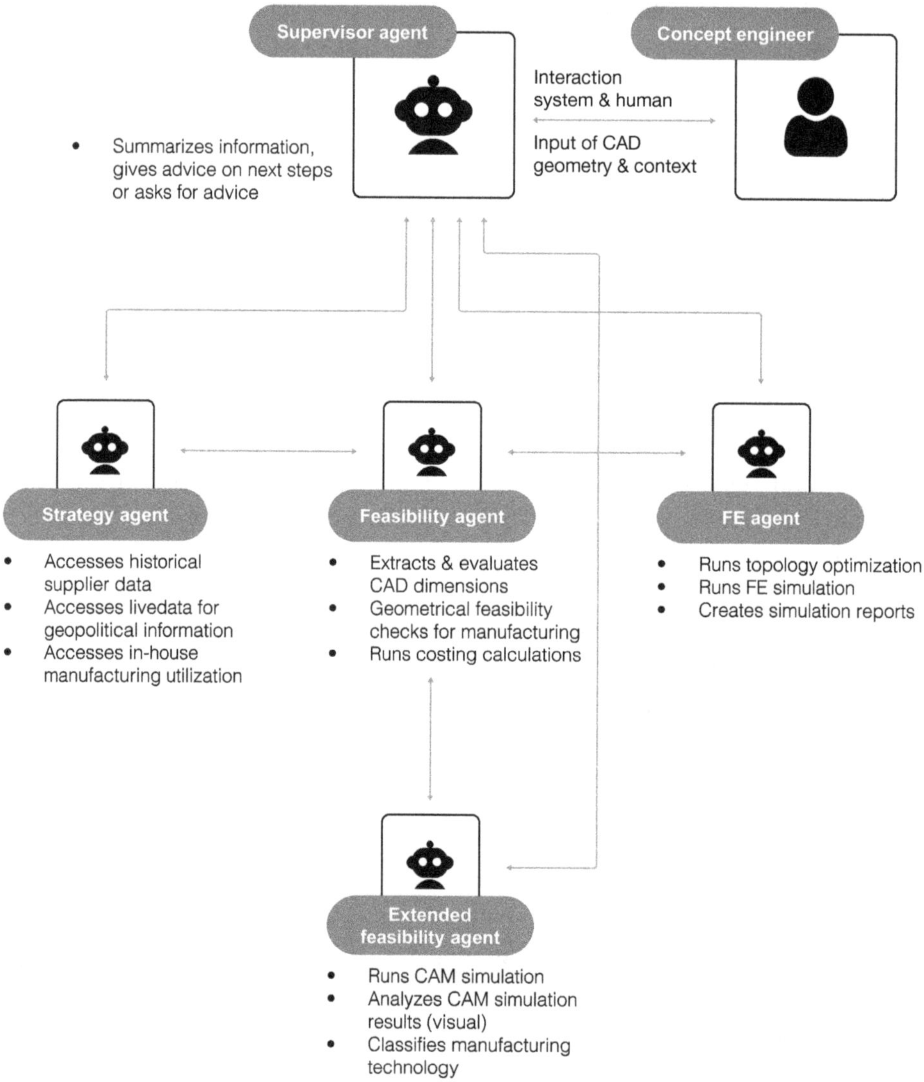

Figure 3.4 A multi-agent system for aerospace component development, where a supervisor agent coordinates a strategy agent, feasibility agent, FE agent, and extended feasibility agent—each handling specialized tasks from CAD analysis to CAM simulation and topology optimization (© Iryna Novoseletska)

The Supervisor Agent: "Tired of waiting for your colleagues? I'm here to help!"

The supervisor agent serves as the central coordinator during the concept phase. It acts as the primary interface for the concept engineer, gathers relevant context, and orchestrates the work of all specialist agents. Rather than generating engineering results itself, its role is to ensure that the right questions are addressed in the right sequence and that output remains consistent across domains.

This agent consolidates simulation results, feasibility assessments, sourcing and strategy constraints, and cost signals into a single, coherent decision package. It actively manages uncertainty by requesting human input when assumptions are incomplete or ambiguous. At the same time, it maintains a traceable record of decisions, data sources, assumptions, and approvals, providing transparency and continuity throughout the concept development process.

This makes the supervisor agent the backbone of coordination and decision integrity within the multi-agent system.

Key functions:

- The agent collects CAD geometry and contextual information from the concept engineer.
- The agent decides which specialist agents to trigger, based on the task type and the current maturity level of the concept.
- The agent coordinates iterations across feasibility checks, simulation activities, and strategy-related inputs.
- The agent summarizes results and explicitly highlights conflicts, dependencies, or trade-offs between domains.
- The agent requests clarification or formal approval when confidence levels are insufficient or assumptions are unclear.
- The agent maintains full traceability of all inputs, assumptions, intermediate results, and final outputs.

Input data from process owner: 3D models, instructions and context via chat interface

Connected tools:

- human chat interface for communication between engineers and the system
- rule-based automation to access and store decision-relevant documents and information in an ERP system or a comparable

The output of the supervisor agent is a consolidated concept decision summary prepared for the engineer. It includes recommended next steps, such as iterating the geometry, switching the manufacturing process, refining assumptions, or requesting missing inputs from other domains. In addition, the agent provides a structured decision package with fully traceable references to all underlying source artifacts, ensuring transparency and auditability throughout the concept phase.

LLM tip: Use a model that is strong in reasoning and context window to ensure accurate analysis and reliable decision support within the automation.

Prompting tip: A supervisor needs to know when to call which agent and in what sequence. If your agents are well prompted, then the supervisor is usually smart enough with a capable model to route to the right agent.

General tip: Try to avoid giving an engineering task to a supervisor. The supervisor's goal is to coordinate and finish a process, not to evaluate designs or concepts.

Special tip: Integrate human-in-the-loop capabilities through prompting. This approach reduces hallucination and ensures the system asks for clarification when information is missing or the next step is unclear.

The Strategy Agent: "I play the devil's advocate."

The strategy agent injects external and organizational constraints into concept decisions. It ensures that engineering concepts are not evaluated in isolation. The agent retrieves historical supplier data, considers geopolitical factors that may influence sourcing, and evaluates internal manufacturing utilization to support build-or-buy decisions.

Its purpose is not to optimize geometry. Its role is to reduce downstream surprises by introducing feasibility constraints early, when design freedom is still high. By bringing in context that typically resides in procurement, operations, or program management, the strategy agent makes this information available to the concept engineer at the moment when key decisions are made.

Key functions:

- It retrieves historical suppliers and sourcing data from ERP systems or comparable databases.
- It pulls live geopolitical signals from internal databases or external information sources that may influence supply risk.
- It checks internal manufacturing utilization and capacity constraints relevant to the concept under evaluation.
- It identifies and communicates red flags and constraints that affect concept selection.
- It suggests preferred process routes based on availability, risk exposure, and organizational strategy.

Input data from other agents: manufacturing technology, should-cost analysis, instructions via text

Connected tools:

- rule-based automation to access supplier databases and historical sourcing records
- rule-based automation to connect to live data feeds for receiving geopolitical or supply-chain risk signals
- rule-based automation to query internal manufacturing utilization dashboards or manufacturing execution system summaries
- rule-based automation to retrieve ERP procurement and category data relevant to sourcing decisions

The output of the strategy agent is a strategy constraints package that includes preferred suppliers, lead time, identified risk flags, and relevant capacity constraints. It also provides sourcing recommendations for each concept option, enriched with clear rationale tags to explain the underlying reasoning. In addition, the agent delivers structured inputs to the supervisor agent, enabling a balanced evaluation of feasibility, performance, and risk during concept selection.

LLM tip: Use a model that is strong in critical thinking and reasoning to ensure accurate analysis and reliable decision support within the automation.

Prompting tip: Capture perspectives that are needed to evaluate other agents but also prompt the agent to think like a critic.

General tip: Balance strategy with a bit of skepticism and goal orientation. A good strategy usually involves analysis of existing challenges and strong focus on goal to go towards.

Special tip: Treat the Strategy Agent to consider multiple technical perspectives. This is different from a supervisor, as the Strategy Agent is still working on by itself.

The Feasibility Agent: "I'm your most motivated and experienced colleague."

The feasibility agent is the primary workhorse during the concept phase. It extracts key dimensions from CAD geometry, evaluates manufacturability constraints using simple mathematical rules, and generates early cost signals. In addition, it can decide to involve an extended feasibility agent when critical areas are identified that fall into a feasibility grey zone and require deeper analysis.

Key functions:

- It extracts and evaluates CAD dimensions and key geometric parameters relevant for feasibility assessment.
- It performs geometric feasibility checks against basic manufacturing rules and constraints.

- It runs early cost calculations and compares the results against defined cost targets.
- It provides manufacturability flags and suggests potential geometry adjustments to improve feasibility.

Input data from other agents: 3D models, manufacturing technology, number of units and manufacturing location, instructions via text

Connected tools:

- rule-based geometry analysis utilities with feature recognition capabilities
- rule-based mathematical calculations to compare extracted feature values against design rules with the correct dependencies applied
- rule-based automation for executing and integrating should-cost calculations

The output of the feasibility agent is a feasibility report that summarizes manufacturability flags, key dimensions, and any identified constraint violations. It also provides an early cost estimate for each concept or variant, including the main cost drivers. In addition, the agent proposes concrete variant actions, such as adjusting fillets, modifying wall thicknesses, changing the manufacturing process route, or altering the build orientation.

LLM tip: Use base or foundation model to ensure computational efficiency and optimize LLM-related costs.

Prompting tip: Use a one shot or few shot prompt technique, wherein you show an agent how you would evaluate feasibility by an example.

General tip: Generate manufacturing-method-specific automations instead of generic, one-size-fits-all solutions. This approach significantly improves result quality, because rules, constraints, and assumptions are tailored to the actual process rather than averaged across multiple manufacturing routes.

Special tip: Do not try to build an overall feasibility agent, as it would conflict with the strategy agent. Try to bake in feasibility based on domain.

Extended Feasibility Agent: "I do the CAM reality check."

The extended feasibility agent deepens manufacturability validation by applying CAM-based simulation. It is activated when basic geometric checks are insufficient or when machining risk is considered high. In these cases, the agent runs CAM simulations to evaluate process-specific constraints such as deep-drawn or hard-to-machine features.

Beyond checking numeric limits, the agent also interprets visual simulation results and assesses whether the proposed manufacturing approach makes sense from a technological perspective. This includes evaluating, for example, filling behavior and process stability rather than relying solely on rule thresholds.

The value of the extended feasibility agent lies in identifying manufacturing risks early, especially for concepts that appear structurally attractive but are difficult or costly to produce. Its outputs remain deliberately focused on feasibility outcomes and on concrete geometry changes that would enable manufacturability, ensuring that concept decisions remain actionable and grounded in real production constraints.

Key functions:

- It classifies the manufacturing technology based on geometry.
- It runs CAM simulations for candidate geometries.
- It analyses CAM simulation results from both a visual and structural perspective.
- It detects manufacturability issues and provides concrete geometry change recommendations.
- It returns manufacturability confidence levels for each concept option.

Input data from other agents: 3D models, material, instructions via text

Connected tools:

- Rule-based automation creates screenshots of the geometry from multiple viewing angles to support part classification and assessment.
- Rule-based automation builds the CAM simulation model and triggers the CAM run, with a dedicated automation required for each manufacturing method.
- Rule-based automation accesses tool libraries and machine envelope definitions to ensure realistic process validation.
- Rule-based automation extracts visual outputs from CAM results and applies simple mathematical rule checks to assess manufacturability feasibility.

The output of the extended feasibility agent is a CAM feasibility report with clear pass, fail, or conditional outcomes. It highlights problematic regions in the geometry and provides specific recommendations for geometry adjustments to resolve manufacturability issues. In addition, the agent delivers an updated manufacturability confidence signal to the supervisor agent, enabling informed decision-making at the concept level.

LLM tip: Since interpreting simulation results and classifying manufacturing methods requires the LLM to process visual information, it is recommended to use a strong multimodal model for this task.

Prompting tip: It is common in our experience that a CAM agent is fed also fed special codes like CNC code. Do not do this in prompting as it is rather unnecessary info that will be processed every time. Such manufacturing specific capability should rather be an AI assisted tool.

General tip: CAM simulation is powerful but time intensive. Use a human-in-the-loop approach via the supervisor agent to trigger CAM simulations selectively.

Special tip: Maintain a library of recurring CAM failure patterns and convert them into reusable checks. A retrieval-augmented generation (RAG) approach can support this by matching new cases against known patterns and surfacing relevant guidance.

FEA Agent: "Creating proposals or proof? No worries, I do both for you."

The FEA agent supports concept-phase validation through fast, standardized simulation. It either runs topology optimization to propose efficient load paths as design guidance for the concept engineer or it performs FE analyses to verify that a concept design meets structural and dynamic targets defined earlier.

The agent is designed around reusable simulation templates so that results remain comparable across variants. It generates short, decision-ready reports rather than detailed solver output. In this way, the FEA agent provides early confidence and helps engineers avoid pursuing concepts that are likely to fail later due to stress, stiffness, or frequency limitations.

Key functions:

- It runs topology optimization to propose efficient load paths and material distribution.
- It runs FE simulations for concept variants using standardized setups.
- It evaluates structural metrics and frequency-related targets relevant to the concept phase.
- It produces simulation reports that enable consistent comparison across concepts.
- It flags target violations and highlights design areas that are sensitive to changes.

Input data from other agents: 3D models, material and load case requirements, instructions via text

Connected tools:

- Rule-based automation triggers topology optimization on a defined design space.
- Rule-based automation builds FE models from existing templates and triggers FE solver runs.
- Rule-based automation performs FE post-processing and generates standardized reports.

The output of the FEA agent includes topology guidance in the form of proposed load paths and concrete design hints. It also delivers a set of FE results, covering stresses, displacements, safety factors, and eigenfrequency metrics. In addition, the agent produces a short simulation report for each concept, complemented by a comparison summary that supports informed concept-level decision making.

LLM tip: Use a base or foundation model to ensure computational efficiency and optimize LLM-related costs.

Prompting tip: Instruct the FEA agent on how to evaluate what kind of topology optimization strategy to use.

General tip: Keep concept-phase FE simulations standardized, using the same templates, mesh targets, and output definitions across all variants.

Special tip: Depending on the interpretation capability of FEA agent, allow FEA agent to directly work with a CAD agent to logically optimize as much as possible.

3.2.5 Measuring the Impact—the Decision to Go All In

Although this section is structured around a specific use case, its purpose extends well beyond the use case itself. The focus is not the bracket in isolation, but the transformation of the entire R&D organization. For this reason, evaluating the impact of agent-based automation requires a broader perspective than simply looking at efficiency metrics alone.

The primary value does not lie in automation as an end in itself. It lies in the ability and speed to make better decisions earlier in the development process and, by doing so, to avoid costly downstream effects caused by early misjudgments. Many of the most expensive issues in product development originate not from execution failures, but from decisions made under time pressure and incomplete information, which can delay whole development programs.

The bracket example therefore serves as a proxy for a wide range of components within the overall product. The underlying idea of value creation is to build an organization that equips engineers with digital coworkers, thereby accelerating product development in a scalable and systematic way. For this reason, the value must be examined from multiple angles in this section. Our approach is to first analyze the cost impact at the level of a single bracket and then to extrapolate this perspective to a broader organizational scale.

At this point, such an analysis inevitably relies on a set of assumptions and hypotheses. This introduces a certain level of imprecision into the results. Accordingly, the following discussion is not intended to be copied directly. Its purpose is to sharpen perspective and to help you translate the underlying principles to your own organizational context.

The largest financial potential likely lies in a faster time to market. Other potential benefits are deliberately left out of this quantitative analysis. You should keep these additional effects in mind as additional positive factors. We therefore begin by examining what it would mean if the typical development time of an aircraft were reduced by 30 percent, while total development costs remained constant. Based on typical product development plans, it is realistic to expect significant time savings through the use of multi-agent systems, especially in the early phases of development. In these phases, decisions are still flexible, iterations are frequent, and much of the effort is spent on coordination rather than deep technical execution. Against this background, a 30 percent reduction in development time represents a plausible and conservative scenario. It reflects the impact of faster concept evaluation, earlier access to cross-functional knowledge, and reduced iteration cycles, rather than assuming radical changes to tooling or certification requirements. The following hypothesis is based on insights drawn from multiple information sources.

For manufacturers such as Airbus, substantial investments are incurred many years before the first revenues are realized, while cash inflows begin only after market entry and the subsequent production ramp-up. For this reason, not only the absolute level of development cost but also the duration of the development phase represents a central economic lever.

For modern widebody aircraft or larger single-aisle programs, total development and industrialization costs realistically fall in the range of USD 10 to 15 billion. In the case of the Airbus A350 XWB, Airbus itself and financial analysts have confirmed program costs in the low double-digit billion range when engineering, industrialization, and ramp-up losses are considered together (Spray 2025). Larger aircraft programs are correspondingly more expensive. For the following analysis, we therefore use a conservative assumption of USD 15 billion in total development costs.

When evaluating such long-term industrial programs, the weighted average cost of capital (WACC) is a critical factor. For aerospace OEMs, financial research typically places the industry WACC between 7 and 9 percent (Damodaran 2026). Airbus has historically operated around 8 percent, which is therefore used as the discount rate in this assessment.

After market entry and ramp-up, successful aircraft programs generate annual operating net cash flows in the multi-billion-dollar range. Large civil aviation programs typically achieve between USD 3 and 6 billion per year once they reach maturity. For a cautious and realistic model, an annual net cash flow of USD 4 billion is assumed.

In the baseline scenario, development takes ten years. During this period, only costs are incurred, while revenues begin in year eleven. In the alternative scenario, development time is reduced to seven years, with identical total development costs and an identical cashflow profile after market entry. As a result, operating cashflows start three years earlier, beginning in year eight.

This time gain has an immediate and material impact on net present value. At a discount rate of 8 percent, cashflows received in year eight have a significantly higher present value than those received in year eleven. Three additional years of operating cashflow, each amounting to USD 4 billion, generate a present value advantage of approximately USD 6 to 7 billion, purely due to reduced discounts. This effect follows directly from the fundamentals of discounted cashflow analysis.

A second effect is often underestimated. The development investment of USD 15 billion is tied up for three fewer years in the accelerated scenario. This reduces the opportunity cost of capital materially. At an 8 percent cost of capital, shortening the capital binding period by three years corresponds to an additional benefit of roughly USD 4 billion in today's value, driven by the time value of money.

Taken together, reducing development duration from ten to seven years creates an additional program value of approximately USD 10 to 11 billion, without saving a single dollar in development cost. This effect is driven entirely by earlier market entry, earlier revenues, reduced capital binding, and a faster break-even point. Additional financial upside from higher sales volumes due to competitive advantage is deliberately excluded from this calculation.

The next step is to contrast this potential value of USD 11 billion with the cost side of implementing agent-based automation. For this purpose, we assume that the aircraft consists of approximately 50,000 distinct components. We begin by estimating the effort required to set up the multi-agent system, including the necessary rule-based automations. Given the large number of components, it is recommended to use an automation platform to enable scalable implementation across the product. This implies that, in addition to internal engineering effort, license costs for the automation platform must also be considered.

Under the assumption that the automation platform already provides the necessary connections to CAx tools and includes an integrated geometry and post-processing kernel, it is realistic to set up a bracket-focused multi-agent system for three manufacturing methods within approximately six months. Many of the developed automations and agent logics can be transferred directly to other components. This creates a strong scaling effect across the product.

Based on experience, building the second multi-agent system requires around 20 percent less effort than the first. This efficiency gain continues with each additional component until the effort stabilizes at roughly 20 to 30 percent of the original baseline effort. To simplify the calculation, we assume an average effort of 70 percent of the initial bracket system effort for each additional component.

This translates to approximately four months of work per component, executed by a single engineer. Since this work requires experienced engineering expertise, we assume an hourly rate of USD 100, based on a 40-hour workweek. This results in labor costs of USD 64,000 per component. License and infrastructure costs for setup are estimated at USD 30,000 to 40,000 per component, leading to a total setup cost of approximately USD 100,000 per component. Assuming an aircraft with 50,000 distinct components, the total investment required to build the full set of multi-agent systems amounts to roughly USD 5 billion.

In addition to setup costs, operating license costs for the multi-agent systems must be considered. Given the scale, this would typically fall under an enterprise agreement. As a simplifying assumption, we estimate annual license costs at 2 percent of the previously identified USD 11 billion value potential. Over a seven-year development period, this results in approximately USD 1.5 billion in license costs. Infrastructure and LLM usage costs must also be included. These are estimated at USD 2 to 3 billion over seven years. This calculation assumes operating costs of USD 10,000 per multi-agent system per year, applied over five years, reflecting the fact that these systems are used less intensively toward the end of development. It is also reasonable to expect these costs to decrease over time as LLM services become more commoditized.

☑ In summary, the total investment for the first aircraft development program is estimated at approximately USD 9 billion, compared to a value potential of roughly USD 11 billion driven solely by reduced development time. Even under conservative assumptions, this strategy can therefore generate a net positive outcome within the first program. For subsequent programs, where only operating costs are incurred, the potential value creation exceeds USD 5 billion per program.

While individual assumptions can certainly be debated and the model is intentionally simplified, the conclusion is clear. This is ultimately a strategic decision. Does an organization believe in a future where engineers work hand in hand with AI agents, or not? If the answer is yes, it becomes essential to allocate capital early and manage the transition risk deliberately. Engineering is moving toward a new era. Organizations that adopt these approaches early stand to benefit disproportionately from the shift. Late adopters, by contrast, risk finding themselves at a significant competitive disadvantage within the next decade.

3.2.6 The 360-Day Plan: Fall in Love with Your Future R&D Organization

The objective of the 360-day program is to systematically de-risk the introduction of agent-based automation within the R&D organization. The focus is not on an immediate full-scale rollout. It is on validating architectural decisions, organizational readiness, and value creation through a sequence of controlled and measurable experiments.

By the end of the program, the organization should have clear evidence of whether a multi-agent system can reliably support engineering decisions in early development phases. It should also be in a position to make an informed decision on whether and how to pursue a broader transformation of its R&D processes.

Phase 1: Understand and Frame (Days 1 – 60)

Goal: Create a shared understanding of the current engineering workflow, identify coordination risks, and clarify where agent-based support can reduce uncertainty without compromising safety or certification.

Key activities:

- Document the current product development process across concept, design, validation, and industrialization phases for a single component.
- Identify decision points with high downstream impact, with a particular focus on early concept phases.
- Map information flows between engineering disciplines, simulation, manufacturing, cost, and program management.
- Identify key risk drivers, such as late changes, over-engineering, long validation loops, and loss of knowledge.
- Define baseline metrics related to iteration time, rework effort, and decision latency.
- Draft an initial hypothesis for how agents could support concept engineers without changing roles or responsibilities.

Deliverables:

- one-page problem statement
- current-state process map and user journey
- preliminary impact hypotheses, such as expected cycle-time reduction or effort savings
- first conceptual view of an agent-supported R&D workflow

Decision Gate A: executive alignment on problem framing and approval to proceed with architectural exploration

Phase 2: Architecture and Governance Design (Days 61 – 90)

Goal: Define the future agentic R&D architecture at a conceptual level and establish governance principles that ensure safety, traceability, and clear human ownership.

Key activities:

- Define the target agent roles for the chosen component.
- Specify responsibilities, boundaries, and hand-off logic between agents and human decision-makers.
- Define data ownership rules, as well as traceability and auditability requirements.
- Design human-in-the-loop checkpoints and clear escalation rules for uncertainty or risk.
- Evaluate build-versus-buy options for orchestration platforms and automation frameworks.

Deliverables:

- An agent architecture one-pager describing roles, data flows, and key decision points.
- A governance model covering responsibility, traceability, and risk management.
- A build-versus-buy decision memo with clear rationale.
- A defined scope for the first experimental use cases.

Decision Gate B: formal approval of the proposed architecture, governance model, and experimental scope

Phase 3: Experimental MVPs and First Tests (Days 91 – 270)

Goal: Run controlled experiments with agent-based workflows in real engineering contexts while minimizing operational risk.

Key activities:

- Implement a first multi-agent system for the selected component, focused on concept-phase tasks.
- Start with read-only integrations to existing databases and engineering systems.
- Use agents to support feasibility checks, early simulation, and decision-making during concept development.
- Integrate human-in-the-loop mechanisms to ensure control, validation, and trust.
- Run multiple test cycles, both on the selected component and on related components within the same product group.

- Compare agent-supported decisions against results from traditional workflows.
- Collect qualitative feedback from engineers and quantitative metrics on cycle time, iteration speed, and decision quality.

Deliverables:

- a working experimental agent system supporting concept-phase activities
- documented test cases and comparison results against traditional workflows
- identified limitations, failure modes, and improvement areas for agent-based support
- a clear understanding of scalability within a single product group
- a refined view of where agents add value and where human expertise must remain dominant

Decision Gate C: executive go/no-go decision on whether agent-based support delivers sufficient value and reliability to justify further investment

Phase 4: Scaling Strategy and Risk Reduction (Days 271 – 360)

Goal: Translate the experimental results into a scalable, risk-managed roadmap for the R&D organization.

Key activities:

- Define clear criteria for scaling agent-based systems to additional components and programs.
- Identify required organizational changes, including skills, roles, training needs, and operating models.
- Estimate the effort and cost needed to move from experimental setups to production-ready implementations.
- Define an integration strategy with certification, compliance, and quality management systems.
- Develop a multi-year rollout roadmap with phased adoption across the organization.
- Build a refined business case based on validated assumptions and experimental results.

Deliverables:

- a scaling and rollout roadmap outlining phased adoption across the organization
- a production readiness assessment covering technical, organizational, and process maturity

- a risk mitigation plan addressing both organizational and technical risks
- a final business case with a clear investment recommendation

Decision Gate D: an executive decision on scaling agentic workflows across the R&D organization

3.2.7 Guest Perspective: From Generative Design to Intelligent Engineering at NASA

Ryan McClelland

The Slow Pain of Traditional Design

The traditional way of designing structures in aerospace has long been painful and slow, even for something as basic as a bracket, much less a complex system like an optical bench. Requirements were often based on conversations rather than consistently documented at the part level, then handed off to a designer who essentially sketches and extrudes shapes driven by past experience and the limitations of the CAD tool.

The designer typically has no simulation or FEA skillset, so designs are shaped by what is convenient to model rather than what performs best. Eventually, the CAD model gets thrown over the fence to the analysis group, which usually has a better understanding of requirements. Analysts then manually create meshes using their own past experience. This process can take weeks, making feedback loops painfully slow, with neither designer nor analyst fully understanding the tools and techniques of the other specialty.

Without much optimization, a design that barely meets requirements eventually gets a drawing and goes to fabrication. There, the feedback loop is even worse. Shops are incentivized to manufacture whatever is thrown their way, and the only signal that a design is difficult to produce comes in the form of high cost and long schedule. Having backgrounds in both design and analysis, this fragmented workflow seemed ripe for disruption.

A COVID-19 Epiphany

The impetus for change came during the COVID-19 shutdown. While searching for ways to use AI in engineering, I came across the Autodesk and JPL Generative Design project from 2016. The concept was compelling: Instead of an engineer manually sketching geometry, computation could explore the design space given constraints, loads, interfaces, and objectives. I eventually met one of the leaders from that team, Dani Grandi at Autodesk Research, and the direction became clear.

The gap I saw was not a lack of powerful CAD or analysis tools. It was the lack of an end-to-end path from intent to verified design that preserved context. Engineers were drawing and re-creating models instead of specifying constraints and letting computation do the exploration. That disconnect is where time, quality, and schedule risk accumulate.

Early Experiments That Changed Everything

The very first time I created a Generative Design for one of my applications, an X-ray mirror mount for the OGRE sounding rocket mission, I was hooked. The complexity and beauty of the design captivated me and clearly felt like the future. I still have the plastic print of that design in my office, even though it was quite rough in retrospect.

This inspired me to keep experimenting, eventually designing the EXCITE Tip/Tilt bracket, which would come to be called a celebrity 3D print even though it was also CNC machined. Its performance was vastly superior to a human benchmark from one of our best designers, Drew Jones, who laid out the original design for the James Webb Space Telescope. The generative design was lighter, stiffer, stronger, and easier to manufacture. I found this approach to be a consistent win against every design challenge I threw at it.

Perhaps the biggest early pivot was away from additive manufacturing. I was surprised to find that CNC machining is far more capable than most engineers realize. The ALICE Optical Bench, eventually featured on the website of the New York Times, demonstrated this clearly. For all our applications, CNC machined parts were stronger, more ductile, easier to inspect, easier to analyze, cheaper, more precise, and faster to produce than their additively manufactured counterparts.

Winning Hearts and Minds

Change is hard. Most engineers use the same tools their entire career, and their identity becomes entangled with specific software products. What ultimately convinced people was delivering and testing hardware, then validating it with existing techniques and tests. It helped that I had done both jobs, design and analysis, on flight projects, so I could speak the language of both communities.

It took patience and answering the same questions for each new project looking to adopt these tools. I had to develop a sales mentality, initially ill-suited to my nuts-and-bolts engineering past. Buy-in from senior management and technology leadership at NASA Goddard was essential, giving me the top cover to seek change. Winning the top and the bottom innovative designers, was easier than winning the middle: product leads who often see new technologies as a risky distraction.

To make successful change, just as happened with drawing boards giving way to 2D CAD and then to 3D CAD, there has to be a huge, obvious win. Something so impactful that once the new tool is picked up, it cannot be put back down because it enables things that were simply not possible before.

Why Engineering Tools Are Still Too Hard

One of the biggest challenges, and what causes tool lock-in and over-specialization between CAD and FEM, is how difficult it is to learn these tools. It often takes thousands of hours to become truly proficient and know where every menu option is and what it does. In short, CAE tools are just too hard to learn. AI copilots and tool-use agents may solve this problem, or workflow automation may largely eliminate it, as processes and best practices become encoded and enforced by default rather than relying on intuition and tribal knowledge.

The real friction shows up when requirements, CAD, analysis, manufacturing feedback, and review artifacts do not flow together. Engineers spend disproportionate time rebuilding models, re-entering parameters, translating data formats, and re-deriving context that already exists somewhere else. Even when individual tools are powerful, the glue work remains the bottleneck, and that glue is often a small number of experienced engineers doing coordination by memory, email, and meetings.

Knowledge That Walks Out the Door

At NASA, subject matter experts build up internal models of what designs and approaches worked on their previous missions and what challenges they encountered. Since spaceflight design cycles are slow, though, most engineers have limited experience across only a few missions and can be biased based on the particular challenges of those missions. We work on such a broad variety of missions, from space telescopes to asteroid sampling, that applying past knowledge is often challenging and sometimes impossible, since many missions are truly unique.

That said, our experts carry a great deal of unique and specialized knowledge. Sometimes it is written down, but often it is tacit, passed down by oral traditions and apprenticeship. When that knowledge is not available, which can be very challenging across a large organization like NASA, teams reinvent the wheel or known issues are not raised until formal review cycles, where late changes are costly.

The Unfulfilled Promise of Digitalization

Modeling and simulation were supposed to make it faster to deliver hardware by reducing the amount of physical fabrication and testing needed. Instead, in my experience, digitalization separated engineering from manufacturing and led to analysis paralysis. Rather than fabricating and testing to answer unknowns, the answer was always more analysis. Given the slowness of the CAD, FEA, and fabrication feedback loop, we did not see the acceleration in hardware delivery we might have anticipated.

Agents as Scalable Engineering Teams

The power of agents is that they are becoming scalable engineering teams that can operate around the clock. One of the unanticipated benefits is that the decision trace, including agent reasoning and input-output logs, can be captured, analyzed, and iterated on. With human designs, decisions are often not captured. They might have been made during a hallway conversation or phone call, causing the context of why decisions were made to be lost. Agentic systems expose those conversations between agents into a trace log available for inspection and review.

I see agents adding the most value as orchestrators of workflows and preservers of context, not just as automation for routine tasks. The real step change is an agent that can translate intent into tool-ready inputs, coordinate across CAD and analysis and data systems, run iterative loops, and produce an evidence package that is reviewable, reproducible, and aligned with engineering governance.

Autonomy, Trust, and Validation

Future engineering workflows will feel like a true human-AI collaboration, as computers go from calculators to collaborators. I expect the pattern to mirror the development of software engineering agents: from one-shot designs that need heavy review and manual tweaking to self-reviewing systems that design and validate iteratively based on input requirements and design standards.

Agents should make decisions autonomously when the problem is bounded, the constraints are clear, and the outcome is testable and verifiable. This includes things like running standard analyses, exploring parameter trade spaces, generating candidate designs under explicit constraints, performing checks, and drafting documentation. Humans must remain in the loop for high-consequence decisions and for anything that involves negotiating requirements, selecting architectures, or balancing mission risk.

We build trust in our systems by using them over a wide range of applications. For agentic systems, this comes in the form of evaluations used to demonstrate that inputs are being transformed into outputs that meet requirements, standards, and verification. As the set of applications grows, challenges arise requiring changes to the workflows and agents. These new edge cases are added to the evaluations, creating a data flywheel and continuous improvement. Ultimately, in engineering, trust comes from robust testing.

The Real Challenge Is People

Getting technology to work and getting the organization to adopt it go hand in hand. Deployment from prototype to production is a journey with many stops, and deployment to the workforce is similarly continuous since people adapt to change at vastly different rates. The keys are to show a clear, undeniable engineering win, make the tools easy to use and get support for, create communities around those tools, and have empathy for the needs and background of new users.

As part of my research on driving adoption, I interviewed the individuals who took NASA Goddard from drawing boards to 2D CAD and from 2D CAD to 3D CAD. The need for a clear win is the same across generations. The need for training and the likelihood that not everyone will make the transition is also the same. What is different this time is the speed at which changes are occurring. Unlike past generations, using one tool for an entire career, or seeing just one paradigm change, is highly unlikely. Curiosity and the willingness to explore new tools and techniques will become a key trait for future engineers.

Bringing Joy Back to Engineering

The key differentiator for choosing between a sophisticated generic agent and a simpler one with deep organizational context is validation. Whichever system creates the superior or more reliable outputs based on the evaluations your organization cares about will deliver more value. You do not need to intuit the answer if you can test it.

As agents take on more coordination and routine analysis, the engineer's role will shift in the same way that software development is being transformed: Writing software is more democratized, and engineers can focus on what and why they are building rather than mostly how.

Success looks like bringing joy to engineering, the joy we had as children building LEGO or tree forts. It is a future where going from idea to prototype is vastly accelerated, and we spend more time thinking about what we build and why rather than the drudgery of how.

3.3 Consumer Goods OEM: Why Good Enough Is Too Expensive

Product development in consumer goods follows economic rules that differ from many other industries. Production volumes are high, margins per unit are often thin, and even small design decisions can have a significant financial impact over the lifetime of a product. At the same time, organizations in this sector vary widely in their product portfolios, manufacturing strategies, and tooling concepts. As a result, even seemingly similar use cases often require very different implementation approaches.

This section therefore follows the same guiding principle as the previous practical use cases. It describes a representative scenario that highlights recurring patterns, without assuming that all consumer goods OEMs operate in the same way. The focus is deliberately placed on injection-molded plastic parts—not because they are the only relevant case, but because they clearly illustrate how small design improvements can scale into substantial economic effects.

The examples presented here should again be understood as inspiration. Your organization may rely on different materials, tooling strategies, or validation workflows. That is more than expected. Take the ideas that fit your products and processes, adapt them where necessary, and extend them where additional constraints apply.

As with all agent-based automation approaches, the decisive factor is not the technology itself, but how well it aligns with real operational and economic drivers. This section acts as a reference model that shows how multi-agent systems can support systematic cost optimization across large product portfolios, while maintaining performance and quality requirements.

3.3.1 Executive Snapshot

Consumer goods OEMs operate in an environment defined by very high production volumes and tight unit margins. Products are often sold in millions of units per year, and even small components can accumulate substantial costs over their lifetime. Injection-molded plastic parts play a central role in this context. They are used across broad product portfolios and are typically produced for many years. Tooling is often replaced multiple times over a product's lifetime, even though the part geometry itself remains unchanged.

In many organizations, these parts are designed to be robust and functionally sufficient but not systematically optimized for minimum material usage or cost. Design decisions are frequently made under time pressure, with a strong focus on performance, quality, and manufacturability. Once a part enters series production, its geometry often remains frozen for long periods, even as production volumes and material costs continue to accumulate.

This leads to a characteristic economic situation:

- Very high unit volumes amplify the financial impact of small design inefficiencies.
- Tool lifetimes are finite, requiring periodic reinvestment in new molds.
- Existing designs are often reused unchanged when new tools are built.
- Engineering capacity is rarely allocated to revisiting parts that already meet functional requirements.

As a result, many consumer goods OEMs carry hidden cost potential within their existing product portfolios. Removing only a few grams of material from a high-volume plastic part can translate into significant savings over the remaining lifetime of the product, without compromising performance or quality. Identifying these opportunities systematically across hundreds of parts, however, is difficult with manual processes alone.

The pressure to address this inefficiency is increasing:

- Material costs and sustainability targets are becoming more critical.
- Product portfolios are expanding, increasing the number of active tools and parts.
- Engineering teams are expected to deliver more optimization without proportional increases in capacity.

These dynamics turn cost optimization of existing parts into a strategic capability, rather than a one-time engineering exercise.

Section Focus

This section shows how a multi-agent system can support systematic cost optimization of injection-molded plastic parts in high-volume consumer goods environments. The focus is on re-evaluating existing designs at the moment when new tooling becomes necessary, and on scaling this capability across many parts and products.

The multi-agent system enables a coordinated optimization workflow:

- geometry analysis to identify material distribution, wall thickness, and structural reserves in existing parts
- manufacturability assessment to validate injection molding constraints and process limits
- performance verification to ensure that functional and quality requirements remain satisfied
- cost impact estimation to quantify material and cycle-time savings per part and across lifetime volumes
- portfolio reuse by applying the same agent logic across multiple parts and product lines

The result is that small design changes translate into large financial impact. Material usage is reduced, cost efficiency improves, and optimization becomes a repeatable and scalable capability, rather than an isolated engineering effort.

3.3.2 Where Cost Efficiency Gets Lost in Daily Doings

Consumer goods OEMs have spent decades optimizing their manufacturing operations. Injection molding processes are highly automated, cycle times are tightly controlled, and scrap rates are continuously monitored. From a production perspective, many organizations operate close to technical excellence. When it comes to product design, however, a different picture often emerges.

Injection-molded plastic parts are typically designed to be robust, manufacturable, and functionally safe. Once these criteria are met and a product enters series production, the design is rarely revisited. Parts that perform reliably often remain unchanged for years, even as production volumes grow and new tools are built to replace molds that reach the end of their lifetime. In practice, design teams move on to the next product, while existing parts quietly accumulate cost with every produced unit.

This creates a structural blind spot:

- Small material inefficiencies remain hidden behind acceptable performance.
- Tool replacements are treated as manufacturing events, not as design opportunities.
- Engineering resources focus on new development rather than systematic optimization of existing parts.

In high-volume environments, this blind spot becomes expensive. Removing one or two grams of material from a plastic part may appear insignificant in isolation. When multiplied by millions or tens of millions of units over the remaining lifetime of a product, these small inefficiencies translate into substantial material, energy, and logistics costs.

Despite this potential, systematic re-optimization rarely takes place. One reason is organizational. Consumer goods OEMs manage thousands of parts across multiple product lines, making manual review impractical. Another reason is methodology. Cost optimization requires balancing multiple constraints at once, including mechanical performance, stiffness, durability, surface quality, manufacturability, tooling limitations, and often sustainability targets. These trade-offs are difficult to assess quickly without structured support.

As a result, optimization efforts tend to be opportunistic rather than systematic. Engineers improve parts when problems arise or when redesign becomes unavoidable, but rarely as part of a repeatable, portfolio-wide process. Even when simulation tools and DFM guidelines are available, their application is selective and heavily dependent on individual experience and available time.

The situation is further complicated by tooling lifecycles. Injection molds have finite lifetimes, particularly in high-volume production. When a tool reaches the end of its life, a replacement is required. In theory, this moment provides a natural opportunity to revisit the part design. In practice, the new tool often replicates the existing geometry unchanged, because schedules are tight and the original design is considered proven. The opportunity for cost reduction is recognized but rarely realized.

Many organizations attempt to address this gap through checklists, design guidelines, or isolated cost-down initiatives. While these approaches can deliver local improvements, they do not scale. They rely on manual effort, fragmented data, and individual motivation. There is no systematic mechanism to continuously screen large part portfolios, quantify optimization potential, and prioritize where engineering effort yields the highest return.

Ultimately, the challenge is not a lack of tools or engineering knowledge. It is the absence of coordination and scalability. Cost optimization in high-volume consumer goods requires a way to apply the same engineering logic repeatedly and consistently across many parts, without overwhelming design teams.

In the following sections, we examine how a multi-agent system can address this challenge by transforming cost optimization from a one-off engineering activity into a scalable and repeatable capability across the product portfolio.

3.3.3 The Art of Not Touching Working Parts

In high-volume consumer goods organizations, injection-molded parts often outlive the projects that created them. A component designed for an initial product launch may remain in production for many years, sometimes across multiple product refreshers, packaging updates, or supplier changes. Over this lifecycle, the central engineering question is rarely whether the part still functions. It is whether there is a justified moment to modify a design that already performs reliably.

In practice, part cost optimization is therefore not a continuous background activity. It is a structured improvement effort that runs alongside regular product development and operations. These efforts are often framed as cost-down initiatives, value analysis or value engineering programs, or continuous improvement campaigns. While organizational labels vary, the underlying logic is consistent. The process must bridge three perspectives that operate on different timelines: engineering design cycles, manufacturing continuity, and financial planning.

Parts typically return to the engineering agenda only when a trigger makes change acceptable or unavoidable. Common triggers include an injection mold approaching the end of its lifetime, a significant increase in projected production volume, shifts in material costs, new sustainability or performance targets, or a supplier change initiated by procurement. These moments create a window in which revisiting a geometry becomes politically and operationally feasible. Outside such windows, the default decision is often to leave the part untouched.

Once a trigger exists, organizations usually begin with a prioritization step. Engineering and controlling teams identify candidate parts based on expected leverage rather than technical curiosity. Annual volume, remaining product lifetime, resin cost, known overdesign indicators, and tooling complexity all influence this selection. At this stage, the objective is not to prove feasibility. It is to decide which parts justify the allocation of limited engineering capacity.

For a selected part, the optimization workflow typically starts by establishing a clear baseline. Engineers collect the current CAD model, tooling assumptions, process windows, quality constraints, and cost drivers. In many organizations, this information is distributed across multiple systems and teams. As a result, a considerable amount of effort is often spent assembling a consistent and complete starting point before any optimization work begins.

With the baseline defined, engineers perform a structured design and manufacturability review. They analyze wall thickness distribution, ribs, bosses, draft angles, and local reinforcements using injection molding design principles. The goal is to identify regions where material could potentially be removed without compromising function, appearance, or process stability. At this stage, several concepts are often explored in parallel, with the understanding that not all will survive further evaluation.

Manufacturing input enters early in this phase. Toolmakers, molders, or suppliers review proposed changes and provide feedback on feasibility. Many cost levers are not purely geometric. They depend on gating concepts, cooling efficiency, ejection strategy, warpage sensitivity, and dimensional robustness. This is often the point where certain ideas are discarded or sent back for revision. A concept that appears attractive from a design perspective may prove impractical from a tooling or process standpoint, forcing engineers to revisit earlier assumptions.

Analytical support is applied selectively. Mold flow simulations are used when changes affect flow length, wall thickness transitions, or surface quality. Structural checks are performed when stiffness, snap-fit behavior, or durability under repeated loading is relevant. These analyses frequently lead to iteration. If results indicate unacceptable risk or degraded performance, engineers return to the design and manufacturability stage to adjust the geometry and reassess feasibility.

The final step is economic evaluation. Material savings are typically straightforward to calculate. Cycle-time effects and scrap sensitivity require closer collaboration with manufacturing. Tooling implications are assessed carefully, since added complexity can quickly offset per-part savings. It is not uncommon for this cost assessment to reveal that a technically feasible change does not deliver sufficient economic benefit. In such cases, the optimization loop either returns to earlier stages to explore alternative concepts or is stopped entirely for that part.

If the combined technical and economic case is strong enough, the change enters the formal engineering change process, including validation planning and a controlled rollout into production. Importantly, this decision is usually the outcome of multiple iterations across design, manufacturing feedback, analysis, and cost evaluation, rather than a single linear pass through the process.

This approach works well for individual parts. It allows experienced engineers to reduce costs while managing risk in a controlled and deliberate manner. At the same time, its iterative nature increases coordination effort. Each loop requires manual alignment, repeated data preparation, and renewed expert attention.

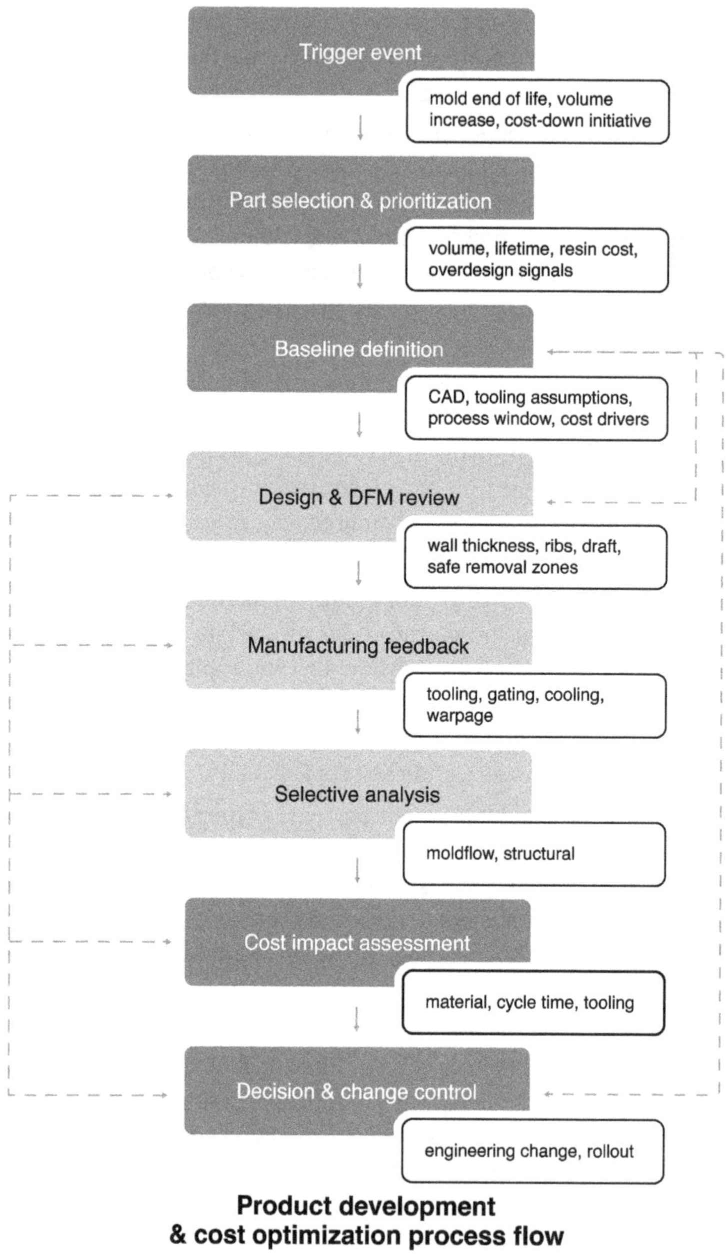

Figure 3.5 The iterative product development and cost optimization process flow, triggered by events such as mold end-of-life or cost-down initiatives, and progressing through part selection, baseline definition, DFM review, manufacturing feedback, selective analysis, and cost impact assessment to a final change control decision (© Iryna Novoseletska)

As product portfolios grow and production volumes increase, this limitation becomes more pronounced. Organizations are aware that significant savings are often hidden in small geometric inefficiencies, yet they lack a repeatable mechanism to explore alternatives systematically, converge efficiently, and prioritize engineering effort across many parts.

This is the point where a different approach becomes relevant. In the following section, we describe how a multi-agent system can explicitly support these iteration loops, reduce coordination overhead, and transform episodic optimization into a scalable, portfolio-wide capability, while preserving engineering judgment and manufacturing robustness.

The simplified process chart in Figure 3.5 summarizes this typical workflow, including the feedback loops that characterize real-world cost optimization in high-volume consumer goods environments.

3.3.4 Making Cost Optimization a Norm

The workflow described in the previous sections reflects how cost optimization of injection-molded parts is commonly handled today. It is driven by experienced engineers, supported by mature design rules, and enriched by manufacturing and quality expertise. When applied to individual parts, this approach delivers reliable results and keeps operational risk under control.

At the same time, a structural limitation becomes evident. Cost optimization is episodic, highly manual, and strongly dependent on individual initiative. Each optimization effort requires engineers to reassemble context, align assumptions across functions, and iterate through design, manufacturing feedback, analysis, and cost evaluation. These iteration loops are essential, but they carry a high cost of coordination. The challenge is therefore not the engineering logic itself. That logic already exists and is well understood. The difficulty lies in applying it repeatedly, consistently, and across many parts without overwhelming the organization. As product portfolios grow and volumes increase, the coordination effort required to run optimization loops scales faster than the savings individual engineers can realistically unlock.

This imbalance explains why many organizations restrict optimization to a small subset of parts, even though significant potential remains elsewhere in the portfolio. The barrier is not technical feasibility. It is the absence of a mechanism that supports iteration, reuse, and prioritization at scale.

A multi-agent system addresses this gap by embedding the existing optimization logic into a coordinated digital workflow. Instead of treating geometry review, manufacturability checks, simulation, and cost assessment as loosely connected steps, the system links them through a shared context and explicit orchestration. Each agent represents a familiar role in the current process and contributes its assessment in a structured and reusable form. Importantly, this does not change how engineers reason about parts. It changes how that reasoning is organized and repeated. Iteration loops remain, but they become faster and more transparent. Assumptions persist across steps. Feedback from manufacturing or analysis is preserved between iterations. Decisions are documented automatically as part of the automation.

Figure 3.6 illustrates how such a multi-agent system can be structured for cost optimization of injection-molded plastic parts. The architecture mirrors today's process, including its iterative nature, while reducing coordination overhead. Existing tools remain in place. CAD, simulation, PLM, ALM, and production systems are connected through the orchestration layer.

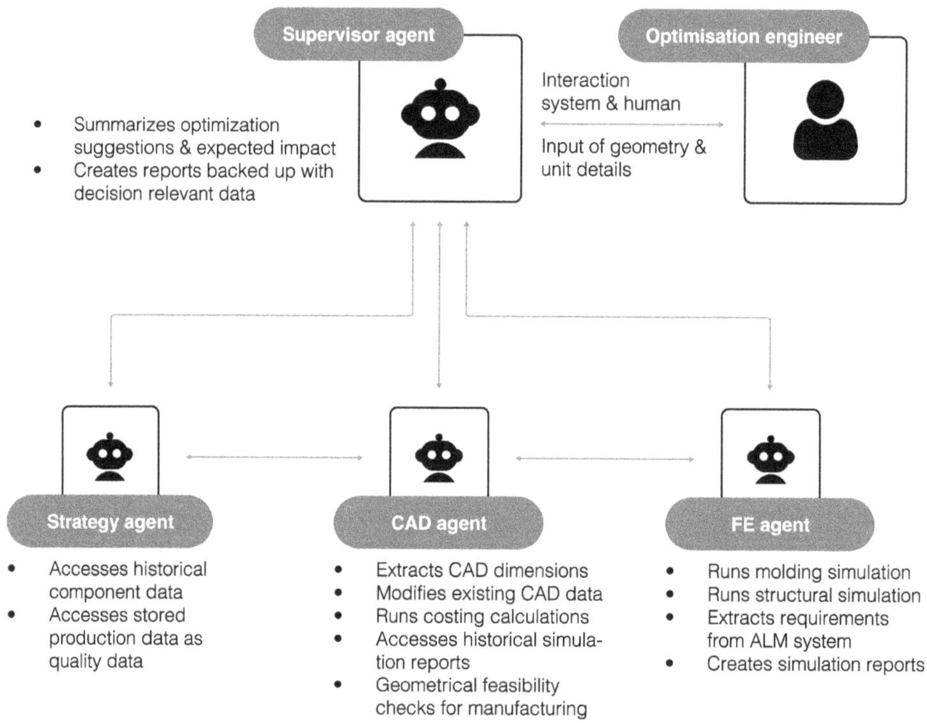

Figure 3.6 A three-agent system for consumer goods optimization, where a supervisor coordinates a strategy agent, CAD agent, and FE agent to deliver data-backed recommendations on geometry, manufacturing feasibility, and structural performance (© Iryna Novoseletska)

The Supervisor Agent: "I can't clone you, but the rest of the team."

The supervisor agent serves as the central coordinator of the optimization workflow and as the primary interface for the optimization engineer. It does not perform geometry changes or simulations itself. Its responsibility is to structure the process, manage iterations, and ensure that all outputs remain decision-relevant. The agent receives the initial input, typically an existing CAD model or part number, along with remaining production volume information and the optimization intent. Based on this context, it determines which specialist agents to activate and in what sequence. Throughout the workflow, it consolidates intermediate results, tracks assumptions, and highlights trade-offs between cost, performance, and manufacturability. By maintaining a consistent decision context, the supervisor agent prevents optimization efforts from fragmenting into isolated analyses. It ensures that every recommendation remains traceable to underlying data, applied rules, and explicitly documented assumptions.

Key functions:

- It accepts geometry and additional context from the optimization engineer.
- It orchestrates CAD, simulation, and strategy agents based on defined optimization goals.
- It manages iteration loops when requirements or constraints are not met.
- It consolidates intermediate and final results into decision-ready summaries.
- It requests human input when confidence levels are insufficient or assumptions are unclear.

Input data from process owner: 3D models or part number, remaining production volume, optimization objectives, instructions and context via chat interface

Connected tools:

- a human interaction interface for clarification, review, and approval
- rule-based workflows for creating standardized optimization reports
- rule-based workflows for storing and distributing reports within the ERP system

The output of the supervisor agent is a consolidated optimization report that summarizes the proposed design changes, the expected cost impact, the level of feasibility confidence, and the recommended next steps for further action.

LLM tip: Use a model that is strong in reasoning to ensure accurate analysis and reliable decision support within the automation.

Prompting tip: Keep the supervisor agent goal- and user-focused. The supervisor usually should be able to ask any agent to change their work depending on user request.

General tip: Treat the supervisor agent as a decision assistant, not as a controlling authority, to preserve creativity within the system. Ensure appropriate control mechanisms through human-in-the-loop integration to maintain oversight and accountability.

Special tip: Integrate human-in-the-loop capabilities through prompting. This approach reduces hallucination and ensures the system asks for clarification when information is missing or the next step is unclear.

The Strategy Agent: "I don't like engineering, I like business!"

The strategy agent injects portfolio-level and business context into the optimization process. It ensures that design decisions are evaluated not only from a technical perspective, but also in terms of production volume, quality history, and operational reality. The agent retrieves historical component data, production metrics, and quality signals from enterprise systems. Its purpose is to identify patterns that influence optimization risk, such as parts with highly stable processes, parts with known quality sensitivities, or parts produced at exceptionally high volumes where even small savings have a significant financial impact. By introducing this context early in the workflow, the strategy agent helps prioritize engineering effort and avoids changes that may appear technically attractive but are economically, operationally, or organizationally questionable.

Key functions:

- It accesses historical components and production data from enterprise systems.
- It retrieves quality and scrap information for existing parts.
- It flags parts with high economic leverage or elevated operational risk.
- It provides portfolio-level context to support prioritization and informed decision-making.

Input data from other agents: remaining production volumes, cost analysis for modified geometry, instructions via text

Connected tools:

- Rule-based automation accesses PLM systems to retrieve historical metadata for components.
- Rule-based automation accesses ERP or MES systems to obtain production, quality, and scrap data.

The strategy agent **outputs** a context summary that highlights volume leverage, expected cost impact, quality risk, and clear prioritization signals for the part under review.

LLM tip: Use a model that is strong in reasoning to ensure accurate analysis and reliable decision support within the automation.

Prompting tip: Since the strategy agent has more reasoning tasks rather than tool calling, instruct the agent to think about business context for the specific component.

General tip: Treat this agent as a risk filter, not a cost optimizer.

Special tip: Try to build and equip the strategy agent with a web search agent so that it can fetch most updated context for business decisions. This will help the businessperson in your organization avoid this additional work.

The CAD Agent: "I'm here to let grams disappear."

The CAD agent is responsible for geometry-centric analysis and modification. It extracts relevant dimensions, identifies overdesigned regions, and applies controlled changes to existing CAD data where appropriate. The agent performs manufacturability checks using simple mathematical rules specific to injection molding and evaluates whether proposed geometry changes remain feasible within process constraints. It can also execute bottom-up cost calculations based on the modified geometry to estimate a holistic financial impact.

Rather than redesigning parts from scratch, the CAD agent focuses on incremental and controlled modifications that preserve functional intent while systematically reducing material usage and cost.

Key functions:

- It extracts geometric attributes, such as wall thicknesses, volumes, ribs, and bosses.
- It identifies candidate regions suitable for material reduction.
- It applies controlled geometry modifications to existing CAD data.
- It performs basic manufacturability checks using injection molding rules.
- It executes bottom-up cost calculations based on proposed geometry changes.

Input data from other agents: 3D models, design rules via RAG, bottom-up cost calculation templates, instructions via text

Connected tools:

- rule-based automation for dimension extraction and comparison from CAD geometry
- a CAD kernel for rule-based geometry analysis and controlled modification of existing designs
- rule-based bottom-up cost calculation based on geometry and material changes
- rule-based access to PLM systems to download current geometry and historical reports

The output of the CAD agent consists of modified geometry variants, each accompanied by associated high-level manufacturability assessments and cost signals.

LLM tip: Since interpreting historical simulation results and analyzing geometry visually requires an LLM with image-processing capabilities, it is recommended to use a strong multimodal model for this task.

Prompting tip: Build a general CAD agent prompt template and then modify it to your specific use case.

General tip: Focus on reversible changes first. Use a retrieval-augmented generation approach to continuously learn from past optimization decisions and improve the agent's recommendations over time.

Special tip: An integrated geometry kernel significantly reduces implementation effort.

FEA Agent: "I'm here to deliver confidence without overkill."

The FEA agent provides analytical support when performance or risk must be validated. It runs structural or molding-related simulations depending on the optimization context and extracts metrics that are directly relevant for decision-making. The agent is designed for reliability and consistency. It retrieves performance requirements from the application lifecycle management (ALM) system and applies them using standardized simulation templates, enabling direct comparison between existing and modified geometries. Results are summarized in concise, decision-ready reports that clearly indicate whether proposed changes remain within acceptable performance limits.

Key functions:

- runs structural or molding-related simulations as required by the optimization context
- evaluates simulation results using both numerical data and visual interpretation
- generates concise simulation summaries focused on decision relevance
- flags performance risks early to prevent late-stage rework

Input data from other agents: modified 3D models, historical part number, material information, instructions via text.

Connected tools:

- Rule-based automation extracts relevant requirements and constraints from the ALM system.
- Rule-based automations execute standardized preprocessing workflows and triggers FE solvers.
- Rule-based automations post-process and visualize simulation results in a consistent manner.
- Rule-based automation builds standardized simulation reports for comparison and decision-making.

The output of the FEA agent consists of simulation summaries that indicate pass, risk, or reject status for each evaluated variant.

LLM tip: Use a strong multimodal model for interpreting plots and images.

Prompting tip: Instruct how the agent must evaluate molding simulations. Generally describing a simulation will not be adequate, it should be more molding specific.

General tip: Keep concept-phase FE simulations standardized, using the same templates, mesh targets, and output definitions across the existing and the new variant.

Special tip: If you have different types of FEA solutions, build separate agents only when these are usually handled by two different engineers in your process. If a single FEA engineer is responsible for both structural and molding simulations, adding communication between agents will create unnecessary communication overhead.

Special Warning: This is not a test!

The multi-agent system described here may appear simpler than the systems presented in other practical sections. In reality, it represents a critical capability. Once implemented, it is universally applicable and delivers recurring cost-saving potential across the entire product portfolio. At the same time, this use case requires particular caution. Unlike early development scenarios, the system intervenes in active, productive products. Any change affects parts that are already in series production. For this reason, the system must operate with absolute accuracy in combination with human oversight. Errors cannot be tolerated. Even small mistakes can lead to significant downstream costs, including quality issues, tooling rework, or supply disruptions. This risk must be explicitly addressed during implementation. Appropriate risk management measures, strict validation steps, and well-defined human-in-the-loop controls are essential to ensure safe and reliable operation.

3.3.5 When One Percent Becomes a Business Case

As demonstrated in the previous sections, large cost effects in consumer goods rarely require radical product redesigns. In high-volume environments, significant economic impact can be achieved through small, systematic improvements applied to components that are produced millions of times. Injection-molded plastic parts are particularly well suited for this type of optimization. They combine relatively high material cost per unit with very large production volumes. This combination creates a strong leverage effect. Even a seemingly marginal material reduction of one percent leads to a direct, measurable, and typically repeatable cost impact. To ground this discussion, consider a representative high-volume consumer goods scenario. Typical examples include household appliances, waste containers, storage systems, or outdoor furniture. These products often contain large plastic components made from materials such as polypropylene (PP) or ABS. Both materials are widely used in consumer goods. PP is commonly selected for robust, cost-efficient components, while ABS is used for higher-quality visible parts with improved mechanical properties.

Market price indices show that polypropylene typically trades in a range of approximately USD 1.1 to 1.6 per kilogram (IMARC 2025a), depending on region and market conditions. ABS prices are significantly higher, for example around USD 2.1 per kilogram in Germany at the time of writing (IMARC 2025b). Prices fluctuate with energy costs, demand, and regional factors. For a conservative and realistic calculation, a blended reference material price of USD 2.0 per kilogram is assumed, covering both PP-heavy and ABS-heavy applications.

In this scenario, assume a single plastic component with a weight of 5 kilograms. Such weights are typical for large housings, containers, interior panels, or structural plastic parts. Assume further a total production volume of 5 million units over the remaining lifetime of the part. These volumes are realistic for globally scaled consumer goods products. The material cost calculation is straightforward.

A component weighing 5 kilograms at a material price of USD 2.0 per kilogram results in material costs of USD 10.00 per unit. A one-percent material reduction corresponds to a saving of USD 0.10 per unit. Multiplied by 5 million units, this results in USD 500,000 in material savings over the lifetime of the component.

The core message is unambiguous. A one-percent material reduction in a single high-volume plastic part generates approximately half a million US dollars in direct material savings, without increasing production capacity, purchasing new equipment, or developing a new product. To assess return on investment, these savings must be compared with the cost of building and operating the multi-agent system described in this section. As in previous sections, organizations face a make-or-buy decision. Given the strong involvement of geometry processing, CAD interaction, and FE and CAM integration, a commercial multi-agent automation platform with built-in CAx capabilities is recommended. This significantly reduces development time compared to hard-coded alternatives and lowers implementation risk. In the initial system version, geometry modification should remain under human control. The optimization engineer applies design changes, supported by human-in-the-loop interaction. The system focuses on generating optimization suggestions and validating their impact.

Based on practical experience, building a production-ready system of this scope requires approximately one full-time equivalent for one year. This effort typically involves multiple roles, including system integration specialists and CAx engineers. Assuming 1,600 working hours at an average blended rate of USD 100 per hour, personnel costs amount to USD 160,000. In addition, license costs for the automation platform are estimated at USD 150,000 per year. Infrastructure and LLM usage costs can be conservatively estimated at USD 10,000 per year. This results in first-year costs of approximately USD 320,000, with ongoing annual operating costs of roughly USD 160,000.

Even under conservative assumptions, the system can amortize within the first year through a single successful optimization project. In ongoing operation, the system can realistically support 20 to 50 optimization projects per year, depending on part complexity and organizational setup.

> ☑ Assuming 25 projects per year and an average saving of USD 500,000 per project, this corresponds to an annual savings potential of more than USD 12 million.

The above calculation deliberately focuses only on direct material savings. In practice, secondary effects often emerge. Reduced material usage can lead to shorter cooling times, lower cycle times, reduced energy consumption, lower scrap rates, or improved transport efficiency. These effects depend strongly on tooling design, process windows, and part geometry and are therefore excluded from this conservative estimate. In many real-world cases, however, they act as additional multipliers.

The defining characteristic of this optimization lever is its immediacy. It scales directly with production volume. In many cases, it is technically achievable using established engineering methods such as wall thickness optimization, rib logic refinement, structural reinforcement strategies, or coordinated geometry and process optimization.

From an economic perspective, this creates a compelling argument for high-volume organizations. A one-percent material reduction is not an innovation gamble. It is a repeatable, operational optimization lever. When applied systematically across a suitable component portfolio, the annual savings potential quickly reaches the multi-million-dollar range.

As in previous sections, individual assumptions can be debated, and the model is intentionally simplified. Its purpose is not to provide a universal formula, but to sharpen perspective. The conclusion remains clear. Organizations that enable engineers to apply small, data-driven optimizations at scale unlock economic impact that far exceeds the cost of the underlying automation.

3.3.6 The 210-Day Plan: From First Agents to Confident Decisions

The objective of the 210-day program is to build and validate a first multi-agent system that delivers reliable and repeatable cost optimization results for injection-molded plastic parts. The focus is not on portfolio-wide rollout. It is on demonstrating that agent-based orchestration can support real engineering decisions under production constraints and deliver measurable economic value.

Unlike RFQ automation or early concept exploration, cost optimization in consumer goods operates close to running production. This significantly raises the requirements for quality, traceability, and trust. For this reason, the program deliberately prioritizes reliability over speed and depth over breadth.

By the end of the 210 days, the organization should be able to answer one clear question: Can an agent-based system consistently support engineers in identifying, validating, and approving small but economically meaningful optimizations in a production environment?

Phase 1: Frame the Optimization Scope (Days 1 - 30)

Goal: Establish a shared understanding of the current cost optimization process and define a realistic MVP scope with clear and measurable success criteria.

Key activities:

- Document the current cost optimization workflow for injection-molded parts, including triggers, decision points, and iteration loops.
- Identify all involved data sources, such as CAx systems, PLM, ERP, tooling information, cost models, and quality feedback.
- Select a small and representative set of parts, typically three to five plastic components with high production volume and remaining lifetime.
- Define clear success criteria for the MVP, for example reliable identification of optimization potential, sufficient validation confidence, and acceptance by engineering teams.
- Explicitly agree on what the MVP will not cover, such as fully automated geometry changes or portfolio-wide optimization.

Deliverables:

- a one-page problem framing that describes today's cost optimization process and its main pain points
- a clearly defined MVP scope with selected parts, assumptions, and explicit boundaries
- initial KPIs such as time to insight, number of viable optimization ideas, and required validation effort
- a first hypothesis outlining where agents can reduce coordination effort and manual overhead

Decision Gate A: management approval of the MVP scope, the selected parts, and the defined success criteria

Phase 2: Architecture and Make-or-Buy Decision (Days 31 – 60)

Goal: Define the future agentic R&D architecture at a conceptual level and establish governance principles that ensure safety, traceability, and clear human ownership.

Key activities:

- Define the MVP agent architecture with clear roles for each agent involved.
- Define responsibilities, hand-offs, and explicit human-in-the-loop checkpoints.
- Decide which rules are implemented as deterministic automation and which tasks require LLM-based reasoning.
- Evaluate build versus buy options with a strong focus on CAx integration effort and long-term maintainability.
- Define data access rules, ownership, and traceability requirements.

Deliverables:

- an architecture one-pager showing agents, connected tools, and data flows
- a make-or-buy decision memo with clear rationale and risk assessment
- an MVP specification describing agent roles, responsibilities, and validation checkpoints

Decision Gate B: formal approval to build the MVP and allocate the required engineering and IT resources

Phase 3: Build the MVP and Establish Trust (Days 61 – 180)

Goal: Implement a working multi-agent system and validate it on real parts with controlled risk.

Key activities:

- Implement the supervisor agent for orchestration, logging, and structured human interaction.
- Build the CAD agent to extract geometrical metrics, identify material reduction opportunities, and calculate cost.
- Integrate the strategy agent to provide volume, remaining lifetime, and risk context.
- Integrate an FEA agent for selective validation where analytical confirmation is required.
- Connect the system to existing enterprise systems to extract relevant data.
- Run multiple test cycles on the selected parts.

- Compare agent-supported results with outcomes from traditional engineering workflows.
- Collect structured feedback from engineers on usability, confidence in results, and decision quality.

Deliverables:

- a working MVP applied to multiple real components
- documented optimization proposals with validated cost impact
- comparison of agent-supported and traditional workflows
- identified limitations and failure modes

Decision Gate C: management decision on whether the MVP delivers reliable and trustworthy results and should be evolved to a production-ready level and scaled to additional part sets

Phase 4: Prepare for Production and Scaling (Days 181 – 210)

Goal: Translate MVP learnings into a realistic, production-ready scaling strategy while systematically reducing organizational and operational risk.

Key activities:

- Identify production-ready gaps and estimate the effort required to close them.
- Determine which parts of the workflow can be reused across additional components.
- Estimate effort and cost for scaling the system to larger part sets.
- Define organizational requirements, including roles, skills, training, and ownership.
- Refine the business case using validated assumptions from the MVP.
- Define a clear roadmap for transitioning from the MVP to production-ready systems.

Deliverables:

- a production, scaling roadmap for cost optimization across part families
- a refined ROI model based on validated MVP results
- a risk mitigation plan covering both technical and organizational aspects
- a clear recommendation for the next steps

Decision Gate D: management decision on scaling agent-based cost optimization beyond the MVP

3.3.7 Guest Perspective: Scaling Engineering Productivity with Context-Aware Agents

Patrick Schmidt

From Models to Systems

My work with AI in engineering began in academia, rooted in classical numerical modelling. Early on, I explored data-driven methods such as neural networks, enabled by increasing computational power and richer datasets. These approaches were effective in clearly defined, supervised settings. Automated parameter fitting and visual data segmentation delivered measurable gains, but their scope was limited.

The perspective shifted when I encountered reinforcement learning. Even simple agents, interacting with artificial environments, could autonomously improve their behavior through feedback. This was the first time it became clear that intelligent systems could move beyond isolated predictions and begin to act within structured environments.

That insight carried directly into my later work in industrial R&D at Miele. With the emergence of large language models, the focus expanded again. The key question was no longer how to build better models, but how to coordinate engineering work across tools, data, and teams.

Why Intelligence Alone Is Not Enough

Early experiments made one limitation very clear. Engineering imposes constraints that differ fundamentally from many other AI application domains. Accuracy requirements are extremely high. Errors are often costly and sometimes irreversible. At the same time, many AI models behave like black boxes. Their results may be statistically sound, but not always explainable.

Another constraint is volatility. Data-driven models are efficient once trained, but training is expensive and validity is limited to the data domain. In environments where requirements, products, or constraints change frequently, purely data-driven approaches lose their advantage quickly.

These limitations explain why generative AI is not valuable as a replacement for deterministic engineering methods. Its real contribution lies elsewhere. Large language models can orchestrate existing methods. They connect simulations, rule-based logic, and task-specific tools into workflows that previously required extensive manual coordination by experts.

Where Productivity Is Actually Lost

Once this orchestration perspective is adopted, the real productivity bottleneck becomes obvious. It is not calculation speed. It is coordination. Many engineering processes still rely on manual handovers, file transfers, and fragmented toolchains. Even when individual tools are highly optimized, lead times grow because information does not flow smoothly between steps.

In our experience, meaningful transformation starts by making this visible. Breaking workflows into individual activities exposes where waiting times accumulate, especially at interfaces between design, simulation, validation, and costing. Digitization must then focus on eliminating non-value-generating work. Given the diversity of engineering tasks, generic platforms, including low-code environments, often scale better than custom integrations-built case by case. At this point, roles begin to change naturally. Engineers spend less time executing steps manually and more time formalizing their expertise so it can be reused consistently across workflows.

Why Context Becomes the Real Differentiator

This shift reveals an important insight. Tools themselves do not create competitive advantage. What differentiates organizations is context: tacit expertise, internal standards, domain-specific trade-offs, and knowledge of how decisions are actually made under real constraints.

Capturing this requires multiple technology layers working together. A reliable infrastructure layer ensures secure and scalable operation. An enabling layer digitizes processes and knowledge through PLM systems, requirements tools, or low-code platforms. On top of this, agents interpret and apply that structured knowledge across connected systems. The agent is not the value. The value lies in the organizational context it can access and apply consistently.

Why Traditional Automation Stops Scaling

Traditional digitalization works well as long as logic can be fully formalized. Rule-based automation excels in stable, clearly defined processes. The limits appear at interfaces. Economic constraints, supplier availability, cross-functional trade-offs, and incomplete information introduce ambiguity that fixed logic cannot resolve. Even when departments automate locally, final decisions still depend on contextual interpretation. This is where many automation initiatives stall. Complexity grows faster than structure. Manual coordination reappears, just in different places.

Where Agents Fit into the Picture

Against this background, the role of agents becomes clearer. Deterministic methods remain essential wherever precision and verification are required. Simulations, tolerance analyses, and validated calculations should not be replaced. Agents add value where coordination and interpretation dominate. They help interpret results, route information across systems, trigger follow-up actions, and prepare decision options within human-in-the-loop workflows. The strength lies in the combination. Deterministic methods ensure correctness. Agents reduce coordination effort and make system-level workflows manageable.

Autonomy Must Follow Risk

Once agents are introduced, the next question is autonomy. Here, risk alignment is critical. We apply a logic inspired by FMEA. Processes with high reproducibility and detectability can tolerate higher autonomy. Orchestration processes allow partial autonomy with human review. Business-critical decisions with high liability must remain fully human-controlled. This framing prevents both extremes. It avoids over-automation where risk is high, and underutilization where automation is safe.

Trust Is Built Through Transparency

Trust follows from this alignment. Evaluation-level outputs are trusted because assumptions and verification paths are clear. Orchestration-level recommendations require transparency in how trade-offs are handled. Business-impacting decisions demand full traceability and explicit accountability.

Across all levels, documentation of both technical outputs and decision logic is essential. Without it, even correct results remain fragile.

Why Adoption Is the Real Challenge

At this point, the main barrier is no longer technical. It is organizational. Generative AI creates high expectations. Without structured change management, those expectations quickly turn into disappointment. Adoption improves when engineers are involved early and see their expertise reflected in the system. These contributors become multipliers across the organization.

How the Engineer's Role Evolves

As coordination and routine analysis are automated, the engineer's role shifts. First, engineers increasingly digitize domain knowledge. They formalize requirements, parameterize geometries, and define workflows that agents can operate on. Second, they govern the system. Validation, continuous improvement, and compliance oversight become core responsibilities. The role moves from executing tasks to designing and supervising engineering processes.

What Success Ultimately Looks Like

Success is not defined by AI sophistication. It is defined by daily work quality. It is defined by less time spent coordinating and more time spent on innovation and high-value decisions. It is defined by knowledge embedded in systems rather than locked in individuals. And it is defined by faster, more consistent, better-informed decisions across the organization. When agents are introduced with this mindset, they do not disrupt engineering work. They make it scale.

3.4 Engineering Service Providers: From Headcount to Leverage

Engineering service providers (ESPs) operate under conditions that differ fundamentally from those of product-owning organizations. Their value creation is not tied to products, platforms, or proprietary toolchains, but to the availability, flexibility, and expertise of their engineering workforce. At the same time, they compete in highly commoditized markets characterized by strong price pressure and a high density of direct competitors.

Projects are typically initiated by customers, not by the service provider. Scope, timing, tooling environments, and delivery models are largely defined externally. As a result, engineering service providers must continuously adapt their capacity, ramping teams up and down with limited advance notice, while maintaining quality and meeting strict cost targets. These dynamics make long-term planning and standardization significantly more challenging than in OEM or tier environments.

This reality has direct implications for automation. Many approaches that work well in product-centric organizations assume stable processes, reusable assets, or long-lived proprietary systems. In the context of engineering service providers, these assumptions often do not apply. Engineers frequently operate directly within customer-owned IT environments, using customer-specific toolchains and workflows. Rule-based automation can therefore become brittle, as even minor variations between customer setups may require substantial adaptation, quickly eroding the business case.

With that, this section follows again the same guiding principle as the previous practical sections. It does not aim to define a universal solution for all engineering service providers. Instead, it outlines a representative scenario that reflects recurring patterns observed across multiple service engagements. The focus is placed on engineering tasks that combine three characteristics. They are well defined, repetitive in nature, and sufficiently decoupled from the customer's core development environment.

The examples presented here should be understood as inspiration rather than instruction. Your organization may serve different industries, operate under different delivery models, or face additional contractual and compliance constraints. Take the ideas that align with your service portfolio, adapt them to your customer context, and extend them where your operational reality demands a different approach.

As with all agent-based automation initiatives, the decisive factor is not the sophistication of the technology. It is its ability to respect the commercial model, contractual boundaries, and flexibility requirements of the organization deploying it. This section therefore serves as a reference model for how multi-agent systems can support scalability, speed, and reliability in engineering services, without requiring ownership of products, platforms, or customer environments.

3.4.1 Executive Snapshot

Engineering service providers operate under conditions that differ fundamentally from those of OEMs or tier suppliers. Their business is project-driven, highly competitive, and strongly shaped by external demand. Project starts are defined by customers, toolchains are prescribed, and engineering capacity must be scaled up or down with very little advance notice. Unlike product-based organizations, ESPs do not accumulate long-term value through platforms or product portfolios. Their primary asset is engineering capacity and the ability to deploy it efficiently across constantly changing projects. Within this environment, simulation services play a central role. In areas such as automotive body-in-white development, a substantial share of engineering effort is spent on preprocessing activities. Geometry interpretation and classification, meshing, model assembly, and solver setup consume significant time and expertise. These tasks are technically demanding, yet they are rarely perceived as differentiating by customers. They are expected to be fast, reliable, and cost-efficient. Errors at this stage can invalidate entire simulation runs and lead to costly rework, schedule delays, and quality risks downstream.

To remain competitive, many engineering service providers have shifted these activities to best-cost-country teams.

While this approach improves hourly rates, it introduces a new set of challenges:

- Ramp-up times at project start increase, especially when context and domain knowledge must be rebuilt.
- Coordination effort rises across locations, organizations, and time zones.
- Dependency on senior engineers grows, particularly for quality checks and troubleshooting.
- Scalability becomes limited when multiple projects start in parallel or when demand spikes unexpectedly.

At the same time, traditional automation approaches offer only limited relief. Rule-based solutions often struggle to scale because customer workflows, modeling standards, and toolchains differ significantly. ESP engineers frequently work directly inside customer-controlled software environments, which restricts the deployment of rigid or deeply integrated automation. Maintaining customer-specific scripts or macros quickly erode the business case, as small deviations require continuous adaptation and support.

Section Focus

Rather than attempting to standardize entire customer-specific workflows, this section shows how a multi-agent system can support engineering service providers by targeting simulation preprocessing and early model validation. The focus is deliberately placed on work packages that are repetitive, well defined, and largely common across customers, even when higher-level development processes differ. In practice, these activities are usually performed in best-cost countries and are often executed outside the customer's core IT infrastructure.

The multi-agent system coordinates a set of specialized agents that address the technical preparation layer shared by most simulation projects:

- geometry classification to derive appropriate meshing strategies and modeling assumptions
- automated meshing and model assembly, including contacts and boundary conditions
- early solver execution through short test runs
- visual and message-based interpretation of solver behavior seconds after start to detect non-physical or unstable models

The result is a preprocessing workflow that becomes faster, more consistent, and easier to scale. Routine setup work is reduced. Obvious errors are detected early, before they propagate into expensive simulation cycles. Engineers remain responsible for validation and approval, but their focus shifts away from repetitive preparation toward interpretation, quality assurance, and problem-solving.

For engineering service providers, this creates a realistic and low-risk entry point into agent-based engineering. The approach does not require ownership of customer systems, nor does it depend on fragile, customer-specific automation. Instead, it strengthens exactly those activities that are executed repeatedly across projects, customers, and industries. In a market defined by volatility, cost pressure, and tight delivery timelines, this form of selective automation becomes a strategic capability rather than a technical experiment.

3.4.2 Engineering by Hand at Scale

Engineering service providers operate at the intersection of deep technical specialization and sustained economic pressure. They are embedded in customer programs, contribute critical engineering work across development phases, and are expected to deliver reliably under tight schedules. Unlike OEMs, however, their competitiveness is not driven by products, platforms, or proprietary intellectual property. It is driven by how efficiently engineering capacity can be deployed, scaled, and redeployed across changing projects. In simulation-driven domains, a substantial share of ESP workloads is concentrated on preparation rather than on analysis itself. Before any meaningful solver run can take place, geometry must be processed, models must be assembled, and simulation setups must be validated. This includes geometry repair, meshing, material and property assignment, contact definition, load and boundary condition setup, and solver configuration. These activities follow established engineering principles. They are not conceptually complex, but they are highly sensitive to detail. Minor inconsistencies can invalidate results, trigger solver instability, or produce non-physical behavior. As a result, preprocessing often consumes a disproportionate share of project time.

Economic constraints intensify this situation. ESPs typically compete in highly commoditized markets with many similar providers, limited differentiation, and constant pricing pressure. Customers expect fast turnaround, predictable quality, and the ability to scale resources up or down with little notice. To meet these expectations, many ESPs distribute preprocessing work across global delivery networks and best-cost-country teams, often outside the customer's core IT infrastructure. While this reduces direct labor costs, it introduces operational friction. Knowledge transfer between teams becomes critical. Model quality depends heavily on documentation quality and implicit assumptions. Senior engineers are required to review and stabilize models prepared elsewhere, often under time pressure. When multiple projects start simultaneously, experienced staff quickly becomes a bottleneck.

Several recurring patterns emerge in this environment:

- Model setup quality varies significantly depending on who prepared it and under which constraints.
- Solver failures or implausible results are often discovered late, after substantial compute time has already been consumed.
- Iteration cycles lengthen because corrections require repeating large portions of the setup process.
- Project scalability depends more on individual experts than on standardized, repeatable workflows.

Attempts to address these challenges through conventional automation have shown limited success. Scripts and macros can accelerate isolated steps, but they rarely survive across customer boundaries. Automation that works well for one customer often needs to be adopted for the next, quickly eroding its economic value. Much of the robustness in current workflows is therefore still provided by human judgment. Engineers visually inspect models, interpret solver messages, and recognize abnormal behavior based on experience. This expertise is essential, but it is difficult to scale. It also slows onboarding and makes capacity planning uncertain. Timing adds another layer of complexity. Indicators of incorrect model behavior often appear very early, sometimes within seconds after a solver starts. Unstable constraints, missing contacts, or unrealistic deformations can be detected almost immediately by an experienced engineer. In practice, however, these signals are not evaluated systematically. They are noticed opportunistically, not as part of a structured, repeatable process. The core issue is therefore not a lack of tools or engineering knowledge. It is the absence of a scalable mechanism to apply that knowledge consistently, early, and across many parallel projects. Engineering service providers need ways to stabilize preprocessing quality, shorten feedback loops, and reduce dependence on individual experts, without violating customer constraints or disrupting established delivery models.

In the following sections, we examine how a multi-agent system can address these challenges. The focus is on supporting geometry classification, model preparation, and early solver behavior assessment in a way that fits the operational reality of engineering service providers and strengthens their ability to scale under sustained pressure.

3.4.3 Where Geometry Becomes Physics

In engineering service provider environments, crash simulation projects typically begin with a complete vehicle assembly supplied by the customer. This dataset represents the current digital state of the vehicle and serves as the common baseline for all downstream simulation activities. The task of the service provider is not to redesign the vehicle, but to transform this highly complex CAD assembly into a numerically stable and physically meaningful finite element model that complies with customer-specific simulation standards. Although toolchains, data structures, and naming conventions vary between OEMs, the underlying preparation logic is remarkably consistent. Crash model build-up follows a well-established, multi-step workflow that combines deterministic preparation rules with continuous expert judgment. The process is not linear. Instead, it evolves through a sequence of preparation steps with frequent feedback loops driven by solver behavior and physical plausibility checks.

The workflow typically starts with the decomposition of the full vehicle assembly into individual parts. Large assemblies often contain hundreds of components. These must be separated into manageable units so they can be classified, simplified, and meshed independently. At this stage, no simulation decisions are made. The focus is purely on structural separation, data hygiene, and manageability.

Once parts are isolated, they are classified into categories. Classification criteria differ by customer but usually combine manufacturing logic and functional relevance. Parts may be grouped by manufacturing method, such as sheet metal, cast components, molded plastics, extruded profiles, or composite parts. In parallel, functional roles are considered. Typical categories include crash-relevant structures, brackets, closures, trim parts, or high-voltage battery components. This classification step is central, because it determines nearly all downstream preparation decisions.

Based on the assigned category, geometry simplification rules are applied. Fine details that do not influence crash behavior, such as small fillets, cosmetic features, or secondary holes, are removed. The degree of simplification depends on both part function and customer guidelines. Primary load-bearing structures are treated conservatively, while secondary components are simplified more aggressively to reduce model size and solver cost. The classification also drives the meshing strategy. Thin-walled components are typically represented with shell elements, while solid elements are reserved for parts where thickness effects, local crushing behavior, or complex geometry require it. At this point, a decision is made whether midsurfaces are needed.

For shell-meshed parts, midsurface extraction is performed. Simple sheet metal components are often handled automatically using preprocessor tools. More complex geometries, such as castings or injection-molded parts, usually require a hybrid approach. Automatic midsurface generation is combined with manual rework to ensure consistent geometry representation and acceptable mesh quality. If required by customer standards, additional geometry is created. This commonly includes representations of weld seams, adhesive bonds, or spot welds. These features are often not present in the original CAD data, yet they are essential for realistic crash behavior and load transfer.

With geometry preparation complete, the workflow moves into meshing. Each part is meshed according to its classification and the customer's meshing guidelines. Automatic meshing functions are used wherever possible to ensure consistency and speed. Manual rework follows where element quality, transitions, or local refinement demand expert intervention. Once meshing is complete, material definitions are assigned to every part.

After individual parts are prepared, they are reassembled into a complete vehicle model. Contact definitions are then applied according to customer specifications. These include tied contacts, sliding interfaces, self-contact, and general contact formulations. At this stage, the model becomes a fully coupled system rather than a collection of independent meshes. Boundary conditions and load definitions are applied next. For crash simulations, this typically includes initial velocities, accelerations, rigid wall definitions, constraints, and prescribed motions. The correctness of these definitions is critical. Even small inconsistencies can lead to non-physical behavior or numerical instability early in the simulation.

The model is then submitted to the solver and the simulation is started. Engineers do not wait for the full load case to complete. Instead, after only a few milliseconds of simulated time, solver output is inspected. This marks the beginning of an iterative validation loop. Engineers visually assess whether the model behaves in a physically plausible manner. They look for unrealistic penetrations, excessive stiffness, unstable contacts, or early numerical instabilities. Solver messages and early result plots provide immediate feedback. If non-physical behavior is observed, contacts or boundary conditions are adjusted and the solver is restarted. This loop is repeated until the model shows stable and realistic behavior in the early phase of the crash event. Only then is the simulation allowed to run to completion. Progress therefore depends less on executing individual steps correctly and more on converging toward a stable and credible system's behavior.

The workflow described in Figure 3.7 has proven robust throughout many customer projects. It enables engineering service providers to deliver high-quality crash models under varying standards and constraints. At the same time, it relies heavily on manual coordination, expert judgment, and repeated iteration. Much of the value creation lies not in performing individual steps, but in navigating the feedback loops between them efficiently.

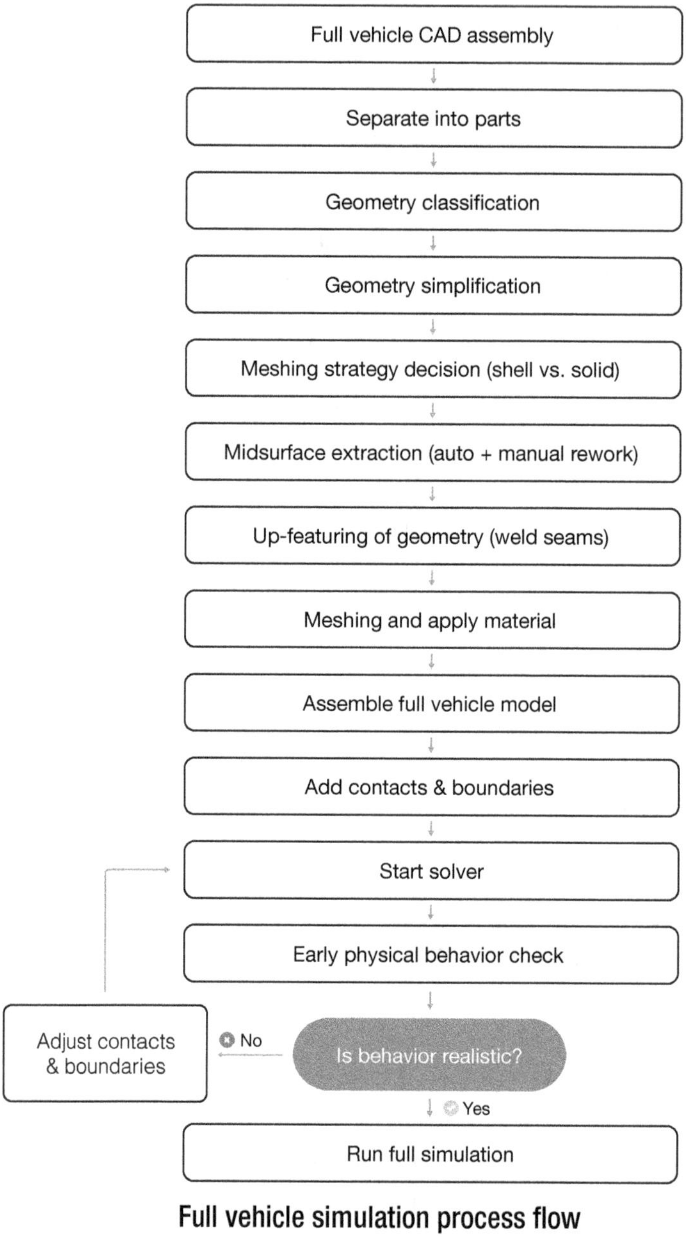

Figure 3.7 The complete preprocessing and simulation workflow for a full vehicle FE model, from CAD assembly separation and geometry classification through meshing, model assembly, solver execution, and a physical behavior validation gate before the final simulation run (© Iryna Novoseletska)

In the next section, we examine how this preparation workflow can be supported by a multi-agent system. The objective is not to replace engineering expertise, but to stabilize and accelerate the iterative loops that dominate real-world crash model preparation.

3.4.4 Embedding Preprocessing Expertise Into a Multi-Agent System

The workflow described in the previous section reflects how full vehicle crash models are prepared today at many engineering service providers. It is a highly structured process, executed by experienced preprocessing engineers, supported by powerful CAE tools and detailed customer guidelines. Each step follows established engineering logic, and the resulting models often achieve a very high level of technical quality. At the same time, this workflow is characterized by strong sequential dependencies and a high degree of manual coordination and effort. Geometry preparation, classification, meshing, model assembly, contact definition, and early solver checks are tightly coupled. Decisions made early in the process propagate downstream. When assumptions later prove incorrect, engineers must manually trace issues back across multiple preparation stages and rework portions of the model.

This creates two defining characteristics for engineering service providers. First, productivity scales almost linearly with the availability of experienced engineers. Second, project-to-project variability and customer-specific standards make it difficult to stabilize throughput without compromising quality. The core challenge is therefore the coordination effort required to repeatedly apply the same preprocessing logic across different vehicle architectures, customer rulesets, and project timelines.

A multi-agent system addresses this challenge by embedding existing preprocessing logic into a coordinated digital workflow. Instead of treating disassembly, classification, meshing, model build, and solver checks as loosely connected manual steps, the system orchestrates them through specialized agents that share context and exchange results continuously while continuously gaining experience. The engineering reasoning itself does not change. What changes is how that reasoning is executed, documented, and iterated. The architecture illustrated in Figure 3.8 shows a representative multi-agent system for full vehicle crash preprocessing at an engineering service provider. It mirrors the current workflow, including its iterative nature, while reducing coordination overhead and increasing robustness. Existing preprocessors, solvers, and visualization tools remain unchanged. They are connected through an orchestration layer that manages data flow, sequencing, and feedback loops.

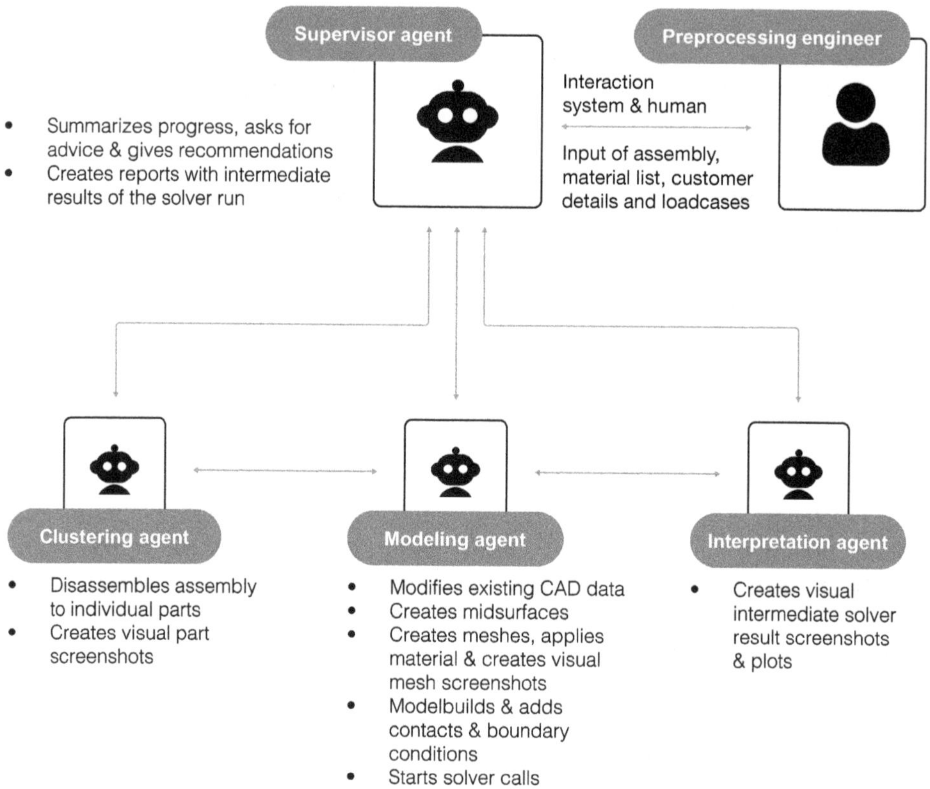

Figure 3.8 A preprocessing-focused multi-agent system in which clustering, modeling, and interpretation agents collaborate under a supervisor to take a full vehicle assembly from CAD disassembly through meshing, model build, solver execution, and intermediate result visualization (© Iryna Novoseletska)

The Supervisor Agent: "My team is here to work for you 24/7."

The supervisor agent acts as the central coordinator and primary interface for the preprocessing engineer. It does not create meshes or define contacts itself. Its responsibility is to structure the workflow, maintain a consistent decision context, and manage iterations across agents. The agent receives the initial inputs, typically a full vehicle assembly, customer-specific preprocessing guidelines, material definitions, and crash load cases. Based on this context, it decides which specialist agents to activate and monitor their progress. As intermediate results become available, the supervisor agent consolidates them into a coherent status view and highlights deviations, risks, or inconsistencies. A critical responsibility of the supervisor agent is iteration management. When early solver feedback indicates non-physical behavior, missing constraints, or unstable contacts, the agent traces the issue back to the relevant preparation stage and re-triggers the appropriate agents with updated instructions. Throughout the process, it maintains traceability of assumptions, changes, and decisions.

Key functions:

- It accepts full vehicle assemblies, customer guidelines, and load cases from the preprocessing engineer.
- It orchestrates clustering, modeling, and interpretation agents based on model maturity.
- It consolidates intermediate results and solver feedback into progress summaries.
- It manages iteration loops when model behavior is ambiguous.
- It requests human input when ambiguity or conflicting signals arise.

Input data from preprocessing engineer: vehicle assembly and part materials, customer preprocessing rules, load cases, instructions via chat interface

Connected tools:

- human interaction interface for clarification and approval
- rule-based workflows for progress reporting and documentation

The output of the supervisor agent is a continuously updated preprocessing status report that includes corrective action recommendations and clear indicators of model readiness.

LLM tip: Use a reasoning-strong model that can explicitly track assumptions, dependencies, and iteration history. Orchestration quality depends more on reasoning robustness than on language fluency.

Prompting tip: Require the agent to always summarize current model maturity, open risks, and the reason for triggering a new iteration. This prevents silent loops and improves trust.

General tip: Treat the supervisor agent as a workflow conscience, not as a decision maker. Its value lies in transparency, not authority.

Special tip: Implement explicit confidence checkpoints where the agent must ask the human engineer whether to continue, revert, or stop iteration. This keeps responsibility clearly anchored.

The Clustering Agent: "It is impossible to be automated. Hold my beer!"

The clustering agent handles early-stage decomposition and classification of the vehicle assembly. It disassembles the full CAD structure into individual parts and generates screenshots from multiple viewing angles. Each part is assigned to predefined categories based on geometry, manufacturing method, and functional relevance. Classification is performed using a combination of metadata, geometrical attributes and visual reasoning within the LLM. For high-quality and customer-consistent results, the agent relies on a retrieval-augmented generation approach. Customer-specific categories and visual reference examples are stored and reused across projects.

Key functions:

- It disassembles the full vehicle assembly into individual components.
- It generates visual representations and metadata for each part.
- It classifies parts by manufacturing type, functional role, and crash relevance.

Input data from other agents: vehicle assembly structure, customer details, material details, instructions via text

Connected tools:

- rule-based automation for assembly traversal and part extraction
- rule-based geometry analysis utilities for feature-based classification
- rule-based automation to create screenshots per part from different viewing perspectives

The clustering agent **outputs** a structured part catalog that includes classifications, simplification rules, meshing strategies, and downstream modeling decisions.

LLM tip: Use a strong multimodal model. Visual classification consistency is essential.

Prompting tip: Always request both a primary and a secondary classification. This improves robustness for ambiguous geometries.

General tip: As an engineer, you probably have different ways of exploding an assembly to better inspect it. Try to capture the intent of this and then craft your tools to support it.

Special tip: Store classification results together with visual screenshots. Over time, this builds a reusable reference library that significantly improves consistency across projects.

The Modeling Agent: "The boring stuff is what I love to do."

The modeling agent is responsible for geometry preparation, meshing, and model assembly. Based on the part catalog, it applies simplification rules, creates additional geometry where required, selects appropriate meshing methods, and generates midsurfaces. For shell-meshed components, the agent combines automated midsurface extraction with targeted refinements encoded as rules. For solid parts, it applies suitable meshing strategies with local refinement where required. The agent assembles all meshes into a full vehicle model and defines contacts and boundary conditions according to customer guidelines. These guidelines are accessed via a maintained retrieval-augmented generation approach. The agent can also trigger solver starts.

Key functions:

- It simplifies or creates geometry based on part classification.
- It selects and applies shell or solid meshing strategies.
- It creates midsurfaces and performs meshing with rule-based refinement.
- It builds the full vehicle FE model including contacts and boundary conditions.

Input data from other agents: part catalog, customer details, material definitions, interpretation feedback, instructions via text

Connected tools:

- rule-based automations to simplify geometries
- rule-based automations to create geometries
- rule-based automation for midsurface and mesh creation controlling commercial preprocessors
- rule-based automation to build the full FE model including contacts and boundary conditions
- rule-based automation to trigger solver calls locally or on an HPC

The output of the modeling agent is a solver-ready crash model that reflects current best practices and remains adaptable to feedback.

LLM tip: Use base or foundation models to ensure computational efficiency and optimize LLM costs. Geometry creation and meshing should remain strictly rule-based.

Prompting tip: Require explicit reporting of applied meshing rules, simplifications, and templates. This is essential for auditability.

General tip: Avoid over-automation in early versions. Stabilize midsurface creation and mesh quality first.

Special tip: An automation platform with an integrated geometry kernel is critical. Without it, CAD and preprocessing automation will dominate implementation risk.

The Interpretation Agent: "Is something awkward? I will figure it out!"

The interpretation agent provides early and continuous feedback from the solver. It evaluates solver messages and intermediate results within the first milliseconds of simulation time. Instead of waiting for a full run to fail, the agent inspects deformation patterns, contact behavior, and energy balance visually and numerically. It compares observed behavior against typical and physically correct model patterns stored in a retrieval-augmented generation system. Non-physical behavior is flagged immediately and reported back to the supervisor agent.

Key functions:

- It generates visual snapshots and concise interpretation summaries.
- It interprets solver messages and intermediate results visually.
- It identifies non-physical responses and unstable model behavior.

Input data from other agents: FE model, instructions via text

Connected tools:

- rule-based automation for reading intermediate solver results and error messages
- rule-based automation to generate screenshots and plots from intermediate solver states

The interpretation agent **outputs** rapid feedback signals that enable immediate corrective action.

LLM tip: Use a strong multimodal model. Early solver interpretation relies heavily on visual pattern recognition. For future, try to build visual language models (VLMs) that can be specific to your company.

Prompting tip: Enforce binary judgments first—physically plausible or not. Detailed explanations come second.

General tip: A rich and distinct visual image is maybe too much for human eyes, but easily recognizable for an LLM. Therefore, try to post-process your images if possible.

Special tip: Build a library of recurring failure patterns such as flying parts, exploding contacts, or energy spikes. Use retrieval-augmented generation to match new cases and suggest corrective actions.

3.4.5 Escaping the Commodity Trap

As in the previous sections, the purpose of this section is not to present a universally valid business case. Engineering service providers differ significantly in customer mix, contractual models, internal cost structures, and regional delivery setups. The following analysis therefore relies on simplified assumptions. Its objective is to sharpen perspective and illustrate how the value of agent-based preprocessing can be assessed beyond short-term cost reduction alone.

To do so, we examine the impact from three complementary angles: a direct financial comparison of manual versus agent-supported work, a scaling and intellectual property perspective, and finally, an outlook on how agent-based capabilities may enable fundamentally different business models for engineering service providers.

(1) Financial Perspective: Manual Effort versus Agent-Supported Preprocessing

We begin with a simplified comparison of a major crash-model design phase, such as the preparation of a full vehicle crash model or a significant model update at a program milestone.

Manual baseline scenario

In a traditional setup, such a phase typically involves several preprocessing engineers working in parallel over multiple months. A representative scenario looks as follows:

- duration: three months
- staffing: four preprocessing engineers
- working time: 40 hours per week
- total effort: approximately 1,920 hours
- average hourly rate: USD 20, reflecting a best cost country setup

This results in direct labor costs of approximately USD 38,400 per major design phase. This figure excludes coordination overhead, rework caused by late error detection, and indirect costs related to delays or extended iteration loops.

Investment to build the multi-agent system

For the agent-based approach, we separate the one-time investment required to build the system from the recurring cost of operating it. Based on practical experience, building a production-ready multi-agent system for crash-model preprocessing is not a small scripting exercise. Given the strong involvement of geometry handling, meshing logic, solver interaction, and result interpretation, the use of a commercial low-code automation platform for building agents with integrated CAx capabilities is strongly recommended.

A realistic setup assumption is as follows:

- development effort: two full-time equivalents for one year
- effort per FTE: 1,600 hours
- blended hourly rate: USD 50, combining best cost country resources and domain experts

This results in approximately USD 160,000 in personnel costs.

In addition, we assume the following:

- annual MAS platform license costs: approximately USD 200,000
- infrastructure and LLM costs during development: approximately USD 20,000

This leads to a total initial investment of approximately USD 380,000 to build the system.

Cost per major design phase using the MAS

Once the system is available, the cost structure per major design phase changes significantly:

- human effort: one preprocessing engineer for one week
- cost: approximately USD 800
- LLM and infrastructure usage per project: approximately USD 1000
- allocated MAS license cost per project: approximately USD 20,000, assuming ten projects per year

This results in a total cost of approximately USD 21,800 per major design phase.

Break-even analysis

Compared to the manual baseline of USD 38,400, the MAS-supported approach saves approximately USD 16,600 per major design phase.

Assuming ten such projects per year, this corresponds to annual savings of approximately USD 166,000 and a payback period of roughly 2.3 years.

From a purely financial perspective, this is not an obvious low-hanging fruit. The numbers alone would not justify immediate adoption in every organization. However, this view ignores two decisive factors: scalability and strategic positioning.

(2) Scaling and Intellectual Property Perspective

The economic picture changes substantially once scalability and knowledge retention are considered. After the multi-agent system is built, its marginal cost no longer scales with headcount. Running one project or one hundred projects in parallel does not fundamentally change the system architecture. The main limiting factors become CAx license availability and compute capacity. Both are significantly easier to scale than human resources.

This has several consequences:

- Capacity can be ramped up or down much faster than with staffing-based models.
- Delivery speed becomes more predictable and less dependent on individual availability.
- Peak loads no longer require emergency hiring or aggressive outsourcing.

Equally important is the intellectual property dimension. In traditional ESP models, core know-how resides primarily in people. When experienced engineers leave, knowledge leaves with them. Agent-based systems fundamentally change this dynamic. Meshing strategies, simplification rules, solver checks, and interpretation logic are encoded in workflows, rules, and agent interactions.

This creates a durable internal asset:

- Knowledge remains inside the organization.
- Competitors cannot easily replicate it by hiring a small number of key individuals.
- The system improves continuously as more projects are executed.

From a customer perspective, delivery speed and reliability become differentiating factors. OEMs are under constant pressure to shorten development cycles. Faster and more robust preprocessing directly supports this objective. In many cases, customers are willing to pay premium rates for predictable delivery and early problem detection.

(3) Future Business Model Perspective

The most profound impact extends beyond cost and scalability. It affects how engineering service providers define their value proposition. Today, most ESPs sell engineering time. Projects are estimated based on expected effort multiplied by an hourly rate. This model scales poorly and remains tightly coupled to human availability.

Agent-based preprocessing opens the door to alternative business models:

- licensing the multi-agent system, or selected components of it, directly to customers
- offering preprocessing as a service with outcome-based pricing
- embedding the MAS into customer environments as a long-term capability

In such scenarios, the ESP no longer sells hours. It sells a system. Internal automation becomes an external-facing product. Margins improve. Revenue becomes less dependent on staffing levels. Knowledge loss due to employee turnover is becoming far less critical.

There is also a compounding effect. Each project execution improves the system. With every iteration, the agents become better at classification, meshing decisions, and early error detection. Over time, this creates a widening capability gap between providers who have invested in such systems and those who rely exclusively on manual execution.

Summary

Viewed in isolation, the financial case for agent-based crash-model preprocessing appears moderate. Its true value emerges only when the perspective is expanded beyond individual projects.

- Financially, the system reaches break-even within a few years under conservative assumptions.
- Operationally, it enables rapid scaling and more predictable delivery.
- Strategically, it transforms human expertise into a durable and defensible asset.

As in the previous sections, the conclusion is not that every engineering service provider will adopt this approach immediately. The conclusion is that organizations that begin building these capabilities early gain strategic options that will be difficult to replicate later. In a market defined by cost pressure, scalability constraints, and talent scarcity, those options may ultimately become decisive.

3.4.6 The 90-Day Plan: From Engineering Capacity to Engineering Capability

The objective of the 90-day program is to validate whether a multi-agent system can reliably support a core engineering service provider's workflow under real customer constraints. The focus is deliberately narrow. Instead of attempting to automate a full vehicle model or multiple subsystems, the program concentrates on a single, complex, and representative subsystem: the high-voltage battery pack.

This choice is intentional. Battery packs combine structural relevance, safety criticality, complex contact definitions, and strict customer-specific guidelines. At the same time, they are typically delivered as clearly scoped work packages and are frequently outsourced to engineering service providers. This makes them an ideal entry point for validating agent-based preprocessing under realistic project conditions.

By the end of the 90 days, the organization should be able to answer three questions with confidence:

- Can a multi-agent system produce preprocessing results that meet customer quality expectations?
- Does the approach reduce manual effort and iteration time in a measurable way?
- Is the solution scalable across projects and customers without undermining the business case?

Phase 1: Scope, Observe, and Stabilize (Days 1 – 15)

Goal: Build a shared and realistic understanding of the current preprocessing workflow for a high-voltage battery pack and define a technically safe MVP scope.

Key activities:

- Select one representative customer project involving a high-voltage battery pack.
- Observe and document the current preprocessing workflow end-to-end, including the following:
  - geometry separation and part handling
  - classification logic for battery housings, modules, brackets, covers, cooling plates, and fasteners
  - geometry simplification rules applied today
  - shell versus solid meshing decisions
  - midsurface creation approaches and known problem areas
  - contact definitions and boundary condition setup
  - early solver checks and typical failure modes
- Identify customer-specific constraints, such as the following:
  - meshing guidelines
  - naming conventions
  - allowed simplifications
  - solver versions and post-processing expectations
- Define quality criteria that determine whether a preprocessing model is considered usable by the customer.
- Select a minimal but representative load case for early solver checks.

Deliverables:

- a documented as-is workflow for battery pack preprocessing
- a clearly scoped MVP definition, for example the following:
  - geometry classification agent
  - meshing and model build agent
  - early solver sanity-check agent
- a list of explicit out-of-scope items for the first 90 days

Decision Gate A: Management and lead engineers agree on scope, quality criteria, and the decision to proceed with MVP implementation.

Phase 2: Architecture and MVP Design (Days 16 – 75)

Goal: Design and implement a first working multi-agent system that mirrors the existing workflow without changing customer interfaces.

Key activities:

- Design the agent architecture for the battery pack use case, including the following:
  - supervisor to orchestrate the workflow and interact with the engineer
  - geometry classification to assign part categories and meshing logic
  - meshing and model build to generate meshes, contacts, and boundary conditions
  - solver checks to monitor early solver behavior and flag non-physical responses
- Implement rule-based logic for
  - part classification based on geometry and metadata,
  - meshing strategy selection per part category, and
  - automated midsurface creation for simple geometries.
- Integrate CAx tools through the chosen low-code MAS platform.
- Design human-in-the-loop checkpoints, especially for
  - complex midsurface decisions,
  - non-standard contacts, and
  - boundary condition validation.
- Ensure all agent actions are logged for traceability.

Deliverables:

- a working MVP capable of preprocessing a simplified battery pack model
- defined handover points between agents and engineers
- first internal test results comparing manual and agent-supported preprocessing

Decision Gate B: approval of running controlled pilot projects on real customer data

Phase 3: Pilot Execution and Validation (Days 76 – 90)

Goal: Validate robustness, quality, and efficiency under real project conditions.

Key activities:

- Run two to three pilot preprocessing cycles using real battery pack data.
- Compare results against manually created reference models with respect to the following:
  - mesh quality
  - contact completeness

  - boundary condition correctness
  - solver stability in the first milliseconds
- Measure key indicators:
  - engineering hours required
  - number of solver restarts
  - time to first stable run
  - number of manual interventions
- Collect structured feedback from engineers using the system.
- Identify recurring failure patterns and update agent rules accordingly.
- Assess scalability:
  - effort required to adapt the system to a second customer guideline
  - parts of the logic that are reusable without modification

Deliverables:

- validated pilot results with quantitative and qualitative metrics
- a refined agent architecture, incorporating lessons learned
- a clear recommendation for next steps, such as
  - expanding to additional battery variants
  - extending to another subsystem
  - preparing for a customer-facing pilot

Decision Gate C: executive decision on whether to scale the approach, invest further, or stop

3.4.7 Guest Perspective: Why Engineering Service Providers Need Automation Now

Felix Klutzny

A Market Under Structural Pressure

The German automotive industry has been under sustained pressure for several years. As a mechanical engineer working for an engineering service provider, I see the effects daily. Projects are paused or cancelled, negotiations have become tougher, and hourly rates for classical services such as design, modelling, and simulation are pushed down to the edge of profitability.

The causes are well known. International competition, particularly from Asian players, is intensifying. Strategic delays in areas such as e-mobility have weakened traditional OEMs. Economic uncertainty adds further strain. The established response model that absorbs cost pressure through highly qualified staff and shifts work to low-wage regions is increasingly ineffective. In domains like body, chassis, interior, model creation, and simulation, this approach is reaching its limits.

Why Automation Is Becoming a Strategic Necessity

Under these conditions, digital engineering is no longer a differentiator. It is becoming a survival factor. Customers expect shorter lead times, lower costs, and higher flexibility, often simultaneously. This is where advanced automation, including multi-agent systems, enters the discussion. MAS are still new in engineering practice, but their potential is real. They can support engineers as intelligent assistants, access internal data and tools, and coordinate workflows across functions. In the long term, they could take over significant parts of development coordination, reducing manual handovers and communication overhead. Initial applications already exist, most notably in RFQ automation. The next logical step is to extend similar principles into core product development.

From Vision to Practical Entry Points

Automating an entire development process end-to-end, at once, is not realistic. The complexity is simply too high. In practice, progress requires a stepwise approach, starting with central engineering activities such as design, simulation, validation, and costing.

A crucial insight is often underestimated. Before agents can coordinate anything, deterministic automation must exist. Agents do not replace these automations. They orchestrate them. In real projects, the majority of effort lies in building robust, rule-based workflows that agents can later control. The agent framework itself is only a smaller part of the total work.

Where Automation Is Most Mature Today

Simulation is currently the most advanced domain. Meshing, job submission to HPC clusters, and post-processing can often be automated reliably. These steps benefit from structured inputs and repeatable pipelines. Advanced preprocessing, however, remains challenging. Boundary conditions, contacts, materials, and load cases must be extracted or inferred correctly. This often requires assumptions based on engineering experience. Rule-based approaches can support this, but implementation effort is high. Result interpretation is even harder. While numerical evaluation can be partially automated, deriving meaningful design improvements still relies heavily on experienced engineers.

Speed, Iteration, and the Role of Machine Learning

Agent-driven workflows require fast feedback loops. This becomes a bottleneck in computationally intensive simulations such as crash analysis, which may take days to run. Machine learning can help accelerate these loops, but only with sufficient data. That data typically comes from structured design-of-experiments approaches. Without this foundation, ML remains more promise than solution.

Why Design Automation Remains Difficult

Design automation poses even greater challenges. Geometry creation and modification must respect functional, structural, and manufacturing constraints simultaneously. Parameter spaces quickly become high-dimensional and difficult to control. Parametric CAD models offer one path forward. Fully automated geometry generation combined with simulation is possible in principle, for example through topology optimization. In practice, however, results usually require extensive manual post-processing to become manufacturable and economically viable.

Downstream Steps Cannot Be Ignored

If the goal is real decision automation, downstream steps such as cost calculation and functional validation must also be automated. These activities are often overlooked, yet they are critical for end-to-end workflows.

Across projects, a consistent pattern emerges. Roughly 80 percent of the effort goes into developing and stabilizing deterministic automations. Only about 20 percent is spent on the multi-agent system architecture itself.

Designing the Agent System

Building an MAS requires clear architectural decisions. How many agents are needed? What roles do they play? How are responsibilities separated? How does communication work?

Workflows must be defined precisely, including inputs, outputs, and escalation paths. This process is rarely linear. It involves iteration, testing, and refinement.

Large language models, often used as the reasoning core, showing limitations in complex technical contexts. Incorrect workflow selection, parameter misinterpretation, and unstable behavior are common, especially as task complexity increases. Text-based reasoning struggles with spatial and visual understanding, which remains central to engineering work.

Hybrid approaches are likely the future. Combining LLMs with strong technical context, deterministic models, and geometry-aware systems could significantly improve robustness.

A Pragmatic Conclusion

Multi-agent systems offer real potential to support engineers, connect data, and automate parts of development work, even for non-standard tasks. At the same time, reliability and result quality are not yet sufficient for full autonomy in complex product development. Until AI systems become truly physics-aware, pragmatic approaches are essential. Focus on automating individual, high-leverage steps such as FE model creation, as discussed throughout this book.

One conclusion is unavoidable. For engineering service providers, investment in automation is no longer optional. Competitive pressure is rising, traditional cost-cutting strategies are exhausted, and delaying action increases strategic risk. Those who start now, pragmatically and incrementally, can improve efficiency, stabilize processes, and position themselves for an industry that is changing rapidly.

4 Organizational Foundations for Agentic Systems

Introducing an agentic system into an organization is not a typical software rollout. It is a structural intervention. Traditional software projects focus on functionality, integration, and user training. Once deployed, the organization adapts only marginally. Agent-based systems behave differently. They interact continuously with engineering workflows, decision-making processes, and responsibility structures. Over time, they influence how work is coordinated, how knowledge is retained, and how authority is exercised.

As a result, the success or failure of an agentic system is determined less by technical capability than by organizational readiness. Agents do not simply automate tasks. They reshape roles, expectations, and interfaces between people, tools, and processes. New questions inevitably arise. Who decides? Who reviews? Who is accountable? What happens when recommendations are wrong? How are learnings captured and reused?

For this reason, implementing agent-based systems cannot be treated as an IT project with a defined end state. It is an ongoing transformation that unfolds over time. The system evolves. The organization evolves with it. Governance, operating models, and trust must mature alongside technical capability.

This chapter focuses on exactly this dimension. It explores how organizations can introduce agent-based systems deliberately, scale them without losing control, and manage the associated risks responsibly. Topics such as pilot selection, IT integration, operating models, change management, maturity levels, and limitations are treated as parts of a single, interconnected challenge.

4.1 Implementing Agentic Systems Without Breaking the Organization

Deciding to introduce a multi-agent system into an organization is not a tactical optimization. It is a strategic, long-term decision that fundamentally reshapes how engineering work is structured, executed, and improved over time. Organizations that treat this step as a short-term efficiency initiative tend to underestimate both the required effort and the potential value. A multi-agent system does not simply accelerate existing work. It changes the way work is coordinated, how knowledge is retained, and how decisions are made.

As stated, multi-agent systems do not behave like conventional software tools. They are not installed, configured once, and then considered complete. Instead, they evolve together with the organization. Their effectiveness grows through repeated use, refinement, and feedback. In this sense, adopting a multi-agent system is closer to building an internal capability than deploying a product. It is comparable to earlier transformations such as the introduction of CAD, PLM, or simulation-driven development. Each of those shifts required patience, learning, and organizational adaptation before their full impact became visible. Even these comparisons fall short. A multi-agent system alters the entire way engineering work is carried out and may represent the most profound change engineering organizations have experienced to date.

One of the defining characteristics of a multi-agent system is that it improves with every interaction. Each project enriches the system with new data, clarified rules, refined prompts, validated assumptions, and documented decisions. Errors are not merely corrected. They become learning signals. Over time, this leads to more robust workflows, more reliable outputs, and a system that increasingly reflects how the organization actually engineers, rather than how processes were once documented on paper. This cumulative learning effect fundamentally changes the economics of automation. Early pilots may deliver only modest gains or feel incomplete. That is normal.

> The real value emerges when the same agents, rules, and orchestration logic are reused across projects, teams, and domains. At that point, the multi-agent system becomes a knowledge-accumulating asset.

Engineering expertise is no longer tied exclusively to individuals or isolated projects. It becomes embedded in the operational fabric of the organization. For this reason, agentic systems must be approached as a marathon, not a sprint. Early phases require deliberate scope limitation, strong human-in-the-loop integration, and a clear emphasis on transparency rather than autonomy. Trust must be built gradually. Knowing failure modes must be understood. Governance structures must mature alongside technology. Attempts to shortcut this process often result in brittle solutions or low adoption, even when the underlying technology is powerful. In the end, it is always people who determine the success of technology, not the other way around.

This section therefore focuses on implementation from an organizational perspective. It does not assume a greenfield environment or a perfect data landscape. Instead, it addresses the realities most organizations face. Heterogeneous IT systems should establish roles and responsibilities, regulatory constraints, and a healthy skepticism toward automation. The following sections provide guidance on how to introduce multi-agent systems in a way that supports long-term success. They cover how to select suitable pilot projects, how to integrate agents into existing IT landscapes, how to structure implementation phases from proof of concept to scaling, and how to prepare the organization for a gradual but lasting transformation. The objective is not to move fast at any cost. It is to move deliberately, learn continuously, and build a system that becomes more valuable with every project it supports.

4.1.1 Defining High-Value Entry Points

Introducing a multi-agent system into an engineering organization is not a short-term experiment. It is a strategic decision that unfolds over years rather than weeks. The first pilot project therefore carries significance far beyond its immediate technical outcome. It shapes expectations, builds or erodes trust, and determines whether agent-based systems are perceived as a practical extension of engineering capability or as an isolated innovation exercise.

Many early MAS initiatives fail for reasons that have little to do with the technology itself. In most cases, the system is technically capable. What undermines success is the choice of use case. Pilots are often too complex, too politically sensitive, or too far removed from day-to-day engineering work. In other cases, the economic impact is too diffuse, or quality criteria are insufficiently defined. When this happens, even solid technical results struggle to gain acceptance. Skepticism grows, adoption stalls, and the organization concludes that agent-based automation is not ready for productive use.

The opposite outcome is just as common when the right pilot is chosen. Even modest agent capabilities can deliver convincing results when applied to a process with clear leverage, real users, and manageable risk. Engineers experience immediate relief from coordination overhead. Decision-makers see faster turnaround and more consistent outcomes. Most importantly, the organization begins to learn. The system improves through use, and teams develop a shared understanding of where agents add value and where human judgment must remain central.

For this reason, the objective of the first pilot is not to demonstrate the full technical potential of a multi-agent System. It is to create a reliable learning environment. The goal is to establish trust, generate tangible value, and build a foundation that can be extended systematically. Selecting the right pilot project is therefore one of the most critical decisions in the entire journey.

Choose Processes with Strong Economic Leverage

A suitable pilot project targets a process where improvement leads to visible and defensible value. This does not necessarily mean selecting the largest or most expensive process. More important is the presence of inefficiencies that are already felt across the organization. Such leverage often appears in processes with long cycle times driven primarily by waiting rather than execution. Engineers may spend days or weeks waiting for inputs, approvals, or cross-team alignment, while the actual technical work takes only a fraction of that time. These delays are rarely visible in cost accounting, yet they represent a substantial operational burden.

Another strong indicator is repetition with variation. Processes that follow the same fundamental logic repeatedly, while differing in parameters such as geometry, materials, load cases, or customer-specific rules, are particularly well suited. In these cases, the engineering reasoning already exists. What is missing is a mechanism to apply it consistently, efficiently, and on a scale.

For early pilots, visibility of impact matters as much as absolute magnitude. Reduced turnaround time, fewer coordination loops, or clearer decision packages are benefits that stakeholders intuitively understand. When value is obvious, discussions move quickly from technical feasibility to broader application.

Choose Processes with High Cross-Functional Involvement

Multi-agent systems deliver the greatest value where coordination dominates execution. Processes that involve multiple engineering disciplines, manufacturing, quality, procurement, and business functions naturally generate friction. Each role contributes essential expertise, but operates with its own tools, assumptions, and priorities.

In such environments, work rarely progresses linearly. Instead, it evolves through iterative back-and-forth loops. Assumptions are refined, constraints are reinterpreted, and partial results raise new questions. These loops are not a flaw in the process. They are a natural consequence of complex decision-making. The challenge lies in how they are managed.

Manual coordination relies heavily on emails, meetings, spreadsheets, and informal agreements. Context is lost between steps. Decisions are revisited because assumptions were not documented. Engineers spend significant time synchronizing information instead of evaluating alternatives.

A pilot project with this level of coordination overhead allows a multi-agent system to demonstrate its core strength. By maintaining shared context, preserving assumptions across steps, and orchestrating interactions between specialized agents, the system reduces friction without changing the underlying engineering logic. Teams continue to reason as before, but with far less effort spent on alignment.

Search for Clear Quality Criteria and Stable Output Definitions

Early pilots often fail because quality expectations remain implicit. When it is unclear what constitutes an acceptable result, every output becomes a point of debate. Technical discussions drift into philosophical ones, and progress slows accordingly. Successful pilot projects are characterized by explicit acceptance criteria. These criteria do not need to be perfect or exhaustive, but they must be clear. Thresholds, tolerance ranges, and defined stop conditions allow both humans and agents to operate with confidence.

Equally important is clarity around decision ownership. Someone must be responsible for determining whether a result is sufficient. Without this clarity, pilots oscillate between endless refinement and premature rejection.

Traceability plays a central role in building trust. Early acceptance of agent-based systems depends less on flawless outputs than on explainability. Engineers need to understand why a recommendation was made, which assumptions were applied, and which data sources were used. When this transparency exists, imperfections are seen as part of a controlled learning process rather than as failure.

A Suitable Data Foundation is Needed

Agentic systems do not require perfect data, but they do require accessible data. Pilot projects should rely primarily on structured or semi-structured inputs such as CAD models, simulation setups, requirement documents, or tabular data. Information does not need to be clean or complete, but it must be locatable and interpretable.

Processes that depend almost entirely on implicit knowledge stored in individuals' heads are less suitable as first pilots. Not because this knowledge cannot be addressed by agents, but because extracting and validating it requires additional organizational effort that can overshadow technical learning.

Stability also matters. When input formats, naming conventions, or system interfaces change frequently, early automation becomes brittle. A pilot should operate in an environment where the fundamentals remain stable long enough to observe learning effects.

Crucially, a human fallback must always exist. Agents should be allowed to ask questions. Experts must be able to clarify, correct, or override outputs. This interaction is not a weakness. It is the mechanism through which the system learns and improves.

Choose Processes With Low Organizational Friction

Early pilots benefit from operating outside highly political or heavily regulated domains. Not because agentic systems cannot eventually support such areas, but because early learning requires room to experiment.

A clearly assigned process owner is essential. This person must have the authority to make decisions, accept temporary imperfections, and protect the pilot from unnecessary interference. Ambiguous ownership almost always leads to stalled progress.

Psychological safety is equally critical. Engineers must not feel that the pilot evaluates their personal performance or threatens their role. When agents are positioned as decision support rather than control mechanisms, openness and collaboration increase significantly.

Choose Real Usage Rather Than an Innovation Showcase

A pilot that exists only as a demonstration is not a pilot. Real learning occurs only when real users apply the system to real tasks under real constraints. From the outset, productive users should work with actual project data. Outputs must feed into existing decision processes rather than parallel shadow workflows. If results are ignored or recreated manually elsewhere, the pilot quickly loses relevance and credibility.

It is also important to define what happens after the pilot. Is the goal scaling, refinement, or a deliberate stop? Without a clear path forward, pilots tend to drift and lose momentum.

A structured learning loop should be established early. Feedback, corrections, and overrides are not failures. They are valuable signals. Capturing them systematically ensures that the system improves with every iteration and that value compounds over time.

Designed for Incremental Learning

The strongest pilot projects allow the multi-agent system to improve through use. Processes with frequent decisions, recurring patterns, and observable outcomes generate natural learning signals. Agent recommendations can be compared with human decisions, differences analyzed, and improvements applied.

Failure modes must be manageable. Errors should be detectable and recoverable. Early pilots should avoid scenarios where a single mistake leads to irreversible consequences. Learning requires room for correction.

Making the First Pilot Count

Selecting the first pilot project is an act of strategic judgment rather than technical optimization. It determines whether agent-based systems are perceived as fragile experiments or as reliable partners in everyday engineering work. This initial choice shapes expectations, influences trust and sets the tone for everything that follows.

The most successful pilots are rarely the most ambitious ones. They are the ones where coordination effort outweighs pure execution, where value becomes visible quickly, and where learning accumulates with each iteration. When these conditions are met, technology itself recedes into the background. What remains is a new way of working that feels practical, credible, and increasingly inevitable.

To support this decision in a structured and transparent way, a pilot project scoring matrix is provided in Section 6.1. It translates the qualitative criteria discussed in this chapter into a comparative framework. Candidate use cases can be assessed across dimensions such as economic leverage, coordination intensity, data readiness, and organizational feasibility. The matrix is not intended to replace judgment. It serves as a decision aid that makes trade-offs explicit and helps to align stakeholders around why a particular pilot was chosen as the starting point.

4.1.2 Integrating Agents Into the Enterprise Nervous System

Introducing a multi-agent system into an enterprise is not a tooling exercise. It is a structural decision that shapes how engineering, IT, and decision-making evolve over many years. Organizations often focus on agent capabilities, reasoning quality, or automation speed. In practice, however, long-term success is determined far more by the surrounding IT landscape than by any individual agent.

A multi-agent system inevitably touches critical parts of the organization. It interacts with systems of record such as PLM, ERP, and ALM. It orchestrates CAx tools and solvers that are license-constrained and tightly governed. It produces outputs that influence engineering decisions, cost assessments, quality judgments, and business commitments. Once deployed, it becomes part of the operational fabric of the company. This makes the IT architecture the enabling constraint. If the landscape is designed thoughtfully, the system can expand safely and continuously. If it is designed poorly, every extension becomes a technical, organizational, and political struggle.

There is also an often underestimated aspect. A multi-agent system improves through use. Each executed workflow generates structured data, assumptions, intermediate artifacts, decisions, and outcomes. Over time, this accumulation becomes a strategic asset. It strengthens reasoning quality, reduces uncertainty, and increases trust. This learning effect only materializes if data, context, and decisions are stored consistently and remain accessible across projects, teams, and time.

For these reasons, IT landscape and integration must be treated as first-order design topics. The objective is not to define a perfect target architecture upfront. The objective is to establish a reference structure that enables safe experimentation, controlled scaling, and continuous improvement over the long term.

Build-Versus-Buy Decision

The decision to build a multi-agent system internally or to rely on a commercial platform is not primarily a technical choice. It is a strategic one. Its consequences extend far beyond the first pilot and directly influence speed, scalability, organizational learning, and long-term risk. The central objective at this stage is to avoid locking the organization into an approach that constrains future development, slows learning, or creates hidden dependencies that only become visible after initial success.

One of the most immediate criteria is time to value. Organizations must assess how quickly an initial idea can be translated into a working system that delivers meaningful results. This includes not only initial development speed, but also the effort required to adapt workflows as insights emerge. Early multi-agent systems rarely remain static. They evolve through iteration, feedback, and refinement. An approach that enables rapid change without extensive redevelopment effort, supports learning and reduces friction during early adoption.

Closely related is the integration effort within the existing CAx landscape. Engineering environments are typically complex and heterogeneous, combining CAD systems, preprocessors, solvers, post-processing tools, as well as PLM, ERP, and ALM systems. The practical question is not whether integration is theoretically possible, but how much effort is required to achieve stable, repeatable automation. The availability of existing connectors, APIs, or automation interfaces plays a decisive role. Automating CAD interactions, meshing workflows, simulation execution, or report generation can quickly become the dominant cost and risk factor if each integration must be built from scratch.

Maintenance and security considerations become increasingly important once a system moves beyond experimentation. Engineering tools evolve continuously, APIs change, license models are updated, security requirements tighten. So organizations must evaluate how update cycles are handled and who carries responsibility for keeping integrations operational over time. Equally critical is the handling of intellectual property, data access, and user permissions. Multi-agent systems operate across multiple systems of record and execution environments. A clear, enforceable security model is therefore essential to ensure compliance, protect sensitive data, and maintain trust.

Another critical dimension is long-term dependency risk. Custom-built solutions often depend heavily on a small number of highly specialized developers who understand the architecture, codebase, and integrations in depth. While this can provide flexibility, it also introduces fragility if key individuals leave or priorities shift. Commercial platforms, by contrast, may introduce vendor dependency, which must be weighed against reduced internal maintenance effort and faster onboarding of new use cases.

> **!** The relevant question is not whether dependencies exist, but whether they are transparent, manageable, and aligned with the organization's risk tolerance.

Finally, the impact on organizational learning should not be underestimated. Multi-agent systems are not static products. They improve through usage. Decisions are refined, edge cases are incorporated, and best practices are encoded over time. Organizations should therefore consider who is able to extend and adapt the system. If every change requires deep software development skills, learning will slow down and innovation will bottleneck. Approaches that allow domain experts to contribute directly, within clearly governed boundaries, tend to accelerate adoption and improve system quality over time.

In practice, the build-versus-buy decision is rarely binary. Hybrid approaches are common. What matters most is that the chosen path supports rapid learning in the early phases, remains adaptable as requirements evolve, and aligns with the organization's long-term vision for agent-based engineering.

Defining a Clear Reference Architecture

Every effective multi-agent system is built around a clear separation of roles. This separation must be reflected not only conceptually, but also technically. Organizations that skip this step often end up with agents that are powerful in isolation but brittle in combination.

At the center of the architecture sits a coordinating entity, often referred to as the supervisor or orchestrator agent. This agent does not perform domain work itself. Its responsibility is coordination and control. It decides which specialist agents are triggered, in which order, and under which conditions. It manages dependencies, retries, escalation paths, and human interaction. Treating this agent as the single entry point for users and the single consolidation point for results simplifies governance and makes system behavior observable.

You should surround the supervisor with domain-specific specialist agents. Each agent represents a narrowly defined responsibility, such as geometry classification, meshing, solver execution, result interpretation, costing, or compliance checking. Enforcing strict responsibility separation at this stage prevents later debates about "which agent owns what" and makes failures diagnosable instead of opaque. Clear input and output contracts are not an implementation detail. They are the mechanism that allows agents to evolve independently.

All agents interact through a shared data and context layer. This layer stores the persistent case context, including inputs, explicit assumptions, intermediate results, decisions, and final outputs. Designing this layer early, even in a simplified form, enables workflows to be paused, resumed, inspected, or replayed. Without it, learning effects remain local and cannot accumulate across projects.

A critical distinction must be made between reasoning and execution. Reasoning tasks such as interpretation, prioritization, and comparison are typically handled by LLM-based components. Execution tasks such as calling CAx tools, solvers, or scripts must remain rule-based and deterministic. Preserving this separation ensures that intelligent behavior does not translate directly into irreversible actions, and it gives organizations a clear control point for audits and approvals.

Separating Systems of Record, Agent Workspace, and Execution Layer

One of the most important integration principles is the strict separation of system types. Ignoring this separation almost always leads to trust issues later. Systems of record such as PLM, ERP, ALM, MES, or QMS remain the official source of truth. They define the official state of products, requirements, costs, and decisions. A multi-agent system must respect this authority. Any organization introducing agents must therefore decide upfront which systems are read-only, which allow proposals, and which support controlled write-back under approval.

To enable fast iteration without operational risk, agents operate in a dedicated workspace. This workspace acts as a sandbox. It contains intermediate geometries, meshes, reports, logs, and temporary results. Establishing such a workspace early allows teams to experiment, fail, and recover without fear of corrupting productive data. Automatic versioning tied to case identifiers turns this workspace into a reliable experimentation environment rather than a temporary scratchpad.

The execution layer complements this workspace. It hosts the tools that perform actual work. CAD systems, preprocessors, solvers, CAM tools, and scripts are invoked from here and treated as services. By triggering tools through defined interfaces instead of embedding logic, organizations preserve flexibility when tools, vendors, or licenses change.

This separation creates robustness. When failures occur, and they inevitably will, recovery remains simple. The system can retry, escalate, or stop without leaving partial or inconsistent states behind. Designing for failure upfront avoids emergency fixes later.

Designing a Progressive Integration Strategy

A frequent mistake is attempting full integration too early. Trust in a multi-agent system must be earned gradually, not demanded. A proven approach starts with read-only access. In this phase, agents retrieve data from PLM, ERP, or other systems and analyze it. They generate insights and recommendations, but do not modify anything. This phase is not wasted effort. It is where teams learn how agents reason and where assumptions must be clarified.

The next step introduces proposal-based workflows. Agents generate suggested changes that are clearly marked as non-authoritative. By explicitly designing this proposal phase, organizations create a safe space for disagreement, correction, and learning. Human review is not a fallback. It is a deliberate training mechanism for both the system and its users.

Only in later stages should controlled writing back be enabled. Even then, permissions must be granular and approvals explicit. Each write-back action should be logged with context, rationale, and approval reference. This staged approach ensures that increased autonomy is a consequence of trust.

From a technical perspective, loose coupling between software systems is essential, rather than low level integrations. Integrations should rely on APIs and service interfaces wherever possible. Designing failure handling explicitly at each interface ensures that the system always fails safely rather than silently.

Standardizing Artifacts, Naming, and Metadata

As workflows scale, inconsistency becomes a hidden tax. Standardization is therefore not a documentation exercise, but a prerequisite for reuse. Naming conventions provides the first layer of structure. Cases, variants, and artifacts should follow consistent, human-readable, and machine-parseable patterns. Defining these conventions early avoids costly refactoring once dozens of workflows exist.

Versioning must be explicit. Engineers need to understand what changed, why it changed, and how to revert. Treating versions as first-class citizens of the system turns iteration history into a learning resource rather than a liability. Metadata acts as the connective tissue. Every artifact should carry identifiers for case, project, customer, product, and maturity level. Confidence indicators and status flags add clarity and reduce ambiguity in decision-making.

Over time, standardized schemas emerge. Investing early in simple, extensible schemas for geometrical metrics, simulation results, or cost breakdowns creates the foundation for portfolio-level insights and cross-project learning.

Building Monitoring and Observability From the Start

A multi-agent system is a living system. Without observability, it quickly becomes opaque and unmanageable. Operational monitoring tracks runtime per agent and per step. This visibility allows teams to identify bottlenecks and prioritize improvements based on evidence rather than intuition. LLM-specific monitoring is equally important. Tracking token usage, cost per workflow, and output drift ensures that reasoning quality and cost efficiency evolve together rather than in opposition.

Business-level metrics close the loop. Cycle time reduction, manual effort avoided, reuse of agent logic, and user adoption provide the signals needed to decide whether scaling is justified. Without these metrics, discussions remain subjective and progress stalls.

Security, Compliance, and Data Protection

Security cannot be added later. Agents require identities, and access must be role-based from the beginning. Central credential management and explicit permissions prevent accidental overreach.

Data isolation is particularly critical for engineering service providers. Customer and project data must be separated by design, not by convention. If knowledge reuse is intended, it must be governed explicitly and contractually.

Auditability underpins trust. Every decision must be traceable and every result reproducible. Designing for auditability early reduces friction later when systems move closer to production use.

Designing for Maintainability and Long-Term Evolution

A multi-agent system is never finished. Agents evolve, prompts improve, and tools change. Organizations must therefore plan for continuous change rather than stability. This requires explicit lifecycle management. Agent logic and prompts should be versioned, tested, and rolled out deliberately. Backward compatibility strategies prevent breaking existing workflows when improvements are introduced.

Scalability must be designed from the start. Systems should scale horizontally and absorb workload peaks without architectural redesign or dependence on individual experts.

Vendor and platform dependence also deserves early attention. Introducing abstraction layers and exit strategies may feel premature, but it preserves strategic flexibility over the long term.

Integration as a Long-Term Commitment

The IT landscape is the foundation on which all agent-based automation rests. A well-designed integration architecture turns a multi-agent system into a trusted, learning, and scalable capability. A weak foundation confines it to a fragile experiment. The guiding principle is simple. Design the IT landscape not only for today's pilot, but for the organization you intend to become over the next decade.

4.1.3 From Proof of Concept to Scalable Capability

Implementing agents should not be understood as classical software deployment. It marks the beginning of a new way of working. Agents do not merely execute predefined scripts. They interpret context, coordinate across domains, and interact continuously with humans, data, and tools. This fundamentally changes how decisions are prepared, how work is synchronized, and how responsibility is perceived inside the organization.

For this reason, a company-wide, top-down rollout is rarely a good starting point. Even if the underlying technology appears mature, the surrounding system is not. People, processes, data, governance, and expectations all need time to adapt. Starting too large amplifies risk in several ways. Technical imperfections become visible at scale before they are understood. Organizational resistance increases when users feel confronted rather than involved. Small failures are quickly generalized and interpreted as proof that the overall approach does not work.

A phased approach avoids these traps. It creates room for learning on multiple levels at the same time: technical, organizational, and cultural. Each phase serves a distinct purpose and has its own definition of success. Skipping phases or blurring their intent usually leads to false conclusions. Either readiness is overestimated, or promising approaches are abandoned prematurely.

The progression from proof of concept (PoC) to pilot to scaling is therefore not a formality. It is a deliberate risk management strategy. It allows confidence to build gradually, while the system itself improves through use. By the time broader rollout is considered, the multi-agent system is no longer perceived as an experiment. It is experienced as a reliable partner in real engineering work.

Proof of Concept: Proving Feasibility, not Value

The proof-of-concept phase exists for one primary reason: to determine whether a multi-agent system can technically function within the given environment. Its scope is intentionally narrow. Attempting to demonstrate business impact at this stage usually creates misleading expectations and unnecessary pressure. At the same time, a PoC is not a two-week experiment. Because environmental integration must be validated, including data access, tool control, and architectural constraints, the PoC often spans several months depending on scope.

A well-designed PoC focuses on a clearly bounded workflow segment. This may be a specific preprocessing task, a document interpretation step, or a limited coordination loop between two domains. The scope is small enough that all assumptions are explicit. Which data is required? Which tools are involved? Which decisions the agent is expected to support?

Integration risk is the central concern in this phase. Can agents access the necessary systems? Can CAx tools be controlled reliably? Do data formats behave as expected? Are there architectural constraints that fundamentally limit automation? These questions must be answered early, before effort is invested in broader concepts.

Iteration speed is critical. Feedback cycles should be measured in days, not weeks. Domain experts must be closely involved, not to validate output quality, but to clarify intent and context. At this stage, misunderstandings are more valuable than polished results. They expose hidden assumptions that would otherwise surface much later.

Equally important is what the PoC does not aim to achieve. It is not a benchmark against human performance. It is not production ready. Error handling may be incomplete. Edge cases are intentionally ignored. Governance, security hardening, and compliance requirements are kept minimal. Treating a PoC as anything more than a feasibility experiment almost always leads to disappointment. A successful PoC ends with clarity rather than perfection. The organization understands what works, what does not, and which risks are manageable. This clarity forms the foundation for the next phase.

Pilot Phase: Turning Feasibility into Trust

While the PoC answers the question whether something can work, the pilot phase answers a more important one: Will it actually be used? The defining characteristic of a pilot is that real users work on real cases. There is no parallel sandbox reality. The multi-agent system becomes part of daily operations, even if only for a limited group. This shift immediately changes the evaluation criteria. Stability, transparency, and usability now matter as much as technical capability.

Measurement becomes meaningful in this phase. Time savings, effort reduction, and quality indicators can be compared against an existing baseline. Equally important is qualitative feedback. Do users trust the system? Do they understand its recommendations? Do they feel supported rather than constrained? Acceptance is not a soft factor. It determines whether scaling is possible at all.

During the pilot, workflows and interfaces are stabilized. Ad-hoc fixes that were acceptable during the PoC are removed. Agent responsibilities are clarified. Output becomes consistent and decision-ready. This is also the phase where organizational bottlenecks surface. Approval chains, unclear ownership, and conflicting incentives often become more visible than technical limitations.

A crucial part of the pilot is moving toward production readiness. This does not mean full enterprise hardening, but it does require discipline. Temporary simplifications are removed systematically. Known edge cases are addressed. Error handling is improved. Escalation paths are defined. The system learns to fail transparently and gracefully rather than silently.

Another key aspect of the pilot phase is observable learning behavior. A well-designed multi-agent system should improve through use. Not through uncontrolled adaptation, but by capturing feedback, comparing outcomes, and refining logic. When users see that the system gets better with each iteration, trust grows naturally.

A pilot is successful when the system no longer feels like a prototype. It does not need to be perfect. It needs to be reliable enough that users are willing to rely on it for real decisions.

Scaling Phase: From Solution to Capability

Scaling is not about doing more of the same. It is about transforming a successful pilot into a sustainable organizational capability. At this stage, the focus shifts from individual use cases to patterns. Agents, workflows, and orchestration logic developed during the pilot should be reusable. New use cases are added through extension rather than reinvention. This reuse is where the real economic leverage emerges.

Governance becomes explicit. Ownership of agents, data, and workflows must be clearly defined. Monitoring expands beyond technical uptime to include performance, cost, and usage patterns. Support structures are established, not to centralize control, but to ensure reliability over time.

Training and onboarding gain importance. New users need more than instructions. They need a mental model of how agents reason, where their limits lie, and when human judgment is required. Narrative matters: Systems positioned as collaborators are adopted very differently from those framed as replacements.

Long-term operation requires preparation: CAx tools evolve, data structures change, and regulations shift. A scalable multi-agent system must adapt without continuous reinvention. Budgeting for licenses, infrastructure, and operational support becomes part of standard planning.

Finally, scaling exposes practical constraints. CAx licenses, solver capacity, and compute resources often become real bottlenecks rather than agent logic itself. Addressing these constraints early prevents artificial limits later.

Human Control Across all Phases

Across all phases, one principle remains constant:
Humans stay in control.

Clear review and approval points are essential. Agents prepare, humans decide. Escalation logic must be explicit, and uncertainty must never be hidden. Traceability is not an afterthought. It is a prerequisite for trust. Engineers need to understand why a recommendation was made, which data was used, and which assumptions applied. When these control points are well designed, imperfections are no longer perceived as failures. They become part of a transparent and productive learning process.

You Don't Scale What You Don't Trust

Implementing agents is the start of a new way of working that evolves over time. The phases described in this chapter provide a structured path to do exactly that. They reduce risk, create space for learning, and ensure that trust is built alongside technical maturity. Organizations that follow this progression experience a clear shift. Agents stop being perceived as experimental tools and start to function as reliable partners in everyday engineering work. At that point, scaling becomes a question of capacity and governance rather than feasibility.

To support this journey in practice, a multi-agent system rollout cheat sheet is provided in Section 6.2. It summarizes the key decisions, checkpoints, and typical pitfalls across all phases, from proof of concept to scalable operation. It is intended as a practical reference to support planning, alignment, and execution as organizations move from first experiments toward long-term adoption.

4.1.4 From Assistive to Autonomous: Managing Agent Maturity

When organizations first encounter multi-agent systems, progress is often framed as a race toward autonomy. The implicit assumption is that higher maturity means less human involvement and faster results. In practice, this mindset creates unnecessary risk and frequently leads to disappointment. Agent-based systems rarely fail because they lack intelligence. They fail because they are introduced faster than the organization can absorb them. Engineering work is deeply embedded in social structures, responsibilities, approval paths, and accountability models that have evolved over decades. Replacing these structures abruptly with autonomous software creates friction long before it creates value.

For this reason, maturity in agentic systems should not be understood as a technical ladder that must be climbed as quickly as possible. It is a progressive alignment between technology, process, and organizational trust. Each maturity level serves a specific purpose. Skipping levels does not accelerate transformation. It destabilizes it.

Learning is another critical dimension. A multi-agent system improves through usage. Its quality depends on feedback loops, validated assumptions, and exposure to real decisions. These learning mechanisms only work when humans remain close to the system in the early stages. Jumping directly to high autonomy deprives the organization of the very insights required to make autonomy safe and effective later on.

The maturity model presented in this section therefore does not describe a single linear roadmap. It provides a shared language to reason about where autonomy is appropriate, where control must remain explicit, and how organizations can expand the role of agents without eroding accountability or trust.

Level 1: Assistive Agents

At the first maturity level, agents function as decision support, not as decision makers. Their role is to reduce cognitive load, structure information, and prepare alternatives for human evaluation. These agents typically operate in read-only mode. They do not modify data in system of record, nor do they trigger downstream actions. Their outputs take the form of recommendations, summaries, comparisons, or risk indicators that help engineers and decision makers work faster and more consistently.

Typical tasks at this level include reading and structuring documents, extracting parameters from geometry, comparing new cases against historical data, or highlighting inconsistencies and missing information. The value comes from speed and coverage rather than from execution automation.

From an organizational perspective, level 1 is central to trust building. Engineers can inspect every output, challenge assumptions, and understand how conclusions are reached. Imperfections are acceptable because they are visible and recoverable. Errors are treated as learning signals rather than failures.

This level is often underestimated because it does not immediately replace work. In reality, assistive agents frequently deliver disproportionate value by freeing experts from repetitive analysis and enabling better decisions earlier in the process. They also create the data foundation and usage patterns required for higher maturity later on.

Level 2 and Level 3: Semi-Autonomous Agents

The second and third maturity level introduces controlled execution. Agents are now allowed to perform clearly defined tasks autonomously, but only within explicit boundaries and under mandatory human approval. At this stage, agents typically automate steps that are well understood, standardized, and already governed by rules or templates. Examples include preprocessing and meshing based on fixed guidelines, execution of simulations using predefined setups, generation of standardized reports, or structured cost calculations.

Human control remains explicit. Approval points are clearly defined, and responsibility for decisions is unambiguous. Agents may prepare results, but humans decide whether these results are accepted, modified, or rejected before any write-back occurs.

These levels are often where organizations experience the first tangible productivity gains. Cycle times shrink, handovers become smoother, and consistency improves. At the same time, the system remains auditable and predictable, which is essential in regulated or safety-critical environments.

Equally important, level 2 and 3 exposes organizational bottlenecks. When agents execute faster than humans can review, gaps in decision ownership, acceptance criteria, or escalation paths become visible. These insights are valuable because they surface process issues that existed long before automation but were previously hidden by manual delays.

Level 4 and Level 5: Largely Autonomous Agents

At the fourth and fifth maturity level, agents gain the ability to iterate independently within predefined guardrails. Instead of executing a single step and waiting for approval, they can explore solution spaces, refine results, and coordinate with other agents until defined targets are met.

Autonomy at these levels is bound, not absolute. It is constrained by policies, thresholds, and escalation rules. Agents act independently as long as results remain within accepted ranges. Human involvement is triggered only when deviations occur, conflicts arise, or uncertainty exceeds defined limits.

Typical capabilities at these levels include autonomous variant generation, optimization loops, multi-step validation workflows, and dynamic task sequencing across specialist agents. The system begins to resemble a digital team rather than a collection of tools.

These levels require a mature data foundation and stable quality definitions. Without clear acceptance criteria, autonomy quickly degrades into noise. For this reason, this stage should only be introduced after sufficient operational experience has been gathered at lower levels.

From an organizational standpoint, the shift is significant. Humans move from supervising individual steps to supervising outcomes. Their role becomes defining boundaries, evaluating exceptions, and improving policies rather than executing routine work.

The Final Level: Organizationally Embedded Agent Systems

The highest maturity level is reached when multi-agent systems are no longer perceived as separate solutions but as part of the operating model. At this stage, agents are embedded into core business processes. They span multiple projects, teams, and domains. Knowledge accumulated in one context becomes available in others. Feedback loops operate not only within a single system but across the organization.

Capabilities expand beyond task execution. Agents support portfolio-level prioritization, identify systemic risks, and surface optimization opportunities that are invisible at the level of individual projects. Learning compounds over time because decisions, outcomes, and corrections are systematically captured and reused.

Governance also evolves. Responsibility shifts from individual agent actions to policies, roles, and oversight mechanisms. Regular audits, performance reviews, and continuous improvement cycles ensure that autonomy remains aligned with organizational objectives.

Reaching this level is not a prerequisite for success. Many organizations generate substantial value at levels 2 and 3. The final level represents the point at which agent-based systems become a durable strategic asset rather than a collection of productivity tools.

A Non-Linear Reality

In practice, organizations rarely operate at a single maturity level. Different processes require different balances between autonomy and control. A safety-critical validation workflow may remain at level 2 or 3, while a high-volume, low-risk preprocessing task operates at level 4 or 5. Assistive agents at level 1 often coexist with more autonomous systems elsewhere. The purpose of this maturity model is therefore not to prescribe an end state. It is to enable deliberate choices. Autonomy should be gained through learning, not assumed through ambition.

Autonomy Is a Decision, Not a Destination

The central question is not how autonomous a multi-agent system can become. The question is when autonomy creates more value than risk. Organizations that respect this distinction progress steadily. Those that ignore it often oscillate between overconfidence and retreat. By treating maturity as an organizational journey rather than a technical escalation, companies create the conditions under which agents can evolve from helpful assistants into trusted partners in engineering work.

4.1.5 Making Agent-Based Automation Operational

Introducing agents into an organization also means introducing a new operational capability that is expected to live for years. Early pilots often focus on feasibility and value creation. Long-term success, however, depends on something more fundamental: a clear operating model.

Without an explicit operating model, agent-based systems tend to drift into one of two failure modes. In the first, they remain fragile experiments. They work as long as a small group of experts is closely involved, but they break down once ownership becomes unclear or key contributors move on. In the second, they degrade quietly. Small changes in tools, data, or models accumulate over time until trust erodes and users gradually stop relying on the system.

Addressing operations early helps prevent both outcomes. It forces the organization to confront necessary questions. Who is responsible when results look wrong? Who decides when rules are updated? Who owns prompts and agent behavior? How are changes tested, approved, and rolled out? These questions are not obstacles to innovation. They are the foundation that allows innovation to scale.

An operating model does not need to be heavy or bureaucratic at the beginning. It does need to exist. Even a lightweight model creates clarity, reduces risk, and signals that the system is intended to become part of everyday work rather than a temporary experiment. The following sections describe core elements of an operating model for agent-based systems that has proven effective across industries and use cases.

Clear Roles and Ownership

The first pillar of the operating model is explicit role definition. Agent-based systems blur traditional boundaries between engineering, IT, and operations. Without clear ownership, responsibility quickly becomes diffused.

At a minimum, three responsibilities must be defined:

- **System operation:** This role is responsible for day-to-day operation. It includes monitoring system health, managing access, and ensuring workflows execute as expected. This is operational stewardship rather than deep development work. In many organizations, this role sits close to engineering operations or digital enablement teams.
- **Rule and logic ownership:** Rules encode engineering knowledge, constraints, and decision logic. Someone must own their correctness and evolution. This responsibility typically lies with senior domain experts rather than IT specialists. The key requirement is authority and understanding of what constitutes a valid engineering decision, not programming skill.

- **Prompt ownership:** Prompts define how agents reason, explain, and interact. They are not static configuration files. They evolve with experience. Prompt ownership includes maintaining clarity, robustness, and alignment with organizational language and expectations. In more mature setups, this responsibility is shared between domain experts and AI-literate engineers.

Separating these roles avoids a common anti-pattern: One person informally owns everything. That approach may work briefly, but it does not survive scaling or staff changes.

Maintenance as a Continuous Activity

Unlike traditional automation, multi-agent systems require ongoing maintenance even when the underlying process remains unchanged. This is not a sign of instability. It is a consequence of operating at the boundary between deterministic systems and probabilistic reasoning.

Maintenance typically falls into three categories:

- **Tool and integration updates:** CAx tools, solvers, APIs, and data sources evolve continuously. Interfaces change, file formats shift, and performance characteristics move. The operating model must define how such updates are monitored, tested, and rolled into the system without disrupting users.
- **Rule evolution:** Engineering rules are not timeless. Standards change. Best practices improve. New failure modes emerge. Rules must be reviewed periodically, especially when agents operate across many projects. A controlled update process ensures that improvements accumulate instead of fragmenting.
- **System refinement:** As usage grows, inefficiencies and edge cases become visible. The operating model should explicitly allow for incremental refinement based on real usage rather than theoretical design.

LLM Model Management as an Operational Discipline

Large language models are not static dependencies. Even when organizations do not actively switch models, behavior can change due to provider updates. This has direct implications for trust and reliability. A mature operating model therefore treats LLMs as living components. Model versions must be explicitly tracked so the organization always knows which model and which version is used in production. Experimental models must be clearly separated from approved ones.

The operating model must also assume that behavior can change without notice. Reasoning style, verbosity, or edge-case handling may shift subtly. Agents that rely on brittle assumptions will fail silently if this is ignored. Revalidation must therefore be part of normal operations. Periodic regression tests using representative real-world cases help detect unintended changes early. These tests aim for confidence rather than perfection.

Prompt robustness plays a critical role. Prompts should tolerate minor behavioral shifts by being explicit about constraints, output structure, and expectations. Overly clever or minimal prompts tend to break first.

Finally, fallback strategies must exist. This may include temporary model downgrades, increased human oversight, or disabling specific agents when confidence drops. The objective is not to avoid change, but to absorb it safely.

Support and Escalation Processes

No system operates flawlessly. What matters is how deviations are handled.

An effective operating model defines clear escalation paths. When an agent produces uncertain or conflicting output, it must be clear who is notified and how decisions are made. Support processes should distinguish between different classes of issues:

- technical failures such as tool crashes or integration errors
- logical issues such as incorrect rule application or outdated assumptions
- interpretation issues where results are technically correct but misleading or poorly explained

Each class requires a different response. Treating all issues as generic errors leads to slow resolution and user frustration.

Long-Term Learning and Resilience

The final element of the operating model is learning. Agentic systems become more valuable over time if the organization allows them to learn systematically. This includes capturing feedback on agent recommendations, comparing outcomes with human decisions, and identifying recurring failure patterns. Over time, this creates an internal knowledge asset that is difficult for competitors to replicate. Crucially, the operating model must ensure that this learning remains inside the organization. Knowledge embedded in rules, prompts, and workflows should not depend on individual employees. When people leave, the system should retain what they helped build.

Building for the Second Year, not for the Demo

A multi-agent system without an operating model is a prototype waiting to fail. A multi-agent system with a clear operating model becomes infrastructure. By addressing roles, maintenance, model evolution, and escalation early, organizations shift the conversation. Instead of asking whether agents can be trusted, they focus on how agents are governed. That shift is subtle, but decisive. It marks the transition from experimentation to a sustainable, long-term capability. To support this transition in practice, a lightweight operational starter cheat sheet is provided in Section 6.3. It summarizes the minimum roles, decisions, and safeguards required to start safely, learn quickly, and avoid fragile early implementations.

4.1.6 What to Remember Before You Scale

Implementing an agentic system is not about deploying a new tool. It is about deliberately reshaping how engineering work is coordinated, how decisions are prepared, and how knowledge is preserved over time. This section showed that success depends on more than technical sophistication. It requires selecting the right entry points, integrating agents into the existing IT landscape, progressing through maturity in a controlled manner, and anchoring the system in a clear and durable operating model.

Organizations that take this path deliberately gain more than short-term efficiency. They build a capability that improves through use, accumulates learning across projects, and remains resilient as tools, teams, and requirements evolve. Organizations that rush toward autonomy or neglect organizational foundations often learn the opposite lesson. Intelligence without structure tends to create fragility rather than advantage.

The central message of this section is straightforward. Agent-based systems reward patience, clarity, and discipline. When introduced thoughtfully, they stop being perceived as experimental technology and begin to function as trusted partners in everyday engineering work. At that point, the question is no longer whether agents fit the organization. It becomes how far the organization is willing to go in building around them.

4.2 The Human Factor in Multi-Agent Systems

When organizations discuss the implementation of multi-agent systems, the conversation often starts with technology: Which models should be used? Which platform should be chosen? How much automation is possible? These questions matter, but they are rarely decisive. In practice, agent-based systems succeed or fail for a much simpler reason. People decide whether they work with them, trust them, and invest their expertise in making them better.

An agentic system does not create value on its own. Value emerges only when engineers rely on agent outputs in real situations, when decisions are shaped by agent-generated insights, and when workflows genuinely change. If agents are ignored, bypassed, or treated as a parallel experiment, even the most advanced system remains irrelevant. Adoption is therefore not a side effect of technical excellence. It is the central challenge.

This makes organizational and change management aspects far more critical than many teams initially expect. Introducing agents alters how work is prepared, how decisions are made, and how responsibility is perceived. Tasks shift from manual execution toward supervision, evaluation, and steering. Engineers move from operating tools to defining goals, boundaries, and acceptance criteria. These changes affect not only processes, but also professional identity, status, and career paths.

Two groups are especially important during this transition. The first are everyday users: engineers, analysts, and specialists who interact with agents as part of their daily work. Their experience determines whether the system feels helpful or intrusive, trustworthy or opaque. The second group is often underestimated: the most experienced domain experts. These individuals hold tacit knowledge that cannot be found in process descriptions or guidelines. They know which assumptions are safe, where rules break down, and which edge cases truly matter. Without their involvement, agents may automate surface logic, but they will fail in real-world situations.

At the same time, these experts often carry the greatest concerns: fear of losing relevance, fear that the system they help build might eventually replace them, and fear that craftsmanship and judgment will be reduced to rules and prompts. These concerns are rational. Ignoring them leads to quiet resistance, superficial adoption, and systems that never mature beyond demonstrations.

Successful organizations address this tension explicitly. They frame agents as force multipliers rather than replacements. They make it clear that expertise does not disappear. It scales. The role of the expert shifts from executing tasks to shaping how decisions are prepared, validating outcomes, and continuously improving the system. In this model, the most valuable engineers are not those who click fastest, but those who can translate judgment into structure, feedback, and learning.

Psychological safety plays a decisive role in this process. Experts must feel safe challenging agent outputs, exposing uncertainty, and correcting mistakes openly. If contributing to the system feels risky, knowledge remains hidden and learning stalls. Trust must be built deliberately, through transparency, explainability, and clear boundaries between agent autonomy and human authority.

For this reason, change management cannot be treated as an afterthought. It must begin before the first agent is rolled out. Organizations need to send clear signals. This is not a headcount reduction initiative. Contribution to the system is recognized and valued. Time spent improving agent behavior is legitimate engineering work. Without this framing, even technically successful implementations struggle to gain traction.

This section focuses on the human dimension of agent-based transformation. It explores how to design effective human-agent collaboration, how to foster acceptance and trust, and how to define governance structures that enable learning without sacrificing accountability. It also addresses emerging roles, training paths, operating models, and incentive structures that support long-term adoption.

Technology enables agentic systems. People determine whether they become a durable organizational capability or a forgotten experiment. The following sections examine how organizations can get this human dimension right.

4.2.1 Designing Productive Human-Agent Collaboration

Agentic systems succeed because people choose to work with them. This distinction is fundamental and often underestimated. Many technology initiatives assume that once a system is powerful enough, adoption will follow automatically. In engineering organizations, the opposite is usually true. The more powerful a system becomes, the more deliberately its relationship with humans must be designed.

Engineering work is not a sequence of isolated tasks. It is a continuous process of judgment, responsibility, and accountability. Decisions carry technical, financial, and sometimes safety-critical consequences. Engineers are trained not only to execute work, but to stand behind outcomes. Any system that interferes with this responsibility without clear boundaries will encounter resistance, regardless of its technical merit.

Human-agent collaboration therefore is the central design challenge of any multi-agent system operating in a real organization. If agents are perceived as opaque decision-makers, engineers disengage. If agents are framed merely as tools that automate clicks, their potential is wasted. The productive space lies in between. Agents must function as digital coworkers that reduce friction, expand perspective, and support better decisions, while authority and accountability remain firmly with humans.

Getting this balance right determines whether agents become trusted partners or quietly ignore background noise. It also determines whether the organization's most capable engineers actively contribute to improving the system or distance themselves from it. The following principles define what sustainable and productive human-agent collaboration looks like in practice.

Agents as Digital Coworkers, Not Autonomous Executors

Agents should be designed to absorb work that consumes time but adds little engineering insight. This includes preparation, coordination, and repetitive execution steps. Typical examples are gathering data from multiple systems, preparing input models, running standardized checks, and synchronizing assumptions across teams. These tasks are necessary, but they distract engineers from evaluating alternatives and exercising judgment.

The guiding principle is simple. Agents prepare. Humans evaluate. Agents should never be positioned as authorities that deliver final answers. Their role is to present structured inputs, comparisons, and recommendations that enable faster and more consistent decisions. When agents act as assistants rather than decision-makers, adoption increases and resistance drops naturally.

Decision Authority Must Remain Explicit

Final responsibility must always stay with humans. This is not merely a legal safeguard. It is a prerequisite for trust. Every automation must clearly distinguish between recommendation and decision. Agents may propose actions, rank options, or highlight risks. The moment a decision has real consequences, a human must explicitly approve it.

Ownership must be visible at all times. It should always be clear who accepted a result and under which assumptions. When responsibility becomes ambiguous, engineers disengage and treat the system as unreliable, even when results are technically correct. This clarity also protects the system itself. Errors are then interpreted as learning opportunities rather than as failures of uncontrolled automation.

Redefining Engineering Roles Deliberately

Introducing agents changes how engineers spend their time. If this shift is not acknowledged explicitly, it creates friction. As agents take over execution and coordination, engineers move toward supervision, evaluation, and exception handling. Their role shifts from operating tools step by step to defining goals, constraints, and acceptance criteria.

This increases the importance of judgment and system-level thinking. Engineers shape workflows, review outcomes, and improve decision logic over time. Tool operation becomes less central. Decision quality becomes more central. Organizations that recognize and communicate this shift early reduce anxiety and resistance. Engineers are not being replaced. Their expertise is being applied at a higher leverage point.

Define Autonomy Boundaries Upfront

Ambiguity about what agents may or may not do is one of the fastest ways to erode trust. For every agent-based system, the following must be explicit:

- Which actions may agents execute autonomously?
- Which actions require human approval?
- Which conditions trigger escalation?

These boundaries must be visible during execution, not hidden in documentation. When agents act, users should immediately understand whether an action is within approved autonomy or awaiting confirmation.

Autonomy should expand gradually, based on experience and demonstrated reliability. Early systems should be conservative by design. Increased autonomy must be gained through stable behavior and clear quality criteria, not assumed from the outset.

Design Interaction for Control, Not Convenience

Interaction design determines whether engineers feel empowered or sidelined. Chat-based interaction works well for intent definition and clarification, but it is rarely sufficient on its own. Engineers also need structured review interfaces that visualize geometry, summarize results, highlight risks, and support decisions explicitly. Execution traces are essential. Users must be able to see what the agent did, in which order, and based on which inputs.

Different roles require different levels of detail. Effective systems support progressive disclosure with high-level summaries for decision-makers and full traces for experts who want to inspect assumptions and reasoning in depth.

Human-in-the-Loop Is a Feature, Not a Fallback

Human checkpoints should be designed into the system intentionally. They are not a workaround for missing automation. They are the mechanism that keeps accountability and learning aligned.

At each critical decision point, agents must expose

- assumptions,
- intermediate results, and
- confidence or uncertainty signals.

Intervention must be easy. Engineers should be able to override results, correct assumptions, and continue execution without friction. These interventions are training signals that improve the system over time. Fallback to manual execution must always remain possible. Knowing that work can continue without the agent reduces anxiety and increases willingness to rely on it.

Actionable Takeaway

Design human-agent collaboration before optimizing automation. If agents reduce cognitive load, preserve decision authority, and make reasoning transparent, they will be used. If they obscure responsibility or remove control, they will be bypassed.

The goal is not fewer humans in the loop. The goal is better humans in the loop, supported by systems that handle preparation and coordination at scale. That is the foundation on which every successful agentic system is built.

4.2.2 Evolving Skills and Roles in Agent-Supported Engineering

Introducing agentic systems changes far more than processes or tools. It changes what it means to be an engineer. Many organizations underestimate this shift. They assume that once agents are technically capable and embedded into existing environments, people will adapt naturally. In practice, resistance rarely stems from missing skills alone. It stems from threatened professional identity.

Engineers invest years, often decades, in building expertise around tools, methods, and execution excellence. Their sense of value is closely tied to knowing how to do things. When agents begin to execute tasks that were previously considered core engineering work, this expertise can feel devalued, even when no such message is intended.

If this psychological dimension is ignored, disengagement follows. Not because engineers cannot learn, but because they no longer see a future role that feels meaningful, respected, and secure. Successful adoption of agentic systems therefore requires deliberate evolution in three dimensions at once: skills, mindset, and professional identity. Treating this purely as a training problem is insufficient. It is a cultural transition that must be shaped intentionally.

From Tool Expertise to System Thinking

Traditional engineering excellence is often measured by tool mastery. Engineers know how to build models, run simulations, debug solver issues, and navigate complex software environments efficiently. Agent-based systems shift the center of gravity. Execution becomes faster and increasingly automated. The scarce capability is no longer knowing how to run a tool, but knowing what should be run, why, and under which assumptions.

This requires a move toward system thinking. Engineers must understand how decisions propagate across domains, how constraints interact, and where uncertainty has the greatest impact. Instead of optimizing individual steps, they evaluate end-to-end outcomes. Organizations should make this shift explicit. Tool skills remain relevant, but they are no longer the primary differentiator. The engineers who create the most value are those who can frame problems clearly, define boundaries precisely, and reason across disciplines.

Prompting, Reviewing, and Steering as Core Skills

Working effectively with agents introduces new, concrete skills. These are not abstract AI competencies. They are practical engineering capabilities that can be learned, practiced, and refined.

Prompting is fundamentally about clarity of intent, not clever wording. Engineers must learn to express goals, constraints, and acceptance criteria explicitly. Ambiguous instructions inevitably produce ambiguous results, regardless of model quality.

Reviewing agent output becomes a central capability. Engineers must assess not only whether a result appears plausible, but whether assumptions are valid, edge cases are addressed, and uncertainty is acceptable. This demands critical thinking rather than blind trust.

Steering agents is the third core skill. Engineers learn to adjust scope, refine constraints, and guide iteration without micromanaging execution. The goal is not to control every step, but to shape the solution space effectively.

These skills do not emerge automatically through exposure. They must be trained deliberately. Organizations that invest early in these capabilities see faster adoption and more robust outcomes.

Letting Go of Manual Execution as the Default

One of the hardest mindset shifts is releasing the need for direct execution. Many engineers instinctively equate quality with manual involvement. If they did not personally run a model or modify geometry, trust in the result decreases. This reaction is understandable. It becomes problematic only when it turns into a bottleneck. Trust in agent-based systems does not come from observing every step. It comes from transparency, consistency, and repeatability. Engineers must learn to evaluate outcomes first, while retaining the ability to inspect details when necessary.

Oversight replaces execution as the default mode of work. Engineers intervene when uncertainty is high, assumptions are unclear, or results deviate from expectations. Otherwise, they move on to higher-leverage decisions. Leaders play a critical role here. Reviewing and steering automated work must be framed as a higher form of professional contribution, not a downgrade.

Redefining What Good Engineering Work Looks Like

As agents take over routine execution, traditional performance signals lose relevance. Productivity can no longer be measured by hours spent in tools or by manual throughput.

Instead, new indicators matter:

- quality of decisions made
- speed and consistency of convergence
- ability to manage uncertainty and trade-offs
- contribution to reusable logic, rules, and workflows

Engineers who improve the system itself create disproportionate value. They reduce future effort not only for themselves, but for everyone who follows. Organizations must reflect this shift in evaluation, recognition, and career progression. If performance systems continue to reward manual heroics, behavior will not change, regardless of technology.

Addressing Fear Without Denial

Fear of replacement is real, even when leadership explicitly denies it. Agentic systems inevitably raise questions about long-term relevance, job security, and status. Avoiding these conversations does not reduce anxiety. It amplifies it. Successful organizations address this tension openly. They clarify that agents change how work is done, not whether expertise is needed. They make emerging roles visible. Agent builders, workflow owners, system stewards, and domain reviewers become critical positions.

> Most importantly, successful organizations involve their strongest engineers early. Those who understand the work best should help shape the system. This improves quality and sends a clear signal. Expertise is being elevated, not erased.

When engineers see their judgment embedded into the system rather than replaced by it, fear shifts toward ownership.

Learning as a Continuous, Shared Responsibility

Skill evolution does not end after initial onboarding. Agentic systems evolve continuously. Prompts improve, rules change, models update, and new edge cases appear. Organizations should establish lightweight but persistent learning loops. Short feedback cycles, shared examples, and visible improvements reinforce engagement. Engineers need to see that their input materially improves the system.

Learning must also be collective. Knowledge captured in prompts, rules, and workflows should be shared across teams rather than remaining local. This reinforces the idea that the system is a shared organizational asset, not a personal shortcut.

Identity Shift as the Hidden Success Factor

Ultimately, the hardest transition is not technical. It is identity related. Engineers move from tool operators to decision shapers, from executing tasks to designing systems, and from individual contributors to contributors to collective intelligence. Organizations that acknowledge and support this shift reduce resistance, accelerate adoption, and retain their most capable people. Those that ignore it risk a different outcome. The technology may work, but the organization will not. Agentic systems succeed when engineers experience themselves not as being automated away, but as being amplified. To support this transformation in practice, a skill, mindset, and identity evolution cheat sheet, dedicated to leaders and HR for evolving roles and skills, is provided in Section 6.4.

4.2.3 Turning Capability Into Adoption

The previous sections described how collaboration should be designed and how roles evolve. This section addresses something more fragile: What makes people actually use the system every day? Most acceptance problems do not originate from abstract fear of AI or general resistance to change. They emerge in everyday interactions. When working with the system feels awkward, risky, or unrewarding, engineers disengage. This happens not because they reject the idea of agents, but because using them does not yet feel like the easiest or safest way to get work done. The focus here is therefore practical rather than conceptual. Acceptance is built through daily experience. The objective is simple. Make working with agents feel useful, predictable, and reversible from the very beginning.

Start With Visible Relief, not Ambition

Acceptance grows when users experience immediate relief in their daily work. Early deployments should deliberately target tasks that engineers already consider low value. Preparation steps, coordination overhead, manual handoffs between tools, repetitive formatting, or routine checks are ideal entry points. These activities require little explanation and generate instant appreciation when they disappear.

Avoid positioning early agents as intelligent or advanced. Position them as helpers that take work off the table. When users feel that a system gives them back time without introducing risk, acceptance follows naturally. A simple rule applies. If the first interaction does not save noticeable time within days, the use case is too ambitious for this stage.

Make Agent Behavior Observable by Default

Do not rely on trust. Make behavior inspectable. Every agent action should leave a visible trace: What was done, in which order, and based on which inputs? This does not require verbose explanations, but it does require consistency. Users should never have to guess how a result came into existence.

Default views should emphasize structure and flow rather than raw detail. Deeper inspection must always be possible on demand, especially for domain experts. This allows quick validation without disrupting the workflow.

Predictability matters more than sophistication. Agents that behave consistently across similar situations are accepted faster than agents that occasionally surprise users with clever but unexplained decisions.

Actively Calibrate How Much Users See

One of the most common design mistakes is showing everyone everything. Different roles require different levels of detail. Engineers validating results need access to assumptions and intermediate states. Project leads need clarity on status, risks, and next steps. Management needs aggregated signals rather than execution detail. Interaction layers should reflect these differences. Start with simple summaries. Allow drill-down when needed. Avoid forcing users to process information that is irrelevant to their role. This calibration is not cosmetic. It directly influences whether agents feel supportive or exhausted to work with.

Embed Feedback Into Normal Work

If feedback requires extra meetings, forms, or documentation, it will not happen. Correction, override, and annotation must be part of normal task execution. When an engineer disagrees with an agent's output, capturing that disagreement should be as frictionless as continuing manually.

Overrides should never be framed as failures. They are expected inputs. Make it visible that corrections are used to improve the system. When users see their input reflected in later behavior, engagement increases quickly.

Recognition does not require formal rewards. Visibility is often enough. Engineers need to see that their feedback shapes the system rather than disappearing into a backlog.

Be Explicit About Limits and Failure Modes

Uncertainty is acceptable. Surprise is not. Agents should communicate clearly what they can do reliably and where they may struggle. Known edge cases should be documented and referenced. This reduces defensive behavior and prevents unrealistic expectations.

Avoid aspirational language in early stages. Do not talk about full autonomy while the system is still learning. Frame progress incrementally. This creates confidence instead of skepticism.

> Clarity about limits helps users decide when to rely on agents and when to intervene.

Design Reversibility Into Every Workflow

Acceptance depends on perceived control. Users must always know how to pause, stop, or bypass automation. Manual fallback paths should be obvious and socially accepted. Engineers should never feel forced to use agents to demonstrate commitment or compliance. Opting out temporarily must not require justification. When people feel safe stepping back during uncertainty, they are more willing to engage when conditions are favorable.

Treat Acceptance as an Operational Metric

Acceptance should be observed, not assumed. Track actual usage rather than availability. Monitor how often agents are used end-to-end, where overrides occur, and when manual fallbacks are chosen. These signals are far more informative than surveys. Declining usage is not a user problem. It is a design signal. Organizations that respond to these signals early adjust faster and avoid silent rejection.

Acceptance Follows Usability, not Persuasion

Trust does not need to be argued about when systems behave well. When agents reduce friction, act predictably, expose their steps, and respect human control, acceptance emerges naturally. When they do not, no amount of communication will compensate.

> The goal is therefore not to convince users to trust agents. It is to design systems that feel safe, useful, and easy to work with.

4.2.4 Finding the Right Personas

When organizations discuss building an agentic system, the conversation often centers on platforms, models, or integration complexity. In practice, none of these factors determine success as much as the people who build the first system. Early personas do far more than implement functionality. They shape how the system reasons, where it draws boundaries, and how it will be perceived across the organization for years to come. They also strongly influence whether problems are treated as solvable challenges or as fundamental showstoppers.

The first agentic system is not neutral infrastructure. It embodies assumptions about what matters, how decisions should be made, and where responsibility lies. These assumptions are rarely written down explicitly. Instead, they are encoded through thousands of small design choices. What gets automated first. What remains manual. How uncertainty is handled. When escalation happens. Whether transparency is prioritized over speed. All of this reflects the mindset of the people building the system.

In addition, early builders must integrate legacy tools and environments. In practice, these tools often lack critical interfaces or clean integration points. Creative workarounds and pragmatic alternative solutions become necessary. How these compromises are made, and how openly their limitations are communicated, again depends on the personas involved.

When the early personas are poorly chosen, two failure modes are common. In the first, the system becomes technically impressive but organizationally fragile. It works in controlled settings, but engineers do not trust it, understand it, or feel represented by it. Adoption stalls. In the second, resistance emerges early. High performers disengage, either because they feel threatened or because the system does not reflect the reality of their work and misses critical integrations. In both cases, the technology is blamed, even though the root cause lies in persona selection.

Getting the personas right from the beginning changes this dynamic. The system reflects how work actually happens, not how it is documented. Decisions feel familiar rather than alien. Engineers recognize their own reasoning patterns in agent behavior. Trust grows faster because credibility is built into the system from day one. Persona selection is therefore not an HR detail. It is a core design decision.

Core Personas Required in Early MAS Development

Building the first multi-agent system requires a small number of clearly defined personas. These are not job titles. They are responsibility profiles. In practice, one person may cover more than one persona, especially in small teams. What matters is that all perspectives are represented deliberately.

The domain expert

The domain expert anchors the system in reality. This person understands the real workflow, not just the documented process. They know where engineers improvise, where rules are bent, and where judgment matters most.

Their primary contribution is sense-making. They can distinguish between how work is supposed to happen and how it actually happens under time pressure, uncertainty, or incomplete information. This distinction is critical. An agentic system that reflects only formal processes will always feel artificial to practitioners.

Credibility is essential. The domain expert must be respected by peers. When others recognize their reasoning embedded in the system, acceptance increases naturally. This also requires a willingness to externalize tacit knowledge. Heuristics, mental shortcuts, and experiential rules must be made explicit.

Equally important is psychological readiness. The domain expert must be comfortable seeing parts of their expertise embedded into a system. This is not a loss of relevance. It is an amplification of impact. Without this mindset, knowledge sharing becomes guarded and the system remains shallow.

The automation-oriented Engineer

This persona connects intent with implementation. An automation-oriented engineer thinks in systems rather than individual tools. They understand workflows across CAD, simulation, data handling, and documentation, and can translate domain intent into structured, executable logic.

Their defining strength is pragmatism. They prioritize robustness over elegance. They care less about perfect abstractions and more about solutions that survive messy inputs, edge cases, and real-world constraints. Curiosity toward automation is essential, as is the absence of fear toward it.

This persona acts as a translator. They prevent domain experts from being forced into technical abstractions and ensure that platforms are not designed in isolation from engineering reality. Without this bridge, teams fragment into “those who know the work” and “those who build the system,” with predictable and damaging results.

The agentic architect

The agentic architect thinks in responsibilities, interactions, and boundaries. Their focus is not on individual agent intelligence, but on how agents, humans, and systems interact as a whole. They design orchestration rather than features. They define what each agent is responsible for, where handovers occur, and how escalation is triggered. Failure modes are a central concern. This persona continuously asks what happens when assumptions break, data is missing, or results conflict.

Restraint is a critical quality. Early-stage systems suffer most from over-automation. The architect deliberately limits autonomy in the beginning while keeping long-term scalability in mind. Short-term pilots are designed so they can grow without requiring complete rewrites.

The product owner

The product owner owns outcomes, not technology. This persona ensures that the system serves real users and real use cases rather than becoming an internal showcase. They balance speed, quality, and organizational readiness. They protect the team from unrealistic expectations, shifting priorities, and political pressure. This protection creates the space required for learning.

The product owner also provides continuity. They hold the long-term vision beyond the first pilot and ensure that short-term decisions do not undermine future scaling. Without this role, many agentic initiatives lose direction after early success.

Characteristics to Actively Seek

Beyond formal roles, certain personal characteristics are especially valuable in early agentic teams. Strong intrinsic motivation to improve how work is done is essential. Early development involves friction, iteration, and ambiguity. Without genuine motivation, progress slows quickly. Comfort with uncertainty matters more than perfectionism. Early systems are incomplete by design. The ability to move forward without full clarity is a prerequisite. A willingness to challenge existing processes respectfully enables progress without alienation. The goal is improvement, not disruption for its own sake.

Clear communication is critical. Complex ideas must be explained to engineers, managers, and skeptics alike. Ambiguity breeds resistance.

Finally, openness to feedback is non-negotiable. Early builders must accept corrections from both humans and the system itself. Learning flows in both directions.

Characteristics to Avoid in Early Phases

Certain profiles consistently create risk in early agentic initiatives. Pure tool specialists without process understanding tend to optimize locally and miss systemic effects. The result is brittle automation.

Highly political actors tend to seek visibility rather than learning to distort priorities. Early agentic work requires patience, not spotlight-driven behavior.

Experts unwilling to externalize knowledge create single points of failure and prevent system learning. Engineers primarily motivated by job protection concerns often block progress implicitly. Fear-driven behavior spreads quickly.

Finally, teams built exclusively from IT or exclusively from engineering lack balance. Successful systems emerge at the intersection of both worlds.

Early Team Composition Principles

Early agentic teams should be deliberately small. Trust and speed matter more than coverage. A clear mandate and protected time allocation are essential. Part-time commitment almost always leads to superficial systems.

Direct access to real users and real problems grounds development. Abstract use cases produce abstract systems. Psychological safety must be explicit. Experimentation requires permission to fail without blame.

> **!** Most importantly, teams should recognize the significance of their work. They are not just building a tool. They are shaping how the organization will work in the future.

The Long-Term Impact of Getting Personas Right

When the right personas are involved from the start, effects compound quickly. Trust builds faster because credibility is embedded. Agent behavior reflects real engineering judgment. Adoption accelerates because peers recognize themselves in the system. Internal capability grows, reducing dependency on external vendors. Knowledge accumulates inside the organization instead of leaking out. Most importantly, the organization does not end up with a one-off solution. It develops durable capability. An agentic system built by the right people becomes more than automation. It becomes a reflection of how the organization thinks, decides, and learns over time.

4.2.5 Embedding Responsibility Into Agent-Based Work

Agentic systems change how decisions are prepared, justified, and executed. They do more than automate tasks. They redistribute responsibility, make assumptions explicit, and expose reasoning that was previously implicit or hidden within individual expertise. This shift makes governance unavoidable.

Organizations sometimes postpone governance discussions out of concern that structure might slow innovation. In practice, the opposite is true. Without clear responsibilities, agent-based systems drift into one of two states. They either remain fragile experiments that depend on a small number of individuals, or they create ambiguity around accountability that erodes trust and adoption. Both outcomes prevent scaling.

Governance in the context of agentic systems is therefore not about control for its own sake. It is about making responsibility explicit in an environment where work is shared between humans and agents. Engineers must know who owns outcomes. Managers must understand where decisions are made. The organization must be able to introduce change deliberately, validate it, and reverse it when necessary. When governance is designed well, it becomes an enabler. It removes ambiguity, allows autonomy to grow without losing accountability, and creates the conditions under which agent-based systems can operate safely in decision-relevant contexts.

Clear Ownership Structures

The foundation of governance is explicit ownership. Agentic systems cut across traditional organizational boundaries. Without named owners, responsibility fragments quickly and decisions fall into gaps. At a minimum, three ownership roles must be established.

The **product owner** for the agentic system owns outcomes rather than technology. This role ensures that the system delivers value to real users, remains aligned with business priorities, and evolves in a direction the organization actually needs. The product owner decides which use cases are in scope, which are postponed, and when the system is ready to move from experimentation into broader use.

The **technical owner** is responsible for the platform, integrations, and operational stability. This includes the orchestration layer, interfaces to CAx tools, data access, security, and runtime reliability. As tools, APIs, and infrastructure evolve, the technical owner ensures that the system remains operable and resilient.

The **domain owners** are responsible for agent logic and validation within their respective areas. They own the correctness of rules, assumptions, and decision logic encoded in the agents. This role must sit with senior domain experts who have both credibility and authority. Governance fails when domain ownership is delegated to people without decision power.

These roles may be held by individuals or small teams, but they must be clearly named. Shared responsibility without clarity almost always results in no responsibility at all.

Decision Authority and Escalation Logic

An agentic system must never leave decision authority implicit. Every automated or semi-automated action requires a clearly defined scope and an explicit owner. Governance begins by defining what agents may decide autonomously, what they may only recommend, and where human approval is mandatory. These boundaries are not static. They evolve with maturity and experience. At any given point, however, they must be unambiguous.

Escalation rules are equally critical. Agents will encounter uncertainty, conflicting signals, or edge cases. When this happens, the system must know when to stop, whom to notify, and which information to provide for human resolution. Escalation should be treated as normal operation, not as failure.

Responsibility chains must be traceable. When an outcome is questioned, it must be possible to reconstruct which agent acted, under which rules, based on which data, and which human approved or overrode the result. This traceability protects both individuals and the organization.

Impact on Informal Power Structures

Governance is not only a technical or procedural topic. It has real organizational consequences. Multi-agent systems reduce dependence on individual knowledge gatekeepers. Expertise that was previously accessible only through specific people becomes encoded, shared, and reproducible. This is one of the system's greatest strengths, but it also reshapes informal power structures.

Some resistance does not stem from fear of automation, but from loss of exclusivity. Transparency makes reasoning visible. Shared logic replaces personal discretion. Governance must acknowledge this dynamic explicitly. Managing this transition requires clarity and fairness. The objective is not to devalue expertise, but to amplify it. Engineers who contribute knowledge to the system increase their influence rather than lose it. Governance should reinforce this message by making ownership visible, recognizing contributions, and ensuring that experts remain central to decision-making even as logic becomes shared.

Documentation as an Operational Requirement

In agent-based systems, documentation is an operational necessity. Governance must require consistent documentation of execution behavior. At a minimum, this includes which agents ran, in which order, and with which outcomes. Data sources and assumptions must be recorded so results can be understood, challenged, and revisited later.

Versioning is critical. Agents, rules, and prompts evolve continuously. Every execution must be traceable to the versions that were active at the time. Without this, learning stalls and incidents cannot be analyzed reliably. This level of documentation supports audits, enables continuous improvement, and protects the organization when decisions are challenged. Over time, it also creates a valuable internal knowledge base.

Change Management for Agent Systems

Agent based systems are living systems. Governance must therefore include explicit change management. Changes to agent logic, rules, or prompts should follow a structured release process. This process does not need to be heavy, but it must be deliberate. Updates should be tested against representative cases, validated by domain owners, and communicated clearly to users.

Rollback mechanisms are essential. Not every change improves the system. The ability to revert quickly prevents loss of trust and limits operational risk. Reversibility should be treated as a core design principle.

Clear change processes allow the system to evolve continuously without destabilizing operations. They also signal professionalism and reliability to users.

Early Involvement of HR and Worker Representation

Governance must extend beyond engineering and IT. Agentic systems reshape how work is structured, how roles evolve, and how value is created. These changes intersect directly with HR policies, career paths, and worker representation frameworks. Early involvement of these stakeholders prevents misunderstandings and late-stage resistance.

HR engagement helps align agent adoption with role development, training, and recognition. Involving worker representation ensures transparency and addresses concerns before they solidify into opposition. This is not about slowing transformation. It is about anchoring it institutionally, so progress remains sustainable.

Governance as an Enabler, Not a Brake

Governance does not constrain agent-based systems. It enables them. When ownership is clear, authority is explicit, and change is managed deliberately, agents can operate with confidence and appropriate autonomy. Engineers know where responsibility lies. Managers understand how decisions are made. The organization retains control over how the system evolves. Without governance, agentic systems remain impressive demonstrations. With governance, they become reliable infrastructure. In the long run, governance is what allows organizations to move from asking whether agents can be trusted to deciding how much autonomy they are prepared to grant.

4.2.6 Operating Models for Sustainable Agent Adoption

Once an agent-based system moves beyond experimentation, questions of structure become unavoidable. Who builds agents? Who maintains them? Who decides how quickly they evolve and where they are applied? These are not technical questions. They are organizational choices that determine whether agent-based systems become a scalable capability or remain a collection of isolated solutions.

The operating model defines how responsibility, expertise, and decision-making are distributed across the organization. It shapes how quickly new use cases can be addressed, how consistently quality is maintained, and how resilient the system remains as people, priorities, and technologies change. When this choice is made too late, friction is almost inevitable. Central teams become overloaded. Domain teams feel constrained. Governance turns reactive rather than intentional.

There is no universally correct operating model. Different organizations adopt different structures depending on size, culture, regulatory context, and strategic ambition. What matters is making the choice explicit and understanding the trade-offs involved. The following models represent common patterns observed in practice. Many organizations move between them over time or deliberately combine elements from several approaches.

Center of Excellence Model

In a center of excellence model, responsibility for agentic systems is centralized. A dedicated team owns standards, governance, architecture, and often a significant portion of implementation. This team acts as the methodological authority for agent-based automation across the organization.

Centralization creates clarity. Standards for agent design, data handling, security, and quality are defined once and applied consistently. Methodological expertise accumulates quickly because the same group works across multiple use cases. This concentration of experience is particularly valuable in early phases, when patterns are still emerging and mistakes are expensive to repeat.

A center of excellence also simplifies governance. Decision authority is clear. Escalation paths are short. Regulatory, security, and compliance requirements can be addressed systematically rather than negotiated case by case. For organizations operating in highly regulated environments, this level of control can be decisive.

At the same time, the model has clear limitations. As demand grows, central teams can become bottlenecks. Distance from day-to-day domain work may slow adaptation to local needs. There is also a cultural risk. Agentic systems may be perceived as something built "by others," which can reduce ownership and dampen adoption within engineering teams.

The center of excellence model works best when agent-based systems are still immature, when consistency and risk control outweigh speed, or when organizational culture favors centralized expertise.

Federated Teams Model

In a federated model, responsibility is distributed. Domain teams build and operate their own agents close to the work they support. Expertise resides where problems occur, and adaptation to local workflows happens naturally. This proximity creates tangible advantages. Domain experts can directly shape agent behavior. Feedback loops are short. Use cases emerge from real needs. Adoption is often higher because teams feel ownership over the systems they use.

Scalability in this model comes from parallelism. Instead of one central team scaling its capacity, many teams innovate at the same time. Once basic capabilities are established, this can dramatically increase speed and coverage. The trade-off is fragmentation risk. Without strong coordination, teams may solve the same problems repeatedly, apply inconsistent standards, or embed conflicting assumptions. Governance becomes more complex, particularly around security, data reuse, and quality assurance.

Federated models require a higher level of organizational maturity. Shared principles must be understood and respected even when implementation is decentralized. Without this foundation, complexity grows faster than value.

Hybrid Models

Most mature organizations converge on a hybrid model. This approach combines centralized and decentralized elements in a deliberate and structured way. Typically, a central team owns the platform, core architecture, governance frameworks, and shared services. This includes identity management, security, data access policies, monitoring, and core agent frameworks. The central function provides coherence, safety, and long-term maintainability.

At the same time, domain teams retain ownership of use cases. They design, adapt, and operate agents within defined boundaries. Responsibility for domain logic, validation, and continuous improvement remains close to the experts who understand the work best.

The hybrid model balances speed and control. It enables local learning and innovation without sacrificing organizational alignment. Dependency risks are reduced. Knowledge is distributed but not fragmented. This balance does require explicit interfaces. Clear definitions are needed for what is centrally governed and what is locally decided. Ambiguity leads to conflict. Clarity enables autonomy.

Choosing and Evolving the Model

Operating models are not static. Many organizations start with a center of excellence to build foundational capability and establish standards. As confidence and competence grow, elements of federation are introduced. Over time, hybrid structures often emerge naturally.

The critical factor is intentionality. The operating model should reflect the current maturity of both the technology and the organization. It should be revisited regularly as usage scales, new domains are added, and agent autonomy increases. What ultimately matters is not which model is chosen, but whether the model supports learning, ownership, and trust. Agentic systems scale through people as much as through software. The operating model is the mechanism that connects the two.

4.2.7 Enabling People to Work with Agents

Introducing an agentic system into engineering without a structured enablement strategy is one of the fastest ways to stall adoption. The technology may work. The architecture may be sound. The use cases may be well chosen. Yet without deliberate training and enablement, the system remains underused, misunderstood, or quietly bypassed.

This is because agent-based systems change how work is done, not just how tools are operated. They shift effort from execution to supervision. They redistribute decision preparation across humans and agents. They expose assumptions, intermediate steps, and reasoning in ways that traditional tools never did. These changes require new skills, new mental models, and in some cases a redefinition of professional identity.

Training for agent-based systems therefore cannot be treated as classical software onboarding. It is not enough to explain which interface to use or which button to click. What people must learn is how to collaborate with agents effectively, when to rely on them, when to challenge them, when to intervene, and how everyday interaction contributes to improving the system over time.

Another critical aspect is differentiation. Not everyone in the organization interacts with the system in the same way or carries the same responsibility. Users, super users, maintainers, and managers engage with agentic systems from fundamentally different perspectives. Enablement must therefore be role-specific, progressive, and tightly connected to real work. The objective is not to turn everyone into an AI expert. It is to ensure that each role understands its responsibilities, control points, and contribution to long-term success.

Enabling Users—Confident Operation and Informed Intervention

End users are the backbone of any agentic system. If they do not trust the system or do not understand how to work with it, adoption stops regardless of technical quality. User enablement must therefore focus on three practical capabilities. The first is operating the system. Users need to know how to instruct the agentic system, provide inputs, review outputs, and navigate the available interfaces. This includes chat-based interaction, structured review screens, and result summaries. The emphasis should be on clarity and predictability rather than completeness. Users should feel confident handling daily tasks without needing to understand the full technical architecture.

The second capability is interpreting outputs. Agent-based systems rarely produce a single definitive answer. They generate recommendations, options, and assessments that must be understood in context. Users need to know what a result represents, which assumptions were applied, and how confident the system is. Effective training therefore includes examples of strong results, borderline cases, and known limitations.

The third capability is knowing when to intervene. One of the most important user skills is recognizing when automation should be paused, corrected, or overridden. This includes identifying missing inputs, unrealistic assumptions, or results that conflict with domain intuition. Users must be encouraged explicitly to intervene. Intervention is not a failure. It is a core learning mechanism that improves the system over time.

User enablement works best when it is closely tied to real cases. Short, scenario-based sessions grounded in actual workflows are far more effective than abstract instruction. Documentation should support daily work, not attempt to replace hands-on learning.

Developing Super Users—Adaptation and First-Line Support

Super users play a critical bridging role between everyday users and the system itself. They are not necessarily developers, but they understand both the domain and the structure of the agentic system well enough to adapt it and resolve common issues.

Their first responsibility is adaptation. As real usage reveals new patterns, edge cases, or inefficiencies, super users help adjust automation within defined boundaries. This may involve modifying parameters, rearranging steps, or refining escalation logic. Their involvement prevents every improvement request from turning into a development task.

The second responsibility is first-line support. Super users answer questions, clarify behavior, and resolve common misunderstandings before issues escalate. This reduces friction and builds confidence across the user base. Their effectiveness comes from understanding both the system's behavior and the practical constraints of daily engineering work.

The third responsibility is translation. Super users translate domain feedback into actionable system improvements and explain system behavior back to users in familiar language. This translation role is essential in early phases, when shared mental models are still forming.

Enablement for super users must go beyond basic operation. It should include automation logic, typical failure modes, and the rationale behind key design decisions. Close connection to maintainers and product owners ensures alignment and prevents local optimization.

Preparing Maintainers—Sustaining Quality and Learning Over Time

Maintainers are responsible for the long-term health of the agentic system. Their importance grows as the system scales and becomes more deeply embedded in daily operations. One core responsibility is rule maintenance. Engineering rules, constraints, and decision logic must be reviewed, updated, and validated continuously.

Standards change. Best practices evolve. New failure modes appear. Maintainers ensure that the system reflects current reality rather than outdated assumptions.

Another responsibility is prompt evolution. Prompts define how agents' reason, explain, and interact. They are not static artifacts. As usage grows, maintainers refine prompts to improve robustness, clarity, and consistency. This includes addressing edge cases, reducing ambiguity, and aligning language with organizational norms.

Maintainers are also responsible for validating model behavior. Large language models can change subtly over time, even without explicit version changes. Maintainers must monitor outputs, run regression tests on representative cases, and detect drift early. When necessary, they coordinate mitigation measures such as prompt updates, increased human oversight, or temporary model adjustments.

Enablement for maintainers requires a combination of domain understanding, system literacy, and operational discipline. They do not need to be AI researchers. They do need to understand how changes propagate through the system and how to validate improvements without disrupting productive work.

Enabling Management—Informed Decisions and Realistic Expectations

Management enablement is often underestimated, yet it is decisive for long-term success. Managers shape expectations, allocate resources, and set the tone for adoption. First, managers must understand opportunities and limitations. Agent-based systems can significantly improve coordination, consistency, and speed. They cannot eliminate uncertainty, responsibility, or the need for judgment. Enablement should therefore clarify what the system is designed to support and where human accountability remains essential.

Second, managers must learn how to interpret system outputs in decision-making. Agent-generated summaries, risk indicators, and scenario comparisons are decision support, not final answers. Managers need to ask the right questions. Which assumptions were used. What alternatives were considered. Where uncertainty remains.

Third, management plays a critical role in expectation setting. Overpromising creates pressure that undermines trust. Underpromising stalls momentum. Enablement should help managers communicate progress realistically, recognize learning, and frame early imperfections as part of a deliberate transformation. Well-enabled managers protect teams from unrealistic demands and give the system time to mature. Poorly enabled managers turn promising initiatives into credibility risks.

Creating and Legitimizing New Career Paths

A structured enablement roadmap also creates space for new roles and career paths. As agentic systems become part of everyday work, new profiles emerge naturally: automation engineers who combine domain expertise with system thinking, agent architects who design workflows, boundaries, and escalation logic, as well as system owners who are accountable for end-to-end performance rather than isolated tasks.

These roles must be visible and legitimate. Without recognition, capable contributors hesitate to invest their energy, fearing that automation work is peripheral or risky. Explicit role definitions, career paths, and recognition mechanisms signal that building and maintaining agent-based systems is valued work. This is particularly important for retaining top performers. When automation work is framed as shaping the future organization rather than replacing oneself, motivation increases and resistance decreases.

Enablement as a Continuous Process

Training and enablement for agentic systems is not a one-time effort. It evolves alongside the system itself. As agents become more capable, interaction patterns change. As autonomy increases, supervision and judgment become more important. As systems spread across domains, shared language and governance gain relevance.

Organizations that treat enablement as an ongoing capability will create a virtuous cycle. Users become more confident. Feedback improves. The system learns faster. Value compounds over time. In the end, the effectiveness of an agent-based system is bound not by its algorithms, but by the organization's ability to learn how to work with it.

4.2.8 Aligning Incentives With Agent-Based Value Creation

Every organization gets the behavior it rewards. This becomes especially visible once agentic systems enter everyday engineering work. Agent-based automation changes how value is created. There are fewer manual steps and less visible effort. More time is spent defining goals, reviewing outcomes, improving logic, and maintaining systems. If success continues to be measured by hours worked, manual throughput, or individual execution speed, the system is undermined from the very beginning.

In such environments, resistance is a rational response. Engineers protect manual work because it remains measurable and defensible. Contributions to automation are postponed because they are harder to justify. Learning slows. Adoption becomes superficial. The system exists, but it never becomes critical to how work is actually done.

This failure mode has little to do with model quality or system architecture. It is a management issue. Organizations ask for a new way of working while continuing to reward the old one. For agentic systems to move beyond pilots, incentives must be realigned deliberately. What gets measured defines what matters. What gets rewarded defines where people invest their effort. If adoption, quality, and reduced coordination are not explicitly valued, they will not emerge organically. Incentives and successful measurements are therefore not a reporting exercise. They are a control mechanism. Designed well, they turn agent-based automation into a self-reinforcing capability. Designed poorly, they silently neutralize it.

Measuring What Actually Matters

Traditional performance metrics tend to focus on activity rather than outcome. In agent-based environments, this approach quickly becomes misleading. A successful system may reduce visible activity while increasing overall impact. Measurement must therefore shift from effort to effect.

One primary indicator is adoption and sustained usage. Initial curiosity does not constitute success. What matters is whether teams continue to rely on the system once novelty fades. Sustained usage signals that the system delivers value under everyday conditions and that trust has reached a level where agent outputs influence real decisions.

Output quality and consistency form the second pillar. Agent-based systems create value not simply by being faster, but by reducing variance. Consistent results across similar cases, transparent assumptions, and predictable behavior matter more than occasional brilliance. Measuring quality requires clear acceptance criteria and tracking how often outputs meet them without extensive rework.

Cycle time reduction is another important metric, but it must be interpreted carefully. The goal is not raw speed at any cost. The relevant question is whether decision-ready results are available earlier and with less coordination overhead. Shorter feedback loops and fewer waiting periods often matter more than absolute execution speed.

Equally important is the reduction of coordination effort. Many engineering processes are slowed not by technical complexity, but by alignment work. Meetings, emails, clarifications, and late rework consume significant amounts of time without appearing in formal metrics. Successful agent-based systems reduce this hidden tax. Tracking fewer handovers, fewer clarification loops, or fewer late-stage corrections provides a more realistic picture of value creation.

Together, these indicators shift attention from individual productivity to system-level effectiveness.

Aligning Incentives With Agent-Based Work

Measurement alone does not change behavior. Incentives do. In agent-based environments, organizations must explicitly value contributions to the system itself. Improving workflows, refining rules, validating outputs, or contributing domain knowledge are all forms of productive work. If these activities remain secondary or invisible, they will consistently lose out to manual execution that is easier to justify.

Rewarding system improvement instead of manual effort represents a fundamental shift. In traditional setups, effort is often equated with value. In agent-based systems, the opposite is frequently true. The highest value contributions are those that reduce the need for future effort. Incentive structures must reflect this by recognizing those who eliminate work, not just those who perform it efficiently.

Protecting time for system improvement is equally important. Without explicit protection, improvement work competes with delivery pressure and usually losses. Organizations that succeed allocate dedicated capacity for refining agents, updating rules, and validating behavior. This time should not be framed as overhead. It is an investment in future throughput and quality.

Crucially, incentive alignment is not limited to bonuses. Career progression, visibility, and influence matter just as much. Engineers who contribute to building and improving agentic systems should gain recognition as system builders and shapers, not as people who stepped away from real engineering.

Avoiding the Trap of Tool-Centric Metrics

A common mistake is treating tool usage as a proxy for success. High usage numbers may look impressive, but they reveal little about value. In some cases, increased usage even signals inefficiency, for example when users compensate for poor automation through repeated manual interaction.

Agentic systems should be evaluated by their outcomes, not by how often they are touched. A mature system may operate largely in the background and surface only when human judgment is required. Low visible interaction can therefore indicate success rather than failure.

For this reason, organizations should resist relying on superficial metrics such as number of prompts, agent calls, or clicks. These indicators are useful for technical monitoring, but they should not drive organizational decisions. The guiding question must always remain whether the system improves how work is done, not how frequently it is used.

Making Success Visible and Collective

Recognition plays a powerful role in shaping behavior. In many organizations, improvements remain invisible because they are distributed across processes rather than tied to individual achievements. Agent-based systems amplify this effect. When work disappears through automation, it can easily go unnoticed. Making improvements visible counteracts this dynamic. Public acknowledgment of contributions signals that this work matters. Highlighting reduced cycle times, avoided rework, or improved consistency translates abstract benefits into tangible outcomes.

Linking agent-based success to team outcomes reinforces the collaborative nature of this way of working. Agentic systems thrive when knowledge is shared and encoded collectively. Recognition mechanisms should therefore emphasize team-level impact and cross-functional collaboration. This visibility also supports trust. When people see concrete examples of how agent-based systems improve outcomes, skepticism gives way to curiosity and engagement.

Designing for Long-Term Behavior, Not Short-Term Wins

Incentives shape behavior over time. Poorly aligned metrics can undermine even the most capable technical systems. Well-designed incentives, by contrast, turn agent-based automation into a self-reinforcing capability.

When success is measured by adoption, quality, and reduced coordination, and when contributions to system improvement are recognized and rewarded, organizations create a virtuous cycle. People invest in making the system better because doing so advances both collective outcomes and individual standing.

The central insight is straightforward. Systems do not create value on their own. People decide whether that value materializes. Incentives and measurements of success determine where attention flows. Getting them right ensures that agent-based automation evolves from an experiment into a lasting organizational advantage.

4.2.9 What to Remember When Everything Else Changes

Agentic systems do not succeed because they are powerful. They succeed because people choose to work with them. This section has revealed a consistent pattern. Technology sets the ceiling. Human behavior determines the outcome. How agents are introduced, explained, governed, rewarded, and embedded into daily work ultimately decides whether they become trusted collaborators or quietly ignored tools. Acceptance is not created through persuasion or mandate. It emerges through tangible relief in daily work, transparent behavior, fair incentives, and respect for professional judgment.

Organizations that treat agent-based systems as a people transformation rather than a software rollout gain a decisive advantage. They move faster without increasing risk. They attract their strongest engineers instead of triggering defensive resistance. Learning becomes a shared organizational asset. Operating models evolve in which agents amplify expertise instead of competing with it.

> **!** In this context, autonomy is not the goal. Trust is—and trust is earned through consistency, clarity, and control.

Ultimately, the most important design decision is not how intelligent the agents become. It is how deliberately the organization changes around them.

4.3 When Intelligence Meets Reality: Risks in Agent-Based Automation

Agentic systems open up powerful new possibilities for engineering work. They accelerate coordination, reduce manual effort, and make complex decision processes more transparent and repeatable. Precisely because of this potential, they also introduce new risks that organizations must address deliberately. The purpose of this section is not to question whether agent-based systems should be adopted. That question has already been addressed in the preceding sections. Instead, the focus here is more practical. What can realistically go wrong? Where are the natural limits of agentic systems? And how can organizations recognize and manage these boundaries without losing momentum or trust?

A common mistake in early agentic initiatives is to treat risk as a purely technical issue. In practice, failures rarely originate from a single malfunctioning model or tool. They emerge from the interaction between probabilistic reasoning, complex tool chains, human expectations, organizational structures, and legal or regulatory constraints. A system can be technically sound and still fail if it is over-trusted, insufficiently observed, misaligned with responsibility structures, or deployed in contexts it was never designed to handle.

Another important dynamic is that many risks increase with success. As agents become faster, more capable, and more fluent, their outputs appear increasingly convincing. This can reduce human scrutiny at exactly the point where scrutiny is still required. Similarly, as agent-based systems scale across teams and projects, small inconsistencies, implicit assumptions, or unclear ownership structures can compound into systemic issues. Risk management in this context is therefore not about slowing adoption. It is about enabling safe and sustainable growth.

This section deliberately avoids repeating guidance on architecture, operating models, or change management. Those topics were covered earlier. Instead, the emphasis here is on categories of risk and limitation that remain even when best practices are applied. Some risks can be mitigated through technical measures such as grounding, monitoring, or staged rollouts. Others require explicit organizational decisions, clear accountability, and conscious expectation management. A few limitations cannot be removed at all and must be accepted as part of working with intelligent, probabilistic systems.

The intent is not to create fear or hesitation. On the contrary, organizations that understand these risks early tend to move faster and with greater confidence. By making limitations explicit, they avoid unrealistic expectations and build trust based on transparency. In this sense, risk awareness is not a counterweight to innovation. It is a prerequisite for making agentic systems a durable and reliable part of everyday engineering work.

4.3.1 Understanding Technical Risks in Agentic Workflows

Agentic systems often appear convincing very early. Even small prototypes can read documents, interpret geometry, trigger tools, and produce well-structured outputs that look remarkably professional. This early success is both a strength and a risk. It creates momentum, builds excitement, and accelerates adoption. At the same time, it can conceal technical fragilities that only become visible once systems are used repeatedly, scaled across teams, or trusted in real decision-making contexts.

Technical risks in agent-based systems differ fundamentally from those in classical software. Traditional systems tend to fail loudly. They crash, raise errors, or refuse to execute. Agentic systems can fail quietly. They may produce outputs that look correct, are well written, and internally consistent, while still being wrong, incomplete, or based on flawed assumptions. In engineering environments, this is particularly dangerous. Many decisions are irreversible or costly to undo. Detecting errors late often means absorbing financial, safety, or reputational impact.

Longevity adds another layer of risk. Agentic systems are not one-off tools. They are designed to evolve, learn, and accumulate knowledge over time. This makes them sensitive to gradual degradation. Small changes in input data, tool behavior, prompts, or rules can compound silently. Without deliberate safeguards, systems that worked well during pilots may slowly drift away from reliability without any obvious breaking point.

For these reasons, technical risk management is not about slowing down innovation. It is about enabling safe learning, preserving trust, and ensuring that increasing autonomy does not turn into uncontrolled behavior. The following sections outline the most relevant technical risk categories that emerge in real-world deployments of agent-based systems.

Hallucination and Incorrect Reasoning

One of the most discussed risks of large language models is hallucination. In the context of multi-agent systems, this risk takes a specific form. Agents may produce conclusions that are linguistically fluent, logically structured, and contextually plausible, while still being factually incorrect or based on false assumptions.

This risk is amplified in engineering environments because agents often operate across multiple domains simultaneously. A single workflow may combine requirement interpretation, geometry analysis, simulation setup, and cost estimation. An incorrect assumption introduced early can propagate across agents and remain undetected until late in the process.

Hallucination does not necessarily mean inventing entirely new facts. More commonly, it appears as overconfident extrapolation. The agent fills gaps in data with assumptions that are reasonable in general but wrong in the specific context. In human work, such assumptions are often challenged through experience or informal checks. In automated workflows, they may pass unnoticed.

Mitigation requires a layered approach. Grounding is essential. Agents should rely on explicit data sources, structured inputs, and rule-based extraction wherever possible. Reasoning must be constrained by clearly defined rules and thresholds for tasks that can be formalized. Validation steps need to be built into workflows rather than added later as manual checks. This includes cross-checks between agents, consistency checks against historical cases, and explicit comparison of assumptions against actual inputs.

> The objective is not to eliminate hallucination entirely. That is unrealistic. The objective is to make it detectable, bounded, and recoverable.

Over-Trust Due to Apparent Competence

A less obvious but equally dangerous risk is over-trust. Agentic systems often communicate through fluent natural language, clean tables, and polished visual outputs. This presentation quality increases perceived correctness, even when underlying reasoning is weak or incomplete. Humans are particularly susceptible to this effect. When outputs look professional, engineers may unconsciously reduce verification effort. This tendency increases under time pressure or after repeated exposure to results that appear reasonable. The risk here is not malicious behavior or obvious technical failure. It is cognitive bias. Fluent explanations and polished visuals create an illusion of certainty. Over time, this can erode critical thinking and reduce the willingness to challenge results.

Mitigation starts with interface design. Systems should make uncertainty explicit. Confidence indicators, assumption lists, and highlighted data gaps help users understand where results are robust and where they are fragile. Comparison views are especially effective. Showing agent-generated results alongside historical cases or manual baselines reintroduces context and anchors judgment.

Deliberate friction also plays a role. For critical decisions, the system should require explicit acknowledgement of assumptions or acceptance of residual risk. This keeps humans mentally engaged and reinforces that agents support decisions rather than replace responsibility.

Data Quality and Availability

Data quality remains a foundational risk for any automated system. In multi-agent systems, this risk has a nuanced character. Large language models are surprisingly robust against noisy inputs. They can filter irrelevant information, infer structure from semi-structured documents, and cope with incomplete data better than many rule-based systems.

This apparent robustness can be misleading. While LLMs can filter some forms of garbage, they cannot reliably detect all inconsistencies, outdated inputs, or missing context. If foundational data are wrong, incomplete, or misaligned with reality, the system will still produce outputs that look coherent and convincing.

A related challenge is that much engineering knowledge is not documented. It resides in the heads of experienced engineers. Assumptions about manufacturability limits, acceptable risk levels, or typical workarounds are often implicit. When these assumptions are not extracted and formalized, agents operate without essential context or within inappropriate process boundaries.

Dependency on external data sources adds another layer of risk. Supplier databases, regulatory documents, material libraries, or cost indices may change without notice. If agents rely on such sources, results may drift over time without any visible system change.

Mitigation requires an explicit data strategy. Critical input must be identified and prioritized. Implicit knowledge needs to be extracted through structured interaction with domain experts. Human clarification must be part of the normal workflow, not an exception. Data sources should be versioned and referenced explicitly so results remain traceable even as inputs evolve.

System Complexity and Emergent Behavior

Multi-agent systems derive much of their power from interaction. Specialized agents collaborate, exchange context, and trigger each other dynamically. This interaction also introduces a form of complexity that differs fundamentally from linear automation.

Debugging multi-agent workflows is inherently more difficult than debugging single scripts. Failures may emerge from interaction patterns rather than from individual components. Small changes in one agent can have unexpected effects elsewhere. Over time, emergent behavior may appear that was never explicitly designed.

There is also a strong tendency toward over-engineering. As systems grow, teams may add more agents, more rules, and more orchestration logic than necessary. This increases cognitive load, reduces transparency, and makes failure modes harder to predict.

Mitigation begins with architectural discipline. Responsibilities must be clearly separated. Each agent should have a narrow, well-defined role. Orchestration logic must be explicit and inspectable. Complexity should be added only when it replaces coordination overhead. Regular simplification is essential. Periodic reviews should remove unused agents, consolidate overlapping logic, and challenge assumptions about what complexity is truly necessary.

Behavioral and Data Drift Over Time

Even when systems are stable at launch, they inevitably change over time. Input distributions evolve. Product portfolios shift. Regulations change. Prompts and rules are refined. Tool behavior is updated. All of this introduces drift. Behavioral drift is particularly subtle. Small prompt changes may alter reasoning style or prioritization. Accumulated rule updates may create inconsistencies. Without periodic revalidation, these effects can slowly erode reliability.

Mitigation requires treating validation as a continuous activity. Representative test cases should be rerun periodically. Outputs should be compared against historical baselines. Deviations must be reviewed deliberately rather than dismissed as noise.

> Drift is not a failure. It is an expected property of living systems. The risk lies in ignoring it.

Tool Instability

Many multi-agent systems interact with engineering tools through user interfaces or APIs that were never designed for automation. Updates to these tools can break workflows unexpectedly. UI changes, renamed commands, or altered defaults may invalidate automation logic overnight.

Capability changes also matter. New solver versions may alter numerical behavior. Preprocessors may introduce new meshing logic. Even when tools improve, automation assumptions may no longer hold.

Mitigation relies on abstraction and monitoring. Tool interactions should be encapsulated behind stable interfaces wherever possible. Automated smoke tests should detect failures early. Dependencies on fragile UI automation should be minimized in favor of supported APIs whenever they exist.

Scalability Challenges

Scalability in agentic systems is rarely limited by reasoning capability. More often, it is constrained by infrastructure. Compute capacity, solver availability, CAx licenses, and queuing effects become bottlenecks as usage grows.

These constraints can distort perceived system performance. Agents may reason quickly, but workflows slow down due to waiting for licenses or compute slots. Without proper observability, users may blame the agentic system rather than the underlying resource limitation.

Mitigation requires explicit capacity planning. Scaling strategies must consider not only agents but also the tools they orchestrate. Queue management, prioritization, and transparent feedback to users help prevent frustration and misinterpretation.

Security Risks

Security risks in agentic systems extend beyond classical access control. Prompt injections are a real threat. Malicious or accidental inputs may alter agent behavior in unintended ways. Uncontrolled tool execution can amplify these risks if agents trigger actions without sufficient validation.

Mitigation starts with isolation. Agents must operate with least privilege. Tool execution should be constrained by explicit rules and approval steps. Input must be sanitized and validated. Sensitive operations should require human confirmation, especially in early maturity stages. Security is not a one-time configuration. As systems evolve, threat models must be revisited continuously.

Lack of Observability

Perhaps the most underestimated technical risk is lack of observability. Without detailed logs, metrics, and execution traces, failures remain invisible. Systems may degrade silently. Costs may increase unnoticed. Trust may erode without a clear cause.

Observability is not only about debugging. It is about learning. Runtime per agent, error rates, fallback frequency, and human overrides provide essential feedback. Without these signals, improvement becomes guesswork. Designing observability from the beginning is far cheaper than retrofitting it later. It turns technical risk from an unknown threat into a manageable engineering problem.

Technical risks are not an argument against agentic systems. They are an argument for deliberate design. Organizations that acknowledge these risks early and design for transparency, control, and learning build systems that remain reliable as they scale. Those that ignore them may enjoy short-term success, but they will struggle to sustain trust over time.

4.3.2 Human and Structural Risks in Agent Deployment

Many automation initiatives fail because the organization is not prepared to work with it. Technical risks tend to be visible and correctable. Human and structural risks are slower, less obvious, and frequently misdiagnosed as technical shortcomings.

Agentic systems intensify this dynamic. They influence decisions, reshape workflows, and alter how responsibility is experienced in everyday work. As a result, success depends less on how intelligent the system is and more on whether people trust it, understand their role within it, and feel confident relying on it. When these conditions are not met, even technically sound systems remain underused or are quietly bypassed.

Lack of Adoption

The most common organizational risk is simple non-use. Systems are deployed, technically functional, and still avoided in daily work. Resistance from engineers is often labelled as conservatism. In practice, it usually reflects rational risk management. Engineers remain accountable for outcomes. If agent behavior is opaque or unpredictable, using the system increases personal risk rather than reducing it.

Perceived loss of control reinforces this reaction. Fluent language, fast execution, and automated steps can make human involvement feel superficial. When engineers feel reduced to approving machine output rather than shaping decisions, engagement drops quickly.

Insufficient change management amplifies both effects. If communication focuses on efficiency gains or cost reduction instead of professional support, uncertainty fills the gap. Without clear framing, agents are interpreted as replacements rather than collaborators.

Adoption improves when agents deliver early, tangible relief. Focus first on removing repetitive preparation and coordination work. Preserve explicit human decision authority. Make reasoning, assumptions, and limitations visible. Position agents clearly as support systems, not evaluators or substitutes.

Unclear Responsibilities

Agentic systems blur traditional boundaries between preparation, execution, and decision-making. If responsibility is not redefined deliberately, accountability gaps emerge. A common failure mode is ambiguity around ownership of outcomes. When agents prepare recommendations and humans approve them, responsibility must be explicit. Without this clarity, failures trigger blame shifting rather than learning.

Another risk is reliance on informal ownership. Early systems often depend on a few individuals who understand everything. This works temporarily but collapses when those people become unavailable or move on. Responsibility must therefore be designed explicitly. Define what agents may decide, what they may recommend, and where human intervention is mandatory. Assign clear ownership for agent logic, approval decisions, and escalation paths. Treat responsibility design as a core part of system design, not as an afterthought.

Skill Mismatch

Agent-based systems introduce new skill requirements. Without deliberate capability development, organizations become fragile. When only external vendors or a small internal group can maintain or adapt the system, improvement slows and trust erodes. Over time, the system is perceived as external technology rather than as an internal capability.

Skill gaps also affect daily usage. Users who do not understand how to steer, review, or challenge agents tend to either over-trust or underuse them.

Mitigation starts with building internal capability early. This does not mean turning everyone into an AI specialist. It means enabling a core group to understand agent behavior, limitations, and evolution. Users must be trained not only in operation, but in interpretation and oversight. Domain experts must be able to contribute to rules and prompts within clear governance boundaries.

Organizational Risks Compound Over Time

These risks reinforce each other. Low adoption hides problems. Unclear responsibility prevents resolution. Skill gaps slow improvement. Over time, confidence declines and the system quietly fades out. The central insight is simple. Organizational readiness is not optional. Agent-based systems change how work is done. Organizations that redesign roles, responsibilities, and capabilities accordingly create the conditions for sustainable success.

4.3.3 Operating Agents Within Legal Guardrails

Agent-based systems differ fundamentally from traditional software in how responsibility, authorship, and decision-making are distributed. Outputs are no longer produced by a single deterministic algorithm or a clearly traceable line of code. They emerge from interactions between language models, rules, data sources, tools, and human input. This shift introduces ambiguity, not only at a technical level, but also in legal terms.

Regulators, auditors, and courts do not evaluate systems based on architectural elegance or innovation potential. They focus on accountability, transparency, and control. Who decided? On what basis? Using which data? Under which safeguards? When organizations cannot answer these questions clearly, legal risk rises sharply, regardless of how advanced or well-intentioned the system may be.

For this reason, legal and regulatory considerations must be treated as design constraints rather than after-the-fact checks. They influence how agents are built, how autonomy is bound, how data is handled, and how human oversight is enforced. Organizations that integrate these aspects early gain two advantages. They reduce exposure, and they avoid costly redesigns once systems are already embedded in critical processes.

Protection of Intellectual Property

One of the most immediate legal concerns in agent-based systems is the protection of intellectual property. Engineering organizations rely on proprietary knowledge. Design logic, simulation setups, cost models, process know-how, and decision heuristics often represent core competitive assets. When agents process, summarize, or transform this information, questions of ownership and leakage inevitably arise.

Training data is the first sensitive area. Organizations must clearly distinguish between models trained externally by providers and proprietary knowledge used at runtime. Internal data should never be incorporated into external training pipelines unless this is explicitly intended and contractually secured. In most engineering contexts, this is unnecessary and undesirable. Runtime inference with strict data isolation is usually sufficient and significantly safer.

Knowledge bases introduce a second layer of complexity. Many agentic systems rely on retrieval mechanisms to access internal documents, design rules, historical cases, or best practices. These knowledge bases effectively encode organizational memory. Their governance therefore becomes critical. Access control, update rights, and usage tracking must be defined explicitly. Without such controls, knowledge that was once tightly managed can become implicitly available to any workflow touching the system.

Prompts deserve particular attention. They are often treated as simple configuration artifacts, yet in practice they encode substantial intellectual effort. Prompts define reasoning structure, decision framing, and interpretation logic. Over time, they reflect how an organization thinks about its engineering problems. Treating prompts as disposable text underestimates their strategic value. They should be versioned, protected, and governed like other forms of intellectual property.

Handling proprietary data in LLM interactions is another critical concern. Even when providers commit not to store or reuse inputs, organizations remain responsible for what they expose. This includes geometry, simulation results, cost information, and customer-specific requirements. Clear data classification policies must define which data may be processed by which agents and under which conditions.

Finally, contractual clarity with platform and model providers is essential. Organizations must understand who owns generated outputs, how data is handled, and what happens if providers change terms or services are discontinued. Vague or overly permissive contracts can transform short-term convenience into long-term legal exposure.

Compliance with AI Regulations

Regulatory frameworks for artificial intelligence are evolving rapidly. Among them, the European Union AI Act represents one of the most comprehensive and influential approaches. Even organizations operating outside the EU may be affected, either through market access, supply chains, or customer requirements. Compliance therefore cannot be treated as a one-time exercise. AI systems and the organizations around must be reviewed continuously against applicable regulations.

Transparency and auditability are central requirements. Organizations must be able to explain how AI-supported decisions are reached. This does not require exposing internal model weights. It requires documenting data sources, applied rules, assumptions, and decision pathways in a way that humans can understand. Multi-agent systems that log intermediate steps and preserve context have a structural advantage in meeting these expectations.

Documentation obligations extend beyond technical descriptions. They include intended use, known limitations, failure modes, and risk mitigation measures. This documentation must evolve as systems change, agents are added, and autonomy increases. Treating documentation as a living artifact rather than a compliance checkbox reduces friction during audits and regulatory reviews.

Human oversight is another cornerstone. The EU AI Act explicitly emphasizes meaningful human control in high-risk systems. This aligns closely with best practices in agent-based engineering. Clear escalation paths, defined approval points, and the ability to intervene or override are not only good system design. They are regulatory safeguards.

Compliance should therefore not be viewed as a barrier to innovation. In many cases, regulatory requirements reinforce sound engineering principles. They promote transparency, robustness, and accountability, all of which increase trust and long-term viability.

Liability and Accountability

Liability is where legal theory meets operational reality. When an agent-supported decision results in failure, delay, or damage, responsibility cannot be delegated to software, regardless of how autonomous it appears. Clarifying responsibility for agent-supported decisions is therefore essential. For each class of decisions, it must be clear whether the agent provides recommendations or executes actions. Where execution is automated, autonomy boundaries must be explicitly defined and documented. Responsibility remains with the organization and, ultimately, with designated human roles.

This is particularly critical in safety-relevant contexts. Engineering decisions related to structural integrity, compliance, or risk mitigation carry legal and ethical weight. In these areas, human oversight must remain explicit and enforceable. Agents may prepare analyses, explore alternatives, or flag risks, but final decisions must always be attributable to accountable individuals.

Accountability also requires traceability. Organizations must be able to reconstruct what the system did, why it did it, and who approved the outcome. This includes version states of agents, rules, prompts, and models. Without such traceability, even correct decisions become legally fragile because they cannot be defended after the fact.

Legal Clarity as an Enabler, not an Obstacle

Legal and regulatory considerations are often perceived as slowing innovation. In practice, clear legal framing accelerates adoption by reducing uncertainty. It enables stakeholders to trust the system, regulators to accept it, and organizations to scale without fear of hidden exposure. Organizations that address intellectual property, compliance, and accountability early do not eliminate risk. They make it manageable. More importantly, they align legal safeguards with technical and organizational design. When this alignment exists, agent-based systems can evolve confidently from experimental tools into durable, compliant, and defensible components of the engineering enterprise.

4.3.4 The Necessary Boundaries of Agent-Based Engineering

Agentic systems deliver the most value when they are treated as amplifiers, not as universal problem solvers. They scale coordination, apply logic consistently, and accelerate decision preparation. They do not replace process clarity, sound engineering judgment, or organizational discipline. When these foundations are weak, automation does not compensate. It exposes the weaknesses faster and at greater scale. Expectation management is therefore not a closing communication task. It is a principle from the start. Organizations that are explicit about what agents can and cannot do create room for learning and trust. Those that promise too much too early often trigger over-trust, defensive behavior, or rejection, even when the underlying system performs reasonably well.

The following limits are not shortcomings of agentic systems. They are structural realities that must be understood and respected.

Not Every Process is Suitable

A common misconception is that enough intelligence can automate any engineering activity. In practice, suitability varies significantly. Agent-based systems work best in processes with recurring decision patterns, high coordination effort, and clear acceptance criteria. Highly exploratory, politically sensitive, or intuition-heavy activities are poor candidates, especially early on. These processes depend on situational context that is difficult to formalize and often change faster than automation can adapt.

Therefore, selectivity is a strength. Choosing where not to apply agents is as important as choosing where to apply them. Organizations that treat agent-based automation as a targeted capability achieve more stable and defensible results than those that attempt blanket adoption.

Agentic Systems do not Fix Broken Processes

Automation does not compensate for unclear ownership, missing inputs, or contradictory objectives. It makes these issues visible. When processes rely on informal agreements, undocumented assumptions, or implicit decision rules, agents struggle because there is nothing stable to reason over. Failures are then attributed to the system, even though the same processes produced inconsistent outcomes long before automation.

This effect is uncomfortable but valuable. Agentic systems act as mirrors. They surface ambiguity, expose hidden dependencies, and force clarification. If acceptance criteria are unclear, agents reveal conflicting interpretations. If responsibilities are blurred, escalation stalls. If data is unreliable, results drift. Expectation management means acknowledging this upfront. Introducing agents must go hand in hand with a willingness to clarify processes and make assumptions explicit. When organizations expect agents to work around structural issues, disappointment is inevitable.

Human Judgment Remains Essential

Agentic systems change how judgment is applied. They do not eliminate it. Agents excel at preparation, comparison, and consistency. They explore option spaces, apply rules without fatigue, and document every step. What they cannot do is assume responsibility. They do not own risk tolerance, ethical trade-offs, or long-term consequences beyond what has been explicitly defined.

Engineering decisions are rarely purely technical. Accountability must remain human. For this reason, successful agent-based systems are designed with explicit control points. Agents propose. Humans decide.

Clear framing matters. Engineers move from executing repetitive steps to supervising outcomes and refining goals. Their expertise becomes more valuable, not less, because it is applied at higher leverage points. When this is understood, agents are seen as multipliers rather than replacements.

Limits as Enablers, Not Constraints

Understanding limits does not reduce ambition. It focuses it. Organizations that respect these boundaries build systems that are credible, trusted, and durable. They scale where structure exists and invest in clarity where it does not. They use agents to support judgment rather than obscure it. Progress becomes incremental, uneven, and sustainable.

Expectation management is therefore not about lowering goals. It is about aligning them with reality. When that alignment exists, agentic systems stop being fragile experiments or inflated promises. They become what they are most powerful as: reliable partners in complex engineering work, improving steadily within well-understood boundaries.

4.3.5 The Playbook to Mitigate Risks

Agentic systems introduce a different risk profile than traditional automation. They combine deterministic execution with probabilistic reasoning, they evolve over time, and they interact with complex tool chains and human decision-making. In this context, failure is not an anomaly. It is an expected part of learning and maturation.

The goal of a mitigation playbook is therefore not to prevent every error. That would be unrealistic and counterproductive. The goal is to ensure that errors remain contained, visible, and reversible. Organizations that succeed with agent-based systems do not eliminate risk. They manage it deliberately.

Effective mitigation creates two forms of safety at once. Technical safety for operations and psychological safety for users. Engineers adopt systems faster when they know that mistakes can be detected early and undone without damage. From an organizational perspective, mitigation turns experimentation into a controlled process rather than a gamble.

The following elements form a practical baseline. They are not advanced practices for mature systems. They should be in place from the first serious pilot.

Sandbox Environments

Sandbox environments provide a protected space where agents can operate without affecting systems of record or production outcomes. Early experimentation should happen here by default. In a sandbox, agents can test workflows, integrations, and assumptions freely. Intermediate artifacts and logs are captured for inspection, but no irreversible actions are taken. This enables rapid iteration without operational risk. Sandboxes also support learning. Engineers can inspect agent behavior, challenge assumptions, and refine rules and prompts without pressure. This phase builds understanding on both sides, human and system.

Staging Before Production

Staging environments bridge the gap between experimentation and real operation. They mirror production as closely as possible while remaining isolated from business-critical decisions. In staging, agents encounter realistic data volumes, tool configurations, and timing effects. Performance bottlenecks, error handling gaps, and integration edge cases often appear here for the first time. Treating staging as optional is a common mistake. For agentic systems, it is essential. It is the last controlled checkpoint before agents influence real outcomes.

Canary Releases

Canary releases introduce change incrementally. New agent logic, prompts, or models are applied to a small subset of cases or users before wider rollout. This limits blast radius. Unexpected behavior affects only a controlled segment, while metrics, logs, and feedback provide early warning signals. Subtle behavioral changes, especially from prompt updates or model switches, often surface only in real usage. Canary releases turn deployment from a binary event into a monitored transition.

Rollback Strategies

Every deployment requires a defined rollback path. This is non-negotiable. Rollback includes more than code. It must cover agent configurations, rules, prompts, and model versions. Organizations need to know which version was active for each case and be able to restore a known-good state quickly. Without rollback, teams hesitate to improve systems. Innovation slows and risk accumulates. With rollback in place, iteration becomes safer and faster.

Dual-Run Phases

Dual-run phases are one of the most effective trust-building mechanisms. The agent-based system runs in parallel with the existing process for a defined period. Both paths produce outputs, but the legacy process remains authoritative at first. Results are compared systematically. Differences are analyzed rather than hidden. This reveals strengths and weaknesses on both sides and surfaces assumptions that were previously implicit.

Dual-run phases validate quality, support learning, and provide concrete evidence for decision-makers. They should not be permanent. Their purpose is to enable a confident transition, after which the agent-based process becomes primary, and the legacy path remains as fallback.

Controlled Risk Enables Progress

A multi-agent system without mitigation mechanisms is fragile. A system with a clear mitigation playbook becomes resilient. Sandboxing, staging, canary releases, rollback strategies, and dual-run phases do not slow adoption. They make it possible. They transform uncertainty into a managed variable and allow organizations to learn faster with less fear.

4.3.6 Operational Safety Nets for Agent-Based Systems

Agentic systems do not fail randomly. When they fail, they tend to fail in recognizable and recurring ways. The same misunderstandings, missing inputs, ambiguous rules, or tool-side limitations appear repeatedly across projects and domains. Treating each occurrence as an isolated incident wastes learning potential and slows maturity.

A failure mode library turns mistakes into assets. Instead of fixing issues ad hoc and moving on, the organization captures failure patterns explicitly, detects them early when they reappear, and responds in a standardized way. This shifts error handling from reactive troubleshooting to systematic risk reduction. Over time, the system becomes more robust not because failures disappear, but because they are anticipated, recognized, and handled consistently. This approach is especially powerful in agent-based systems. Agents operate at scale and across many cases. A single unresolved failure pattern can propagate quickly. Conversely, a single well-understood countermeasure can improve reliability across dozens or hundreds of automations.

Collecting Recurring Failure Patterns

The foundation of a failure mode library is a structured collection of known failure patterns, described in practical, operational terms rather than abstract technical language.

Typical examples include the following:

- misinterpretation of ambiguous requirements
- missing or inconsistent input data, which leads to plausible but incorrect outputs
- tool-side failures such as solver crashes, licensing issues, or unstable preprocessing
- logical errors caused by outdated rules or conflicting assumptions between agents
- overconfident recommendations in situations with insufficient data

Each failure mode should be documented with a short description, typical symptoms, affected agents or tools, and known triggers. The objective is recognizability, not exhaustive root-cause analysis. Engineers and operators should be able to answer quickly: Have we seen this before?

Automated Detection

A failure mode library delivers value only if patterns can be detected reliably. Wherever possible, detection should be automated.

This may include the following:

- rule-based checks for invalid states or missing inputs
- pattern recognition in logs, outputs, or execution traces
- threshold-based alerts for deviations from expected ranges
- consistency checks that flag contradictory conclusions across agents

Detection does not need to be perfect. Its purpose is early warning, not final judgment. Even partial automation significantly reduces time to resolution and prevents repeated manual diagnosis of the same issues.

Standardized Countermeasures

For each documented failure mode, a standardized response should exist. This is what turns the library from documentation into an operational safety net.

Typical countermeasures include the following:

- requesting additional input from a human reviewer
- falling back to a simpler or more conservative workflow
- re-running steps with stricter constraints or alternative parameters
- escalating the case to a defined role or expert group
- blocking autonomous continuation until conditions are clarified

Consistence matters. When teams respond differently to the same failure, trust erodes and learning will be fragmented. Standardized countermeasures create predictable behavior and make agent responses easier to understand and accept.

Reuse Through Retrieval-Augmented Generation

As the failure mode library grows, simple lookup mechanisms become insufficient. This is where retrieval-augmented generation becomes valuable.

By connecting the library to the agents' reasoning process, agents can

- match current situations against known failure patterns,
- surface relevant past cases and applied countermeasures,
- explain why a safeguard or escalation was triggered, and
- propose mitigations based on prior successful resolutions.

This does not replace rule-based safeguards. It complements them. RAG allows agents to reason with organizational experience in a controlled way, without relying on generic external knowledge. Over time, this creates a compounding effect. Each issue resolved strengthens the system. Failures become less disruptive, response times shorten, and confidence increases.

From Error Handling to Institutional Learning

A failure mode library formalizes a critical mindset shift. Failure is no longer an exception to be hidden or worked around. It becomes a source of structured learning. Organizations that invest in such safety nets move faster with less risk. They do not avoid mistakes. They absorb them. With each absorbed failure, the agentic system becomes more predictable, more trustworthy, and more aligned with how the organization works.

4.3.7 Managing Vendor Lock-in and Exit Strategy

Agentic systems are long-term capabilities, not short-term tools. Once agents are embedded into engineering workflows, they accumulate knowledge, assumptions, rules, and operational history. This creates lasting value, but it also creates dependency. If that dependency is tied too closely to a single vendor, platform, or proprietary interface, strategic flexibility erodes over time.

Vendor lock-in is rarely the result of one poor decision. It emerges gradually. Early convenience shortcuts, missing abstraction layers, and implicit assumptions about tool availability compound quietly. Years later, organizations discover that change has become expensive, risky, or politically difficult.

> Designing an exit strategy does not signal mistrust toward vendors. It signals maturity. It ensures that the organization retains control over its knowledge, data, and operating model, even as technologies, providers, and priorities evolve.

Ensuring Data Portability

The most critical asset in an agentic system is not the agents themselves. It is the data they produce and consume. Context, intermediate artifacts, assumptions, decisions, logs, and outcomes must remain accessible independent of any specific platform.

This requires explicit ownership of data schemas and storage formats. Case data, agent outputs, and learning artifacts should be stored in formats that can be exported, interpreted, and reused without proprietary tooling. Even when commercial platforms are used, the organization must be able to retrieve its full operational history in a usable form.

Portability also applies to knowledge assets. Rules, prompts, and decision logic should be documented and versioned so they can be migrated or reimplemented if needed. Knowledge that exists only inside opaque configuration layers is knowledge that cannot be reclaimed.

Abstraction Layers for Tools

Tight coupling between agents and specific tools increases fragility. When a CAD system, solver, or automation interface changes, deeply embedded logic breaks. Abstraction layers reduce this risk. Instead of binding agents directly to tool-specific calls, tools are accessed through clearly defined service interfaces. These interfaces describe what is done, not how it is done. Meshing, simulation execution, or report generation become capabilities rather than hard-coded interactions.

This approach adds some upfront design effort, but it pays off quickly. Tools can be replaced, upgraded, or parallelized without rewriting agent logic. Over time, abstraction becomes a key enabler of resilience and scalability.

Use of Open Interfaces

Open interfaces are the practical foundation of portability. APIs, standard data formats, and documented protocols reduce dependency on undocumented behavior or brittle UI automation. Wherever possible, integrations should rely on stable, supported interfaces rather than screen scraping. This is especially important in CAx environments, where UI changes are frequent and outside the organization's control.

Open interfaces also enable hybrid architecture. Organizations can combine commercial platforms, in-house components, and specialized tools without being locked into a single ecosystem. This flexibility becomes increasingly valuable as agent-based systems scale.

Documented Migration Paths

An exit strategy only exists if it is explicit. Even if migration is unlikely in the near term, organizations should define how it could happen.

This includes the following:

- identifying vendor-specific versus portable components
- defining how data, rules, and prompts could be extracted
- estimating effort for partial or full migration scenarios
- reviewing assumptions periodically as the system evolves

The goal is not to prepare for immediate departure. It is to ensure that departure remains possible. This knowledge alone improves negotiation leverage, reduces long-term risk, and increases internal confidence in the sustainability of the approach.

Strategic Flexibility as a Design Principle

Organizations that treat exit strategies as part of system architecture retain strategic freedom. They can adopt new technologies, respond to market shifts, and evolve their operating model without being constrained by early decisions.

> **!** Vendor lock-in is not avoided by rejecting commercial platforms. It is avoided by designing for choice.

4.3.8 Risk Is Not a Reason to Stop

Agentic systems introduce new risks, but they do not introduce uncertainty into engineering organizations. That uncertainty has always existed. What changes is how visible, scalable, and consequential it becomes.

The risks outlined in this section are not edge cases. They are structural. Hallucination, over-trust, data drift, organizational resistance, unclear accountability, and regulatory exposure are not signs of immature technology. They are natural consequences of introducing systems that reason, act, and learn inside complex organizations.

The critical distinction is this. These risks are manageable, but only when they are addressed deliberately. Organizations that treat agentic systems as ordinary software tend to encounter their limits too late. Organizations that treat them as socio-technical systems, design safeguards early. They define boundaries, preserve human judgment, build observability, and plan for change rather than assuming stability.

Risk management in this context is not about eliminating failure. It is about making failure visible, recoverable, and instructive. Sandboxes, staged rollouts, dual-run phases, failure mode libraries, and exit strategies are not defensive overhead. They are mechanisms that make learning safe and progress repeatable.

The most successful organizations are not those that avoid risk. They are those that understand where autonomy creates value, where it creates danger, and how to move deliberately between the two. When this balance is achieved, agent-based systems stop being perceived as fragile or threatening. They become reliable instruments for scaling engineering judgment without losing control.

A practical checklist covering the most important risk considerations when starting to build agentic systems can be found in Section 6.5.

5 Outlook—Engineering in the Age of Intelligent Systems

The previous chapters have examined what agentic AI systems are, how they work, and how to implement them in engineering organizations. We have discussed the technical foundations of large language models, tool integration, memory architecture, and the practical considerations of deployment, governance, and team building. Technology does not exist in isolation, though. The engineering organizations that deploy these systems operate within economic pressures, organizational traditions, and technological ecosystems that will shape how agentic AI evolves and what it ultimately delivers.

This chapter looks forward—not with the certainty of prediction as no one can forecast with precision what the next five to ten years will bring, but with the structured uncertainty of scenario analysis. We will examine the forces that will shape the trajectory of agentic AI in engineering: technological advances in models and architectures, economic pressures from venture capital and consolidation, organizational dynamics as established practices confront new capabilities, and the individual experience of engineers whose work will be transformed. We will consider both optimistic and pessimistic scenarios, not because truth lies in the middle, but because the range of possibilities is wide and the outcome depends on choices yet to be made.

Some of you may find this chapter more speculative than the rest of the book. That is intentional. The goal is not to tell you what will happen, but to help you think about what might happen, and what you can do to prepare for and influence it.

5.1 The Two Futures

Ask different experts about AI's trajectory and you will get dramatically different answers. The CEOs of the leading AI companies like OpenAI, Google DeepMind, or Anthropic have all predicted that artificial general intelligence could arrive within five years. Meanwhile, prominent skeptics like Gary Marcus argue that current AI approaches have fundamental limitations that will prevent them from achieving reliable, trustworthy performance in domains where correctness matters.

Both camps make valid points. The optimists can point to extraordinary progress: Capabilities that seemed years away arrive months after being dismissed as impractical. The skeptics can point to persistent failures: hallucinations, brittleness to small changes, inability to reliably follow constraints, and fundamental unreliability in contexts requiring ground truth.

For engineering leaders, the question is not which camp is right, it is how to operate productively when both could be right in different respects. Engineering applications require reliability and verifiability. They also benefit enormously from capabilities that are advancing rapidly. The strategic challenge is capturing value from what works while maintaining appropriate caution about what does not.

The Acceleration Scenario

In the acceleration scenario, the trends of 2024–2025 continue. Models become more capable, more reliable, and cheaper. Context windows expand to handle complete engineering datasets. Reasoning capabilities improve to the point where agents can handle multi-step engineering problems with minimal human oversight. Agent architectures mature, with standard patterns emerging for coordination, memory, and tool integration. The infrastructure layer will commoditize and make sophisticated agent systems accessible to organizations without dedicated AI teams.

Under this scenario, by 2030–2031, engineering organizations would routinely deploy level 4 and level 5 agentic systems that learn from experience and collaborate with humans as team members. Design cycles would compress dramatically. The traditional V-model of systems engineering with its sequential phases of requirements, design, implementation, and verification would transform into something more iterative and concurrent, with agents continuously validating design choices against requirements and simulating outcomes in real time.

The economic implications would be profound. Organizations that successfully deploy these systems would achieve productivity gains of 5- to 10-times in engineering-intensive activities. Those that lag would find themselves unable to compete on either speed or cost. The workforce implications would be equally significant: Fewer engineers would be needed for routine work, but demand would surge for engineers who can orchestrate agent systems, capture organizational knowledge, and handle the genuinely novel problems that require human creativity and judgment.

The Plateau Scenario

In the plateau scenario, current approaches hit fundamental limits. The scaling laws that have driven improvement begin to plateau as training data is exhausted and compute costs become prohibitive. Reliability problems persist despite engineering efforts. Hallucinations and reasoning failures, tolerable in creative applications, prove intractable in engineering contexts where precision matters. The gap between impressive demos and reliable production systems remains wide.

Under this scenario, agentic AI delivers meaningful but bounded value. It handles well-defined tasks within established domains but struggles with novel situations and cross-domain reasoning. Organizations invest heavily in guardrails and human oversight, capturing perhaps 20 to 30 percent productivity improvements but never achieving the autonomous operation that optimists envision.

Gary Marcus and other skeptics argue this is the more likely outcome. They point out that current AI systems are fundamentally limited: They learn correlations, not causation, they lack true understanding of physical laws, and they cannot reliably follow constraints or verify their own reasoning. These are not merely engineering challenges to be solved with more data and compute, and they may reflect architectural limitations that require fundamentally different approaches.

The Strategic Implication

The prudent engineering leader prepares for both scenarios. This means making investments that deliver value under plateau conditions while preserving optionality to capture acceleration benefits if they materialize. Concretely: Build the context capture and integration infrastructure that agents need to be useful, as this investment pays off regardless of how capable the models become. Develop organizational capabilities for human-agent collaboration leading to these skills becoming more valuable as agents improve, not less. Maintain engineering expertise and judgment. If acceleration fails to materialize, humans remain essential; if it succeeds, the ability to evaluate agent outputs and handle exceptional cases becomes premium expertise.

5.2 Technological Trajectories

Several technological developments will shape what agentic AI can accomplish in engineering over the next five to ten years. Understanding these trajectories helps organizations make informed bets about which capabilities to build toward and which to wait for.

Physics-Informed Foundation Models

The current generation of large language models learned from text. They understand engineering concepts because engineers wrote about them, but they have no direct experience of physical reality. They know that $F = m \cdot a$ because physics textbooks say so, not because they have ever observed mass accelerating under force.

A new class of models is emerging that incorporates physical knowledge more directly. Physics-informed neural networks (PINNs) embed differential equations describing physical behavior into their training process, ensuring that learned solutions respect conservation laws and boundary conditions. These models require less training data because physics provides constraints that narrow the solution space. They extrapolate more reliably because physical laws bound what is possible. They are more interpretable because the physics component is transparent even when the learned component is not.

Current PINN applications are narrow, which involve solving specific differential equations for specific domains. However, researchers are working toward physics foundation models that would generalize across physical phenomena. NVIDIA's PhysicsNeMo framework provides infrastructure for training such models at scale. Recent work on models like PhysiX and GPhyT demonstrates that a single model can learn to simulate diverse physical systems and generalize to phenomena absent from training data.

By 2030, we may see hybrid architectures where large language models handle natural language understanding and high-level reasoning while physics-informed models handle physical simulation and prediction. An engineer could describe a design in natural language, have the language model interpret the description and formulate simulation parameters, then have the physics model predict behavior—all within an integrated agent system. This would combine the flexibility of language models with the physical grounding that pure LLMs lack.

World Models and Spatial Intelligence

Current AI excels at language but struggles with space. Large language models can discuss the properties of a mechanism, but they cannot visualize how it moves. They can describe a manufacturing process, but they cannot simulate the physical transformation of material through operations. World models aim to change this. These systems learn internal representations of how the physical world works, not just what objects exist, but how they move, interact, and change over time. Fei-Fei Li's World Labs and Yann LeCun's new venture AMI Labs are pursuing what Li calls "spatial intelligence," the capability that links imagination, perception, and action.

The implications for engineering are substantial. An agent with true spatial intelligence could examine a CAD model and intuitively understand how it would behave under load, how it would move through an assembly process, and how it would interact with adjacent components. It could simulate not just through explicit calculation but through learned intuition, in the same way experienced engineers "see" problems that novices miss.

Research on embodied AI, systems that learn through interaction with physical environments, provides another path to spatial intelligence: robots learning to manipulate objects and developing implicit understanding of physics that purely language-trained models lack. As techniques for transferring this embodied knowledge to broader AI systems mature, the capabilities available to engineering agents will expand significantly.

The Context Expansion

Context windows, the amount of information a model can consider at once, have grown from thousands to millions of tokens in just a few years. This trend will continue. Within five years, models may be able to hold entire product development databases in context: every specification, every design decision, every test result, and every lesson learned.

This matters because engineering decisions require context. The right material choice depends on manufacturing capabilities. The right tolerance depends on assembly sequence. The right design depends on lessons from past failures. Human engineers carry this context in their heads, accumulated over years of experience. Agents with sufficiently large context windows could carry it in their active memory, accessing it instantly without retrieval delays or lossy summarization.

The practical challenge shifts from whether agents can access context to whether organizations can provide it. The models are ready for more context than most organizations can supply in structured, consumable form. This is why context capture, the systematic encoding of organizational knowledge, becomes the differentiating investment.

Simulation Acceleration

Traditional engineering simulation is expensive. A single finite element analysis might take hours; a full optimization study might take weeks. This computational cost shapes engineering practice. Decisions are made with incomplete simulation data because time and cost prohibit exhaustive analysis.

AI-accelerated simulation is changing this equation. Surrogate models trained on simulation data can predict results orders of magnitude faster than running the full simulation. Companies like PhysicsX, Neural Concept, and Pasteur Labs offer platforms that turn weeks of simulation into minutes of inference. The global simulation software market, projected to exceed USD 20 billion by 2025, increasingly incorporates these AI acceleration capabilities.

For agentic systems, simulation acceleration enables real-time design feedback. Instead of proposing changes and waiting for overnight simulation runs, agents could evaluate thousands of design variants in the time a human engineer takes to sketch an alternative on a whiteboard. This transforms the role of simulation from validation to exploration.

5.3 Economic Forces

Technology does not develop in an economic vacuum. The trajectory of agentic AI in engineering will be shaped by investment flows, market dynamics, and consolidation patterns in the software industry.

The Venture Capital Ecosystem

AI has become the dominant theme in venture capital. Global private AI investment reached USD 252 billion in 2024, with generative AI funding alone hitting USD 34 billion—eight times higher than 2022 levels. Foundation model companies account for roughly 40 percent of global AI funding. The scale is unprecedented: A single AI deal in Q1 2025 was USD 40 billion, larger than the total venture investment in most years.

Engineering software specifically is attracting substantial investment. PhysicsX raised USD 135 million in 2025 to accelerate physics simulation through AI, with strategic participation from Siemens and Applied Materials. The involvement of industrial giants signals confidence that AI-native engineering is becoming foundational. Smaller players like Neural Concept, Pasteur Labs, Synera, and many others are pursuing specialized applications from generative design to manufacturing process optimization.

This investment creates both opportunity and risk. Opportunity because well-funded startups will push the boundaries of what is possible, creating tools that engineering organizations can deploy. Risk because venture-backed companies face pressure to grow quickly, sometimes prioritizing impressive capabilities over reliable operations. Engineering leaders must evaluate whether a vendor's technology is truly production-ready or whether it remains an impressive demo supported by venture dollars.

Incumbent Consolidation

The established engineering software vendors, Siemens, Dassault Systèmes, Autodesk, PTC, and Synopsys, are not standing still. They acquire AI capabilities aggressively and integrating them into their platforms. Siemens acquired Altair for USD 10 billion in 2024, adding AI simulation capabilities to its already comprehensive portfolio. The company has enhanced Teamcenter and NX with autonomous agents for digital twin lifecycle management and simulation orchestration.

The PLM and engineering software market grew to USD 31 billion in 2024, with the top ten vendors holding 85 percent market share. This concentration is likely to increase. The incumbents have data gravity as decades of customer designs, simulation results, and manufacturing data represent irreplaceable training assets for AI models. They have distribution channels and trust relationships with enterprise customers. In addition, they have the capital to acquire promising startups before those startups can challenge their position.

For engineering organizations, this consolidation has mixed implications. On the one hand, it means AI capabilities will be integrated into familiar tools, reducing the friction of adoption. On the other hand, it means reduced competition and potentially slower innovation as the market becomes more concentrated. The strategic question is whether to commit deeply to a single vendor's ecosystem, which could lead to gaining integration benefits but accepting lock-in, or to maintain flexibility through multi-vendor architectures at the cost of integration complexity.

The Cost Curve

AI inference costs are falling rapidly, by roughly 10-times per year according to some estimates, with recent analyses indicating that the decline may be even steeper. The cost to run a model performing at GPT-3.5 level dropped over 280-fold between November 2022 and October 2024. This trend will continue as hardware improves, models become more efficient, and competition intensifies.

Falling costs change what is economically viable. Capabilities that are too expensive for routine use today may be affordable for every engineering decision tomorrow. The hybrid architecture described in earlier chapters using expensive models for complex reasoning and cheap models for routine tasks become less necessary as even powerful models become affordable. This shifts the bottleneck from inference cost to integration effort and context quality.

5.4 Organizational Transformation

Technology and economics set the boundaries of what is possible. Organizational dynamics determine what actually happens within those boundaries. The adoption of agentic AI in engineering will be shaped by existing practices, professional identities, and the inherent conservatism of industries where errors have serious consequences.

The V-Model Under Pressure

The V-model of systems engineering, that outlines requirements flowing down through design and implementation, while verification flowing up through integration and validation, has governed complex system development for decades. It emerged from aerospace and defense, spread to automotive and industrial equipment, and shaped how engineering organizations structure their work.

The V-model assumes that certain activities must precede others. Requirements must be defined before design begins. Design must be complete before implementation. Implementation must be finished before integration testing. Each phase produces artifacts that feed the next phase. The sequential structure provides governance and traceability at the cost of rigidity and long cycle times.

Agentic AI challenges these assumptions. If agents can simulate design performance against requirements in real time, the clean separation between design and verification blurs. If agents can explore thousands of design alternatives in the time traditional processes allow for one, the rationale for committing early to a single design weakens. If agents can maintain continuous traceability across all artifacts, the formal phase gates that exist primarily to ensure documentation completeness become less necessary.

This does not mean the V-model will disappear. The underlying logic that complex systems require systematic decomposition and verification remains valid. What may change is the implementation: more concurrent activities, faster iteration, continuous verification rather than phase-gate verification, and human attention focused on the genuinely difficult decisions rather than routine compliance checking.

Professional Identity and Resistance

Engineers build identity around expertise. Mechanical engineers know how mechanisms work. Structural engineers understand how loads flow through structures. Manufacturing engineers know how to make things. This expertise, accumulated over years of education and practice, defines who they are and what they contribute.

Agentic AI threatens this identity. If agents can perform tasks that previously required years of experience, what is the engineer's role? If junior engineers with agent assistance match the output of senior engineers without, what is expertise worth? These are not merely economic questions, but they are questions of professional meaning that will generate resistance regardless of technical capability.

The resolution lies in reframing what expertise means. The engineer's role shifts from executing analysis to defining what should be analyzed, from generating designs to evaluating generated designs, from performing routine tasks to handling the exceptions that agents can't. This is genuinely valuable work as agents need human direction to be useful, and the quality of that direction depends on engineering expertise. However, the transition requires engineers to embrace a new conception of their contribution, which not all will do willingly.

Safety and Liability

Engineering exists in a regulatory and liability framework designed for human decision-making. When a product fails, responsibility flows to the engineers who designed it, the managers who approved it, and the organizations that released it. This framework assumes humans made the relevant decisions and can be held accountable for them.

Agent involvement complicates this framework. If an agent recommends a design that fails, who is responsible? The engineer who accepted the recommendation? The organization that deployed the agent? The vendor that built it? The regulatory frameworks for these questions remain unsettled, creating uncertainty that may slow adoption in safety-critical applications.

The practical resolution, at least initially, is clear human accountability. Agents recommend, humans decide. Agents analyze, humans approve. Agents generate, humans validate. This preserves the existing liability framework while capturing agent benefits. Over time, as agent reliability improves and trust develops, the boundary between agent recommendation and human decision may shift, but for the next five to ten years, maintaining clear human accountability will be both legally prudent and practically necessary.

5.5 The Individual Engineer

Behind organizational and technological change are individual engineers whose careers will be shaped by these developments. What should an engineer expect, and how should they prepare?

Skills That Appreciate

Some skills become more valuable as agents become more capable. Judgment, which could mean the ability to evaluate agent outputs, identify errors, and recognize when situations exceed agent capabilities, becomes more valuable as agent involvement increases. The engineer who can tell when an agent is wrong is more valuable than the engineer who can do what the agent does, because wrong agent output at scale is worse than no agent output at all.

Systems thinking approaches involving understanding how components interact, how requirements flow through designs, and how changes propagate across systems become more important as agents handle component-level work. Someone needs to see the whole picture, and agents working on local problems cannot replace that integrative view.

Communication skills like explaining technical concepts to non-technical stakeholders, translating business requirements into engineering specifications, negotiating trade-offs across competing objectives continue to remain distinctively human. Agents can draft documents, but they cannot build the relationships and shared understanding that effective engineering requires.

Creativity, identifying problems worth solving, imagining solutions that do not exist yet, making intuitive leaps that bypass systematic search, are the nature of tasks and domain where human advantage persists longest. Agents can explore defined spaces efficiently. Humans define which spaces are worth exploring.

Skills That Depreciate

Routine analysis that involves running standard simulations, checking designs against known rules, performing calculations that follow established procedures, is exactly what agents do well. Engineers whose primary contribution is executing well-defined analytical processes face displacement. This is not speculation, it is already happening in some domains.

Information retrieval tasks like knowing which specification applies, finding the relevant test data from past projects, and locating the expert who solved a similar problem are what agent memory systems are designed to replace. The engineer whose value lies in knowing where to find things rather than what to do with them is vulnerable.

Documentation tasks pertaining to writing reports, maintaining records, producing the paper trail that engineering governance requires is being automated rapidly. Agents can generate first drafts of most engineering documents. Humans will review and approve, not write from scratch.

The Career Trajectory

For junior engineers entering the field, the path to expertise is changing. Traditional apprenticeship with years of routine work building toward independent judgment may compress or disappear. Agents handle what junior engineers used to cut their teeth on, leaving fewer opportunities to learn through doing. The challenge is developing judgment without the repetitions that traditionally built it.

For mid-career engineers, the question is adaptation. Those who embrace agent collaboration like learning to prompt effectively, evaluate outputs critically, and direct agent work strategically, will find their effectiveness multiplied. Those who resist or ignore the transition will find their skills devalued gradually and then suddenly.

For senior engineers approaching retirement, the situation is complex. Deep expertise remains valuable as input to agent systems and as check on agent outputs. However, the organizational patience for manual processes may diminish as agent-enabled competitors demonstrate what faster cycle times can achieve. The late-career engineer may find the runway shorter than expected.

5.6 Scenarios for 2030 – 2035

Bringing together the technological, economic, organizational, and individual threads, we can sketch scenarios for what engineering might look like in five to ten years.

Scenario A: The Transformed Organization

In this scenario, agentic AI fulfills its promise. Engineering organizations deploy sophisticated multi-agent systems that handle most routine work autonomously. Design cycles that once took months complete in weeks. Simulation that once constrained design exploration now enables it. Engineers focus on the genuinely difficult problems like defining requirements, making trade-offs, handling exceptions, while agents handle execution.

The organization has 30 percent fewer engineers than it did in 2025, but they accomplish three times as much. New roles have emerged: agent architects who design the multi-agent systems, knowledge engineers who capture and encode organizational context, and validation specialists who ensure agent outputs meet standards. The traditional engineering hierarchy has flattened as agents democratize capabilities that once required years of experience.

The V-model has evolved into something more concurrent. Requirements, design, and verification happen simultaneously, with agents maintaining consistency across the threads. Formal phase gates have been replaced by continuous validation, with human review focused on key decision points rather than routine approvals.

Scenario B: The Augmented Status Quo

In this scenario, agentic AI delivers meaningful but bounded value. Agents handle specific, well-defined tasks effectively like design rule checking, documentation generation, simulation setup, but struggle with novelty and cross-domain reasoning. Human engineers remain essential for most substantive work, with agents serving as capable assistants rather than autonomous collaborators.

The organization has similar headcount to 2025, but productivity has improved 20-30 percent through targeted automation. Engineers spend less time on paperwork and routine analysis, more time on design and problem-solving. The fundamental structure of engineering work done via the V-model, the phase gates, the review processes remain intact, with agents embedded at specific points rather than transforming the overall flow.

Investment in agentic AI has moderated from the frenzied levels of 2024–2025 as the gap between promise and delivery became apparent. Organizations have settled into steady, incremental adoption, capturing value from proven applications while remaining skeptical of more ambitious claims.

Scenario C: The Bifurcated Industry

In this scenario, agentic AI creates winners and losers. Leading organizations master the technology and achieve dramatic competitive advantages. Lagging organizations fail to adapt and find themselves unable to compete. The middle ground hollows out as moderate adoption proves insufficient.

The engineering software market has consolidated around two or three dominant platforms that control the AI infrastructure. Organizations that committed early to these platforms benefit from continuous improvement; those that delayed face difficult migration decisions or permanent capability gaps. The context moat which contains the accumulated organizational knowledge that makes agents effective proves to be decisive. Organizations that invested in capturing and structuring their knowledge have agents that understand their specific needs. Those that did not have generic agents that provide generic value.

Engineering talent has polarized. A small number of highly paid engineers orchestrate sophisticated agent systems. A larger number of lower-paid engineers handle the work that agents cannot. The traditional middle or experienced engineers doing substantive, but routine work has largely disappeared.

5.7 Preparing for Uncertainty

No one knows which scenario will materialize. The honest answer to questions about AI's future is uncertainty. Uncertainty does not preclude preparation, though. Organizations and individuals can take actions that improve their position across multiple scenarios.

For Organizations

Invest in context capture. Whatever happens with AI capabilities, agents will need organizational knowledge to be useful. The work of documenting design rules, capturing lessons learned, and structuring institutional knowledge delivers value regardless of how capable the models become. This is the investment that compounds.

Build integration infrastructure. Agents need to connect to your CAD systems, simulation tools, and PLM platforms. The connections you build for current agent's capabilities will serve future capabilities. Avoid building narrow integrations for specific use cases. Build flexible infrastructure that can support use cases you have not yet imagined.

Develop human capabilities. Train engineers to evaluate agent outputs, to recognize when agents are wrong, and to direct agent work effectively. These skills become more valuable as agent capabilities increase, not less. The organizations that develop them will capture more value from whatever capabilities emerge.

Maintain strategic flexibility. Avoid deep commitment to a single vendor, a single approach, or a single scenario. The landscape is changing too rapidly for long-term lock-in to be prudent. Build capabilities that can be redirected as the future becomes clearer.

For Individuals

Develop the skills that are valued, such as judgment, systems thinking, communication, and creativity. These are the capabilities that remain distinctively human and that become more valuable as routine work is automated.

Learn to work with agents. Not as a technical specialty, but as a core engineering skill. The ability to prompt effectively, evaluate outputs critically, and integrate agent capabilities into your work will be as fundamental as CAD proficiency is today.

Embrace the transition. The engineers who thrive will be those who see agents as amplification, not threat. They will be curious about new capabilities, willing to experiment, and quick to adapt their practice as the technology evolves.

Maintain domain expertise. Agents are tools. Expertise makes tools valuable. The engineer who deeply understands their domain can direct agents effectively. The engineer who relies on agents without understanding cannot evaluate their outputs or recover from their failures.

5.8 The Choice Ahead

The future of agentic AI in engineering is not predetermined. It will be shaped by technological progress, but also by the choices that organizations and individuals make. How aggressively do companies pursue automation? How thoughtfully do they capture context? How wisely do they invest in human capabilities alongside AI capabilities? How seriously do they take safety and reliability? The answers to these questions, aggregated across thousands of organizations and millions of engineers, will determine which scenario materializes.

The AI 2027 project and similar forecasting efforts remind us that transformative change can happen faster than expected, but they also remind us that the path to transformation is not automatic. It requires solving hard problems, making difficult choices, and navigating genuine uncertainty. The organizations that recognize this will prepare for multiple futures while working to shape the future they prefer.

This book has provided the foundations for that preparation. We have examined what agentic AI systems are and how they work. We have explored implementation patterns and organizational considerations. We have discussed what works today and what remains experimental. This chapter has looked at what might come next.

The rest is up to you. The technology is available. The patterns are established. The investment is flowing. What remains is execution. The hard work of capturing your organizational context, building the integrations, developing the capabilities, and managing the transition.

The tools will be available to everyone. The context is organization specific. The question that determines your future remains: **What will you teach your agents?**

6 Appendix

6.1 Pilot Project Scoring Matrix

Table 6.1 shows a pilot project scoring matrix.

Table 6.1 Pilot project scoring matrix

Criterion	Guiding Question	1 – Weak Fit	3 – Medium Fit	5 – Strong Fit	Weight
economic leverage	Will improvement be clearly felt?	low volume or impact barely noticeable	moderate time or cost impact	high leverage on cost, time, or capacity	20 %
repetition & similarity	Does the process repeat structurally?	mostly one-off, unique work	partial repetition with many exceptions	highly repetitive with parameter variation	15 %
cross-functional coordination	How much coordination dominates today?	single function, linear flow	several teams, some back-and-forth	highly iterative, many dependencies	15 %
quality & acceptance clarity	Is "good enough" clearly defined?	subjective or implicit acceptance	partial KPIs, some ambiguity	clear KPIs, thresholds, and ownership	15 %
data accessibility & stability	Can agents work with the data?	fragmented, implicit, unstable	mixed structure, manual interpretation	structured or semi-structured, stable	15%
organizational risk & friction	How risky is experimentation here?	high regulatory or political exposure	manageable exposure with care	low-risk learning environment	10 %

Table 6.1 Pilot project scoring matrix (*continued*)

Criterion	Guiding Question	1 – Weak Fit	3 – Medium Fit	5 – Strong Fit	Weight
real usage commitment	Will it be used in real work?	demo or showcase only	limited pilot usage	real users, real decisions	5 %
learning & improvement potential	Will the system improve with use?	rare feedback, little learning	some repetition and feedback	frequent feedback, clear outcomes	5%

6.2 Multi-Agent System Rollout Cheat Sheet

(1) Proof of Concept (PoC)

Goal: Prove technical feasibility, not business value.

Purpose: Answer the question "Can a multi-agent system technically work in our environment?"

Scope & focus: narrow and clearly bounded workflow; one or two agent interactions; limited data sources and tools; minimal governance and hardening

What to validate: tool integration (CAx, solvers, data access); data availability and format stability; agent orchestration logic; core assumptions about automation feasibility

What not to optimize: output perfection; edge cases; performance benchmarks; organizational rollout questions

Success indicators: Agents can reliably execute the core workflow, integration risks are understood, technical constraints are visible and manageable, and there is a clear decision on whether to proceed to pilot.

Typical pitfalls: scope creep; trying to demonstrate ROI too early; treating PoC results as production quality

(2) Pilot Phase

Goal: Establish trust and usability in real work.

Purpose: Answer the question "Will people actually use this system?"

Scope & focus: real users working on real cases; limited but complete workflow; human-in-the-loop by design; stable interfaces and outputs

What to validate: time, effort, and quality impact; user acceptance and trust; transparency and explainability; organizational bottlenecks and friction

Production-readiness activities: remove PoC simplifications; handle known edge cases; improve error handling and escalation; stabilize data flows and interfaces

Success indicators: system used voluntarily in daily work; measurable improvements vs. baseline; clear ownership and acceptance criteria; observable system learning over time

Typical pitfalls: treating the pilot as demo; ignoring feedback; over-engineering before adoption is proven

(3) Scaling Phase

Goal: Turn a solution into a sustainable capability.

Purpose: Answer the question "Can this be expanded without breaking trust or control?"

Scope & focus: extension to additional use cases or domains; reuse of agent logic and workflows; formalized governance and support; long-term operational stability

What to establish: clear ownership and responsibilities; monitoring performance, cost, and usage; training and onboarding for new users; maintenance and update strategy

Scaling constraints to watch: CAx license availability; compute and solver capacity; data governance and access rights; change management bandwidth

Success indicators: new use cases added faster than the first; consistent quality across teams; reduced dependency on individual experts; agents perceived as normal collaborators

Typical pitfalls: scaling before pilot maturity; underestimating operational costs; losing transparency as complexity grows

6.3 Operational Starter Cheat Sheet—The Minimum You Need at the Beginning

> Remember this:
> You don't need a perfect operating model. You need a visible one.

(1) Name the Owners (Non-Negotiable)

Before the first pilot goes live, answer three questions:

- Who runs the system day to day?
- Who decides if logic is correct?
- Who approves changes?

One person may hold multiple roles at the beginning, but no role should be implicit.

(2) Keep Humans in Control

At the start, it is important that you keep humans in control:

- Agents prepare results.
- Humans decide.
- Nothing writes back automatically.

If users don't trust the system yet, that is expected.

(3) Expect Change (And Make it Safe)

Do only this—that's enough for the start:

- Keep old versions.
- Change one thing at a time.
- Be able to roll back.

(4) Treat LLMs as Unstable Components

You don't need deep AI governance yet, just remember the following:

- LLM behavior can change.
- Results may drift slightly.
- When in doubt, ask a human.

Visibility beats control at this stage.

(5) Define a Simple Escalation Rule

When something looks wrong: Stop, ask, document the correction. If users don't know what happens when agents fail, trust disappears.

(6) Capture Learning Early

For every pilot, collect

- where agents helped,
- where humans overruled, and
- why was override necessary.

This is not overhead. This is how the system improves.

(7) One-Question Health Check

Ask regularly: If the main expert leaves tomorrow, does the system still make sense? If the answer is no, slow down and stabilize before scaling.

Final Thought

Early operating models are not about control. They are about clarity. Define metrics for adoption and agents in production systems. This will help you measure and adapt your overall agentic strategy and use case selection. Get clarity first. Everything else can mature later.

6.4 Skill, Mindset, and Identity Evolution Cheat Sheet—What to Consider First

(1) What Leaders Must Understand First

Multi-agent systems (MAS) don't reduce headcount needs by default. They change where human value is created:

- less value in manual execution
- more value in judgment, oversight, and decision quality
- Expertise shifts, it does not disappear.

(2) Why the Smartest People Matter Most

The most critical risk is not resistance from average performers, it is losing or disengaging top experts:

- High performers may fear loss of relevance.
- Deep domain knowledge is essential for building good agents.
- Without expert involvement, MAS quality degrades quickly.

Key insight: The best engineers must see MAS as a career accelerator, not a threat.

(3) How Engineering Roles Will Evolve

From: tool operators; individual problem solvers; execution-focused contributors

To: decision architects; system supervisors; exception handlers; knowledge curators

This shift impacts

- job descriptions,
- performance criteria,
- career paths, and
- training programs.

(4) New Roles That Will Emerge

Organizations should name and legitimize new roles early:

- **Automation engineer:** builds and improves agent workflows
- **Agent architect:** designs responsibility boundaries and orchestration
- **Workflow owner:** owns quality, escalation logic, and outcomes
- **Domain guardian:** ensures engineering rules remain valid and safe

(5) Skills HR Should Actively Develop

These are the high-priority skills:

- systems thinking
- decision evaluation
- reviewing and validating AI output
- defining constraints and acceptance criteria
- cross-functional collaboration

These skills have lower priority than before:

- tool-specific manual expertise
- repetitive execution skills

(6) Cultural Risks to Address Early

These are common failure patterns:

- agents framed as replacements
- automation treated as cost-cutting only
- learning mistakes punished instead of used

These are leadership actions that help:

- Explicitly state that humans retain decision authority.
- Reward contributions to system improvement.
- Make learning visible and psychologically safe.
- Avoid overpromising automation outcomes.

(7) Incentives and Measurement

Do **not** measure success by

- the number of automated steps,
- tool usage, and
- reduced human involvement alone.

Measure success by

- adoption and trust,
- decision quality,
- cycle-time stability,
- reuse of knowledge across projects, and
- reduced dependency on individuals.

(8) What HR and Leadership Should Do First

- Involve HR early in MAS initiatives.
- Update role descriptions proactively.
- Create visible career paths linked to MAS.
- Position MAS work as high-impact, not side work.
- Communicate openly about change and uncertainty.

One Sentence to Remember

Multi-Agent Systems don't replace engineers. They redefine what it means to be a great engineer.

6.5 Practical Checklist for Responsible Agent Deployment

(1) Technical Risk Controls

Reasoning and hallucination

☐ Are all critical agent conclusions grounded in explicit rules, data, or calculations?

☐ Is there a clear separation between reasoning and execution?

☐ Are validation steps in place before any irreversible action?

Over-trust prevention

☐ Are uncertainty signals shown explicitly in outputs?

☐ Can users compare agent results with alternative or baseline views?

☐ Are agents framed as recommendations, not authorities?

Data quality and availability

☐ Are input data sources defined, versioned, and monitored?

☐ Is outdated or conflicting data detectable?

☐ Is implicit expert knowledge progressively externalized into rules or prompts?

Drift management

☐ Are prompt and rule changes versioned and documented?

☐ Is periodic revalidation of behavior planned?

☐ Are real-world cases reused as regression tests?

Tool and platform stability

☐ Are dependencies on CAx UI or APIs monitored?

☐ Is there a fallback if a tool or capability changes unexpectedly?

Scalability constraints

☐ Are compute capacity and queue effects monitored?

☐ Are CAx license bottlenecks visible and planned for?

Security

☐ Are prompt injection risks considered and mitigated?

☐ Is tool execution strictly controlled and permission-based?

Observability

☐ Are agent steps, decisions, and failures logged?

☐ Can failures be detected before users notice wrong outcomes?

(2) Organizational Risk Controls

Adoption and trust

☐ Do engineers experience tangible relief early?

☐ Is transparency prioritized over apparent intelligence?

☐ Are agents positioned as assistants, not replacements?

Responsibilities and accountability

☐ Is it always clear who decides and who is accountable?

☐ Are escalation rules explicit for uncertain cases?

Skill readiness

☐ Is there internal capability to maintain and evolve the system?

☐ Is vendor dependency understood and intentionally accepted?

(3) Legal and Regulatory Safeguards

Intellectual property

☐ Are ownership of prompts, rules, and knowledge bases clarified?

☐ Is proprietary data protected during LLM interaction?

☐ Are contracts with platform and model providers explicit?

Regulatory compliance

☐ Are transparency and auditability requirements fulfilled?

☐ Is human oversight formally defined?

☐ Are legal regulations considered where applicable?

(4) Limits and Expectation Management

☐ Is the use case genuinely suitable for agentic automation?

☐ Are broken processes fixed before automation?

☐ Is human judgment preserved where it adds value?

(5) Risk Mitigation Mechanisms

☐ Are sandbox environments available?

☐ Is staging used before production?

☐ Are canary releases supported?

☐ Is rollback always possible?

☐ Is dual-run operation planned where risk is high?

(6) Learning and Resilience

☐ Are recurring error patterns collected?

☐ Can failures be detected automatically?

☐ Do standardized countermeasures exist?

☐ Is knowledge reused via RAG or similar mechanisms?

(7) Vendor Lock-in and Exit Strategy

☐ Is data fully portable and owned by the organization?

☐ Are abstraction layers used for tools and integrations?

☐ Are open interfaces preferred?

☐ Is a documented migration path available?

Key Reminder

Risk does not disappear with experience. What changes is how early it is detected and how safely it is handled.

---

7 References

Anglara: 10+ High-Impact AI Agent Use cases for finance. Anglara Digital Solutions, November 19, 2025. *https://anglara.com/blog/ai-agent-use-cases-for-finance-industry*

Berylls Strategy Advisors GmbH: Top 100-Zulieferer-Studie 2025. Der nächste Rückschlag für die Zuliefererindustrie. 2025. *https://www.berylls.com/wp-content/uploads/2025/08/TOP-100-Zulieferer-Studie-2025-DE-Digital-Final-compressed.pdf*

Borden, B.: AI transformation in financial services: 5 predictors for success in 2026. Microsoft Industry Blogs, December 18, 2025. *https://www.microsoft.com/en-us/industry/blog/financial-services/2025/12/18/ai-transformation-in-financial-services-5-predictors-for-success-in-2026*

Brown, T.: New research shows how AI agents are driving value for financial services. Google Cloud Blog, September 30, 2025. *https://cloud.google.com/transform/new-research-shows-how-ai-agents-are-driving-value-for-financial-services*

Bulwark Health: Why AI agents in healthcare are a C-Suite priority in 2025. Bulwark Health, August 20, 2025. *https://www.bulwarkhealth.info/blogs/ai-agents-in-healthcare*

Chen, X./Yi, H./You, M./Liu, W./Wang, L./Li, H./Zhang, X./Guo, Y./Fan, L./Chen, G./Lao, Q./Fu, W./Li, K./Li, J.: Enhancing diagnostic capability with multi-agents conversational large language models. In: npj Digital Medicine, 8 (1), 159, March 13, 2025. *https://doi.org/10.1038/s41746-025-01550-0*

Damodaran, A.: Cost of Equity and Capital (US). January 2026. *https://pages.stern.nyu.edu/~adamodar/New_Home_Page/datafile/wacc.html*

IMARC Group: Polypropylene Price Trend, Index and Forecast. 2025a. *https://www.imarcgroup.com/polypropylene-pricing-report*

IMARC Group: Acrylonitrile Butadiene Styrene (ABS) Price Trend, Index and Forecast. 2025b. *https://www.imarcgroup.com/acrylonitrile-butadiene-styrene-pricing-report*

Jannelli, V./Schöpf, S./Bickel, M./Netland, T./Brintrup, A.: Agentic LLMs in the supply chain: towards autonomous multi-agent consensus-seeking. In: International Journal of Production Research, December 21, 2025, pp. 1–31. *https://doi.org/10.1080/00207543.2025.2604311*

Lungren, M.: Developing next-generation cancer care management with multi-agent orchestration. Microsoft Industry Blogs, May 19, 2025. *https://www.microsoft.com/en-us/industry/blog/healthcare/2025/05/19/developing-next-generation-cancer-care-management-with-multi-agent-orchestration*

Moolchandani, J.: LLMs and Multi-Agent Systems: The Future of AI in 2025. Classic Informatics, September 26, 2025. *https://www.classicinformatics.com/blog/how-llms-and-multi-agent-systems-work-together-2025*

Morell, J. A./Swiecki, B. F./Andrea, D. J./Center for Automotive Research/Altarum Institute: Automotive suppliers and the revenue acquisition process: What's working, and what's not? Altarum Institute,

September 2002. *https://www.cargroup.org/wp-content/uploads/2017/02/Automotive-Suppliers-and-the-Revenue-Acquisition-Process.pdf*

Pan, M. Z./Arabzadeh, N./Cogo, R./Zhu, Y./Xiong, A./Agrawal, L. A./Mao, H./Shen, E./Pallerla, S./Patel, L./Liu, S./Shi, T./Liu, X./Davis, J. Q./Lacavalla, E./Basile, A./Yang, S./Castro, P./Kang, D./Ellis, M.: Measuring Agents in Production. arXiv.org, December 2, 2025. *https://arxiv.org/abs/2512.04123*

Spray, A.: The Airbus A350 development timeline. Simple Flying, January 25, 2025. *https://simpleflying.com/airbus-a350-development-timeline*

[x]cube LABS: Multi-Agent System: top industrial applications in 2025. [x]cube LABS, August 28, 2025. *https://www.xcubelabs.com/blog/multi-agent-system-top-industrial-applications-in-2025*

Index

D

E

P

Q

R

S

www.ingramcontent.com/pod-product-compliance
Lightning Source LLC
LaVergne TN
LVHW060313240926
848814LV00006B/36
9781569905623